PRISMATIC PERFORMANCES

TRIANGULATIONS
Lesbian/Gay/Queer ▲ Theater/Drama/Performance

Series Editors
Jill Dolan, Princeton University
David Román, University of Southern California

Associate Editors
Ramón H. Rivera-Servera, University of Texas Austin
Sara Warner, Cornell University

RECENT TITLES IN THE SERIES:

Queer Nightlife Edited by Kemi Adeyemi, Kareem Khubchandani, and Ramón H. Rivera-Servera

Translocas: The Politics of Puerto Rican Drag and Trans Performance by Lawrence La Fountain-Stokes

Prismatic Performances: Queer South Africa and the Fragmentation of the Rainbow Nation by April Sizemore-Barber

Ishtyle: Accenting Gay Indian Nightlife by Kareem Khubchandani

The Bodies of Others: Drag Dances and Their Afterlives by Selby Wynn Schwartz

Charles Ludlam Lives! Charles Busch, Bradford Louryk, Taylor Mac, and the Queer Legacy of the Ridiculous Theatrical Company by Sean F. Edgecomb

Memories of the Revolution: The First Ten Years of the WOW Café Theater edited by Holly Hughes, Carmelita Tropicana, and Jill Dolan

Murder Most Queer: The Homicidal Homosexual in the American Theater by Jordan Schildcrout

Butch Queens Up in Pumps: Gender, Performance, and Ballroom Culture in Detroit by Marlon M. Bailey

Acts of Gaiety: LGBT Performance and the Politics of Pleasure by Sara Warner

Performing Queer Latinidad: Dance, Sexuality, Politics by Ramón H. Rivera-Servera

A Menopausal Gentleman: The Solo Performances of Peggy Shaw edited by Jill Dolan

Lady Dicks and Lesbian Brothers: Staging the Unimaginable at the WOW Café Theatre by Kate Davy

Bulldaggers, Pansies, and Chocolate Babies: Performance, Race, and Sexuality in the Harlem Renaissance by James F. Wilson

Queering Mestizaje: Transculturation and Performance by Alicia Arrizón

PRISMATIC PERFORMANCES

Queer South Africa and the Fragmentation of the Rainbow Nation

April Sizemore-Barber

UNIVERSITY OF MICHIGAN PRESS
Ann Arbor

First paperback edition 2021

Published in the United States of America by
the University of Michigan Press
Manufactured in the United States of America
Printed on acid-free paper

First published in paperback October 2021

A CIP catalog record for this book is available from the British Library.

ISBN 978-0-472-13205-8 (hardcover : alk. paper)

ISBN 978-0-472-12698-9 (ebook)

ISBN 978-0-472-03879-4 (pbk. : alk. paper)

Cover: Athi-Patra Ruga in *The Future White Woman of Azania*, performed on the streets of Makhanda (Grahamstown) South Africa for an exhibition curated by Ruth Simbao, *Making Way: Contemporary Art from South Africa and China* (2012). Photo by Ruth Simbao. In the photo a person covered head to hip by multicolored balloons walks in high-heeled shoes and bright pink stockings down a dirt road with low buildings on either side. Looking on with a degree of fascination are a tall man, hands in pockets, and a toddler hanging on to the man's jeans.

Contents

Acknowledgments vii

INTRODUCTION 1

ONE. A Queer Transition: Prismatic Whiteness in Postapartheid Drag Performance 22

TWO. Living in the As-If: Queering *Ikultcha* with the Chosen FEW Soccer Team 47

THREE. In-Hypervisibility: Aesthetic Displacement and "Corrective" Rape 75

FOUR. When Jason Kissed Senzo: Prismatic Soap Opera Fandom on *Gensblog* 106

Conclusion 136

Notes 145

Bibliography 169

Index 177

Digital materials related to this title can be found on the Fulcrum platform via the following citable URL https://doi.org/10.3998/mpub.10192303

Acknowledgments

Prismatic Performances could not have come to fruition without my South African collaborators generously sharing their time, energy, and stories with me. This book is therefore dedicated to the following people: the fearless activists affiliated with the Forum for Empowerment of Women, especially those who played for the Chosen FEW soccer team, including Phindi Malaza, Tumi Mkhuma, Matshidiso Mofokeng, Thuli Ncube, Dikeledi Sibanda, Bakhambile Skhosana, and Pinky Zulu, among many others; the archivists and advocates who provided me with a home base at Johannesburg's Gay and Lesbian Memory in Action (GALA), including Linda Chernis, Anzio Jacobs, Gabriel Hoosain Khan, Genevieve Louw, Anthony Manion, John Marnell, Skye Martin, Noma Pakade, and Graeme Reid; the generous colleagues who provided community during my time as a visiting researcher, including Catherine Burns, Nicky Falkof, Pumla Gqola, Tish Lumos, Zethu Matebeni, Warren Nebe, Hamish Neill, and Natasha Vally (in Johannesburg) and Veronica Baxter, Mark Fleishman, Carla Lever, Talia Meer, Mbongeni Mtshali, Alex Müller, Lindy-Lee Price, and Clare Stopford (in Cape Town). Last, but not least, I dedicate this book to the pathbreaking artists who have discussed their work with me over the years: Sibulele Gcilitshana, Janice Honeyman, Dean Hutton, Mwenya Kabwe, Makgano Mamabolo, Zanele Muholi, Mamela Nyamza, Jay Pather, Athi-Patra Ruga, Malcolm Purkey, Andrew Putter, Jane Taylor, Pieter-Dirk Uys, and Mlondolozi Zondi.

This project received generous financial support from Georgetown University's faculty research fund and The Harvard Mellon School of Theatre and Performance Research. It also greatly benefited from a UK Arts and Humanities Research Council-funded postdoctoral fellowship in Drama at Royal Holloway, University of London.

I have learned from many brilliant teachers who have profoundly shaped both my thinking and my own pedagogy. At Oberlin College, I experienced the importance of both radical empathy and creative curiosity firsthand in classes taught by professors Phyllis Gorfain and Caroline Jackson Smith. At Berkeley, I gained an appreciation for the entwinement of theory and practice working closely with my dissertation committee members Gillian Hart and Paola Bacchetta. Most of all, I am grateful for ongoing support of my chair Catherine Cole. Her ethical and rigorous critical voice, generous mentorship of emerging scholars, and commitment to the field of African performance studies has had a profound influence on this book and on my evolution as a scholar.

Intellectual generosity is a rare and precious gift. I am immeasurably lucky to be in conversation with a far-flung community of interlocutors—colleagues, friends, and collaborators—who helped enrich the echo-chamber of the writing process. I am especially grateful to Gibson Cima, Ashley Currier, Laura Edmonson, Lindsay Green-Simms, Casey Golomski, Caitlin Marshall, Brenna Munro, and T.J. Tallie for their invaluable feedback on earlier drafts of this manuscript. So too, members of the American Society for Theatre Research's *Performance in/from the Global South* working group have provided insightful critiques workshopping several of the book's chapters. David Donkor, Ryan Hartigan, Kellen Hoxworth, Kat Leider, Megan Lewis, Lakshmi Padmanabhan, Karin Shankar, Josh Williams, and so many others have made attendance at ASTR a yearly intellectual homecoming. Warmest thanks also go to my Berkeley Performance Studies comrades: Michelle Baron, Marc Boucai, Shane Boyle, Ashley Ferro-Murray, Katie Horowitz, Paige Johnson, Iván Ramos, Scott Wallin, and Brandon Woolf. The initial seeds of this endeavor were nurtured across seminar tables and over hoppy Jupiter quaffs through their encouragement and solidarity.

Finally, I thank my big queer family—Roy Barber, Elese Sizemore, and Gary Raymond—for their love and support throughout my life. I could not do the work I do today without my father's deep conviction about theatre as a tool through which a new world can be shaped, my mother's brilliance and endless empathy, and Buppy's quiet strength and cutting wit. Nevermore has the triangulated, prismatic phrase *umuntu ngumuntu ngabantu*—a person is a person through other people—seemed more apt. I am who I am today because of you.

Chapter 1 is a revised version of an article that appeared in earlier form as "A Queer Transition: Whiteness in the Prismatic, Post-Apartheid Drag Performances of Pieter-Dirk Uys and Steven Cohen," in *Theatre Journal* 68, no. 2 (2016): 191–211.

INTRODUCTION

Prelude: Cause for Celebration?

In October 2012, Johannesburg marked its twenty-third annual Gay and Lesbian Pride Parade. Twenty thousand people of all races, genders, and sexual orientations converged to watch the parade wind through the walled streets in the wealthy suburb of Rosebank. House music blasted from passing floats as revelers cheered and waved rainbow flags superimposed with the South African flag's distinctive Y-shaped design. To all appearances, Joburg Pride was the "Pride of Africa" (as its organizers boasted), a space of hope and tolerance on a continent where same-sex attraction and identity still remain largely criminalized. South Africa's 1996 progressive postapartheid constitution explicitly protected sexual orientation as part of a larger national commitment to human dignity.[1]

Gay antiapartheid activist Simon Nkoli had articulated the need for an intersectional struggle at Johannesburg's first pride in 1990: "This is what I say to my comrades in the [antiapartheid] struggle when they ask why I waste time fighting for '*moffies*' (queers); this is what I say to gay men and lesbians who ask me why I spend so much time struggling against apartheid when I should be fighting for gay rights: I am black and I am gay. I cannot separate the two parts of me into secondary or primary struggles."[2] Convened six months after Nelson Mandela's release from twenty-seven years of imprisonment, the first parade reflected a mix of defiance and trepidation. Held in Johannesburg's diverse inner city, only several hundred participants attended the march, some wearing bags over their head for fear of being recognized, as sodomy was still illegal under apartheid law. Yet the day was an expression of liberation and belonging at a time when national narratives were daily being rescripted, a preview of future victories in a more accepting country. Through strategic visibility and political maneuvering, activists like Nkoli ensured that South Africa's LGBT citizens would be important actors in shaping the New South Africa.

Between the 1990 and 2012 parades, much had improved for South Africa's sexual minorities. Bolstered by the constitution, progressive legislation had decriminalized sodomy (1998) and legalized same-sex adoption (2002). When same-sex marriage became the law of the land in 2006, far earlier than in much of the so-called progressive West, many activists saw this triumph as clearing the final hurdle to full citizenship. Yet the string of legal successes had resulted in a certain amount of complacency and lack of political will among many LGBT people. Where the first pride march wore its political agenda on its sleeve, framing the struggle for equality as inseparable from the larger fight for racial justice, organizers of Joburg Pride in 2012 seemed content to simply throw a party. The 1990 march had ended with an inner-city rally where activists strategized how to face the struggles ahead. By contrast, the 2012 parade's destination was a specially constructed "community village" in the nearby Zoo Lake Park, where partiers were encouraged to trade their cash for "Pink Rands." Organizers consigned political activity to the nongovernmental organization (NGO) tables on the perimeter of the fenced-in party zone, alongside booths hocking energy drinks and rainbow gear.

After a decade plagued by financial challenges, Joburg Pride finally became solvent due in large part to local and international corporate sponsorship. Modeled on the careful choreography of what might be called the celebratory pride script, images from the day—drag queens, LGBT families, and floats advertising gay clubs—were interchangeable with similar celebrations across the globe. The 2012 Pride's primary engagement with its South African context was a defensive one. Its theme, "Protecting Our Rights," was crafted in response to a movement from the all-black Congress of Traditional Leaders to remove references to sexual orientation from the constitution. On its website, Pride organizers urged "South Africa's LGBTI community [to] stand together as one," against this outside threat, with the proviso that "Joburg Pride will—as always—offer a frisky mix of fun, flair and finesse, rounding out its important messaging."[3]

Halfway through its route, however, Joburg Pride became the scene of a resistant performative intervention with effects and affects echoing far beyond that October day. In a coordinated action, around twenty young, primarily black and queer women wearing bright purple T-shirts broke through the sidelines to unfurl banners reading "No Cause for Celebration" and "Dying for Justice." With the help of life-sized, straw-stuffed mannequins, the protestors—later revealed to be members of the feminist direct-action group the One in Nine Campaign—staged a die-in across the road, effectively halting the parade in its tracks. The women called for a minute of silence to commemorate LGBTI South Africans, particularly

Fig. 1. No cause for celebration: One in Nine Campaign's Joburg Pride 2012 die-in. Photo: Heather Mason.

black lesbians, who had lost their lives to violence the previous year. They passed out leaflets naming the dead, explaining that the action was meant to draw attention to Joburg Pride's break from its activist roots and its economic and geographic inaccessibility for most nonwhite LGBTI people.

The reaction to this unexpected intrusion was immediate and visceral: as the majority-white marchers picked their way over the prone bodies, some looked uncomfortable. Others aggressively snapped rainbow flags in the faces of those holding the signs, flashed middle fingers, kicked at the bodies, and told the protestors to "go back to your *lokshins*! [townships]."[4] As the One in Nine members held their position and the parade's floats began to back up, the Jackson Five's bouncy "I Want You Back" clashed with the call-and-response harmonies of the protestor's "Siyaya Nobakubi," a song repurposed from the antiapartheid struggle. Irate members of Joburg Pride's all-white board arrived at the scene to threaten and attempt to physically remove the women. The parade marshals finally forced the activists to retreat by driving motorcycles into the banners. The women were eventually moved to the side of the road; disruption resolved, the parade continued to the party site, back on track.

If the organizers hoped that this physical containment would render the protesters out of sight and out of mind, however, they would be disappointed, as the reactions provoked by the intervention merely expanded to virtual spaces. By the end of the day, One in Nine had released the footage as a heavily edited YouTube video, featuring voice-over selections of the press release intercut with the most violent interactions between the marchers and the protesters. Over the next days and weeks, hundreds of YouTube commenters weighed in on the effectiveness of One in Nine's tactics, the politics of Joburg Pride's board of directors, and the essence of LGBT pride itself. Marchers who had witnessed the protest took to the internet to give alternate accounts and attempted to explain the extreme negative reaction many had toward a cause that, at least in theory, everybody could support. As noted by South African queer activist and academic Nyx Mclean, social media's fluid temporality and uncensored polyvocality both expanded and destabilized the initial "event" of the protest.[5] The striking visual and audio footage circulated widely on blogs outside of its initial geographic context, reframing the South African intervention within larger transnational critiques of homonationalism and pinkwashing.[6]

The clash of queer bodies on the very site where unity had been the scripted order of the day violently revealed the unspoken, yet palpable tensions among South Africa's various racial, ethnic, and sexual communities two decades into its democracy. The unity called for by the pride committee intentionally, if superficially, echoed the oft-repeated self-image of postapartheid South Africa as the Rainbow Nation, a country "united in its diversity." When marginalized queer South Africans threatened to wrest control of the pride narrative, however, the pride committee contained and removed their bodies. This reaction to One in Nine's protest created the impression that queer blackness was acceptable only if it could pay the price of entry to the community village; Africanness appeared desirable if it added flavor to the prix fixe menu, a strand of colorful beads or a bottle of the cheekily named lubricant *Assegai*. The Rainbow Nation rhetoric of inclusivity provided a patina of the local in the global space of corporatized pride. One in Nine's intervention dragged Joburg Pride, with its global aspirations, back to its South African context, where sexual violence and poverty are stark realities for the majority. The Pink Rands spent on a double gin and tonic in the grounds of the Community Village could feed an entire family living in the nearby Alexandra Township. The unrehearsed, visceral responses by those confronted with unwanted black bodies and the economic and spatial legacies of apartheid made clear that old narratives had merely taken new forms.

Queering African Performance, Performing Africa Queerly: Enter the Prism

Prismatic Performances analyzes such evocative moments of disruption and affective exchange between queer bodies, their audiences, and the physical-symbolic terrain of postapartheid space. South African gays and lesbians exist within a paradoxical relationship to the nation-state: protected legally and often cited as examples of the country's pluralistic modernity, they have been consistently scapegoated for the larger failures of the democratic project. The political interventions, theatrical and artistic representations, and everyday self-understandings of LGBT South Africans discussed in this book provide what I term a prismatic lens on contradictions of postapartheid and postcolonial space. At turns reflecting and challenging the narrative of multiculturalism that defined the first two decades of the country's democracy, these performances reveal the shifting borders of national belonging.

The performances charted within this book take place within the years between Nelson Mandela's triumphant 1994 election and his 2013 death, a period that captured the rise and fall of the Rainbow narrative. These two decades saw an initial enthusiastic embrace of a nonracial national identity gradually give way to widespread disillusionment and resentment toward the government's failures. The Rainbow Nation metaphor, popularized by Archbishop Desmond Tutu and referenced frequently by Nelson Mandela during his presidency (1994–1999), was at once seductive and illusory, evoking a desired unity that did not actually exist. Feminist scholar Pumla Gqola, writing in 2001, critiques what she terms "rainbowism" for its implicit promises of equality and success while maintaining the same material economic power structures that had thrived under apartheid.[7] An ascendant LGBT movement mirrored this national narrative arc, initially benefiting from a cultural moment where, Brenna Munro argues, the *idea* of gay rights made South Africans "feel modern and magnanimous as they watched, or took part in, multiple dramas of acceptance."[8] Yet these early legal gains have subsequently been undermined by widespread discontent with modernity's failure to deliver economic transformation; LGBT citizens, already subject to uneven access to de jure rights across racial and class lines, became easy targets for popular anger.

Each chapter of *Prismatic Performances* illuminates a different facet of queer performance—theatrical, quotidian, material, and virtual—to reveal the tensions within and between multiple visions of the postapartheid nation. The book draws on a diverse dramatis personae from the first two decades of South Africa's democracy. Pieter-Dirk Uys and Steven Cohen, two white gay male drag artists grappling with racial and societal transformation in the 1990s, found that drag served to prismatically critique and refract whiteness as a queer form of Africanness. A team of black lesbian soccer players in Johannesburg—briefly visible on the global stage as a 2010 FIFA World Cup human interest story—challenged their communities' conviction of homosexuality's inherent "un-Africanness" by embracing a complex configuration of overperformed personas and everyday actions. Choreographer Mamela Nyamza and photographer Zanele Muholi, in their multigenre representations of sexual violence experienced by black lesbians, developed aesthetics to displace and refract the impossible representational paradox (simultaneously invisible and hyperexposed) on their complicit audiences. Finally, the melodramatic postings and self-images of members of the primarily heterosexual online soap opera fandom Gensblog.co.za provided an unlikely real-time account of gay representation in popular and virtual media, as both a source of disruption and (tentative) assimilation into what Munro terms South Africa's "queer family romance."[9] The different, yet oft-overlapping, scales of the performances under discussion animate the intersection of "queer" and "South African," making visible a wide variety of presumptions about race, gender, and citizenship held by South Africans twenty years after the fall of apartheid.

Prismatic Performances argues for the importance of performativity in understanding queer nationalisms more generally. Unlike many countries in the global South, South Africa has incorporated sexual orientation and nonheterosexual bodies as a key element in the country's self-image as a new progressive postcolonial state. Just as this inclusion signaled expansive optimism in the earliest days of democracy, the disillusionment with the African National Congress government by the time of Mandela's death (and continuing into the present) has engendered widespread antigay sentiment and broader normalization of violence as a source of discipline and gendered authority. A 2013 Pew Research poll, conducted seven years after same-sex marriage had been legalized, indicated that 61 percent of South Africans surveyed still thought homosexuality should not be accepted by society.[10]

Despite the government's proclamations of postapartheid rainbows and African renaissances,[11] the gap between haves and have-nots has continued to grow. The majority of South Africans are now economically worse off than they were during apartheid. South Africa consistently registers the world's highest Gini coefficient—the ratio between richest and poorest—a wealth disparity that remains deeply racialized.[12] High levels of inequality and the legacies of colonial and apartheid trauma have kept the black communities that make up over 80 percent of the population in positions of sustained precarity. As a 2014 Oxfam report bluntly stated: South Africa's "extreme inequality corrupts politics, hinders economic growth and stifles social mobility. It fuels crime and even violent conflict. It squanders talent, thwarts potential and undermines the foundations of society."[13] This deep cultural destabilization has contributed to a rate of sexual violence that is among the highest in the world. As One in Nine's Joburg Pride intervention sought to publicize, black lesbians are particularly vulnerable to targeted sexual assault by members of their communities, some of whom strategically use rape and, at times, murder as a performative method of intimidation and even affirmative masculinity.[14]

One in Nine's protest and its various counter-performances provide a rich illustration of how performance can both reveal and disrupt the complex and shifting power relations between sexual, racial, and national identities in postapartheid South Africa. The mass-produced spectacle of Joburg Pride—where organizers encouraged the "Gay Community" to be "together as one"—reflected a particular, neoliberal presumption of what gay South Africa was supposed to look like: wealthy, Westernized, mostly white, gender normative, and centered around male sexuality. By placing the (stand-in) bodies of dead black lesbians at the feet of the LGBT community's most public performance, One in Nine made the event's exclusionary politics explicit and unavoidable to its audiences. One in Nine symbolically called both those marching and those watching to account for their social position in relation to the lives (and deaths) of those bearing the greatest burden of the community's quest for visibility. Though subsequently accused by the Joburg Pride board of fostering racial division, the One in Nine protesters merely revealed the deep fractures that already existed.

If the rainbow is both a symbol of gay pride and postcolonial multiculturalism, this book offers its titular prism as a situated framework to unpack this weaponized metanarrative. Its inquiry is animated by two key questions: If postapartheid society is already fractured, how do queer performances draw attention to the fracture, animate it, and evoke an emotional and critical response from their audiences? And, if we were to view performance as a method of refraction—of seeing differently—allowing us to disentangle unexamined emotional responses and attachments, what do queer South African performances do and show us in this field?

Beyond being merely a rhetorical device, the prism provides an animated, multidimensional way to think through the embodied, deconstructive work performances do. Where a prism deconstructs light into its many-hued parts, creating a flattened image of a rainbow (nation), a prismatic *performance* reflects and refracts the emotional investments projected onto it by varied audiences. What remains is not a clearly defined spectrum, but an often messy and ambiguous assemblage of conflicting viewpoints that forces both audience members and performers to encounter their own most deeply held beliefs and desires anew. Rather than focusing on performances as flat representations (or critiques) of South Africa during the rainbow era, a prismatic framework emphasizes the multiplicity of meaning and affects generated by the artists' provocations; it acknowledges that meaning is not foreclosed and that the projected futures enacted at one moment are just as readily refracted and rejected through the lens of hindsight.

Staging South Africa from the "Bad Old Days" to the Rainbow Nation: Genealogies

The New South Africa, as the post-1994 democratic regime was popularly known, defined itself through symbolic and performative gestures of reconciliation and rebirth.[15] The national motto, *!ke e:/xarra//ke* ("Diverse people unite"), for instance, reanimated the nearly-extinct Khoisan language of the indigenous !Xam people to imagine a unified future outside of the ossified racial and cultural divisions of the past. The revamped national anthem was similarly polylingual and performative, combining the antiapartheid struggle hymn "Nkosi Sikelel' iAfrika" ("God Bless Africa," sung in a mix of iXhosa, isiZulu, and Sesotho) with the previous regime's anthem "Die Stem van Suid Afrika" ("The Call of South Africa," in Afrikaans), and a new verse written in English calling for unity. The rainbow metaphor, as strategically employed by Desmond Tutu and Nelson Mandela, also performed interpolative work, turning South Africa's multiracial citizens into a singular united nation, metonymically marking a break with forty-five years of racial apartheid and three hundred years of colonial rule.[16]

Only white South Africans held full citizenship under apartheid, while the nonwhite South Africans that comprised over 80 percent of the country's population competed for rights and resources in a racialized hierarchy. Minority populations—Indians and so-called *Coloureds* (people of mixed-descent)—were banned from certain spaces and jobs. Black Africans, banished to invented tribal homelands (Bantustans), were effectively denied citizenship in their own country. Grand Apartheid, as it came to be known, administered by Dutch-descended Afrikaners and upheld by English-descended white South Africans, was consolidated via incarceration, segregation, forced land expropriation, and the sexual criminalization and control of nonwhite and black bodies. Homosexual relations, primarily those between races and among whites, were criminalized as threatening the purity of the white race and threatening the family unit central to reproducing white supremacy. Apartheid, euphemistically defended by its architect Hendrik Verwoerd as a policy of "good neighborliness," was most visible in its biopolitical control of the black body. Yet images and cultural production of nonwhite bodies in literature, media, theater, television, and film were equally policed in a parallel regime of cultural censorship.[17] Where the state economically depended on the complete control of black bodies and labor, it equally depended on white complicity cultivated via propaganda.

Apartheid censors focused on print and visual media, underestimating the live, performing body's capacity to galvanize opposition. In the 1980s, while cracking down on community theater groups in black townships, the apartheid government made a goodwill gesture to demonstrate its tolerance of dissent to an increasingly skeptical global community: certain theatrical productions, developed in limited locations such as Johannesburg's Market Theatre, were allowed to tour internationally. The logic behind this decision is unclear; perhaps the government assumed that, unlike an image or a text, bodies could not be copied or reproduced outside of their control. By every estimation, however, this gambit was a colossal miscalculation. Between 1980 and 1990 numerous South African plays—among them *Woza Albert*, *Asinamali*, *Bopha*, *Born in the RSA*, *You Strike a Woman You Strike a Rock*, and *Sarafina*—toured Broadway, London's West End, and regionally. In their unflinching depictions of state suppression and resistant black humanity, Marcia Blumberg and David Walder argue, these productions played a key, "intermittent and indefinable" role in the international struggle against apartheid.[18] At a time when economic and cultural boycotts effectively cut South Africa off from the rest of the world, these stories became the world's primary window into the country.

Whether witnessing the individual performer's sweat-drenched virtuosity in air-conditioned theaters or experiencing the raucous spectacle of thousands toyi-toying[19] in the street on television, international audiences were assured that the struggle was a just one, and that the tide of democracy was unstoppable. Yet as David Graver has pointed out, the restaging of the pieces for Western audiences often undercut the specificity of their political critique, so that "performances designed to participate in resistance and revolt were reduced to images of resistance and revolt served up for the audience's inconsequential pleasure."[20] With few other examples of African performance available on Western stages, critics often unthinkingly reproduced colonial narratives in their embrace of so-called struggle theater's alleged authenticity.[21] These performances tended toward the didactic, leaning heavily on the self-evident immorality of a white supremacist government that ruled by divide and conquer. The Manichaean dramaturgical framework, though effective as both dramatic device and political motivator, had the unintentional long-term effect of presenting South Africa's story as one of good versus evil and white versus black, with little room for ambiguity or nuance. For a global audience that consumed this narrative, Nelson Mandela's 1994 ascension to the presidency amounted to one of the oldest and most superficially satisfying dramatic tropes: the happy ending.

Life, however, continued beyond this convenient narrative endpoint. As the West elevated Mandela to the pantheon of modern-day saints, South Africa's new government assumed the often-banal and dirty business of nation-building.[22] The subsequent ANC-party presidencies of Thabo Mbeki (1999–2008), Jacob Zuma (2009–2019), and Cyril Ramaphosa (2019–present) have not lent themselves to the same easy moral typecasting.[23] Postapartheid South Africa reflects a number of contradictions and extremes: legally progressive but socially conservative; the highest GDP on the African continent alongside the highest Gini coefficient; communist and worker parties that maintain central roles in an aggressively neoliberal government; the government's embrace of an ethos of reconciliation and *ubuntu* (shared humanity) versus its early AIDS denialism resulting in the unnecessary death of hundreds of thousands of its citizens.

These contradictions have increasingly fragmented and undermined the Rainbow Nation narrative, revealing it to be, at best, an aspirational project. At worst, it can be seen as an intentional diversion, a pretty, kaleidoscopic light-show to distract audiences from deepening structural inequalities. In the first two postapartheid decades covered by this book, theater in South Africa, for all its historical efficacy as a tool of popular critique, had largely invested in this nation-building project. With a few exceptions (notably, the biting satirical plays of Mike van Graan), the industry continued to struggle for a collective vocabulary—and sometimes, an audience—to interrogate the ambiguities of democracy. Instead, much like the country itself, performance has increasingly Balkanized and re-formed to serve different audiences, often looking backward toward its protest past in a gesture Gibson Cima has termed *postconflict nostalgia*: yearning for an imagined "freedom" that never quite arrived.[24] For some, particularly underfunded community theater-makers, this urge has manifested in repurposed struggle aesthetics to address the newer enemies of HIV and endemic violence.[25] For perennially precarious institutions, such as Johannesburg's Market and Cape Town's Baxter and Fugard Theatres, revenues are increasingly dependent on popular revivals of "struggle classics" and British-American musical theater productions to remain solvent and appeal to audiences who largely still consist of white liberals. The postapartheid government, as part of a larger shift toward free market neoliberalism, has limited funding available for the arts, thus encouraging theater-makers to seek funding within the private sector.[26]

As theater struggled to reinvent itself in the country's new image, it has had to compete with other, newly emergent representational media. During apartheid, theater's only competition had been government-controlled newspaper, radio, and (after 1976) television. South Africans currently coming of age—the so-called Born Free Generation—have grown up alongside television programing mandated to represent the diverse nation. The state-owned South African Broadcasting Corporation (SABC), initially under the rainbow-hued slogan *Simunye* (we are one), produces nightly multiracial and multilingual soap operas, which have from the earliest years of democracy included gay and lesbian characters. While much scholarship on Africa and technology still frames the continent in terms of lack and "digital divide," the internet and cheap data-based texting applications such as Mx-It and WhatsApp have increasingly become a central source of information and entertainment for a young population. As I illustrate in chapter 4, in relation to the *Gensblog* soap opera online message board, South Africans simultaneously negotiate a variety of media spaces. With the majority now able to access (and create) global mediascapes through mobile phones, South Africans have become curators, performers, and audiences to the drama of social media.[27]

If scarcity and segregation defined apartheid's visual and performance cultures, excess and proliferation increasingly characterize the postapartheid public sphere, challenging South African theater scholars to expand their understanding and theorization of performance in this context. Noting that much postapartheid performance has, paradoxically, fixated on the (im)possibility of capturing "South Africanness" via performance, Anton Krueger posits that rather than rejecting constructions of race outright—in the embrace of multicultural sameness—postapartheid artists and practitioners have explored the limits of these inherited identity categories in order to see them from new angles. What forms do these performances take? What visions of nation, self, and other do they enact?

Prismatic Performances contends that an analysis of LGBT/queer identities provides one such necessary counterpoint to the overdetermined, primarily racial and ethnic, divisions that have consumed much of South African cultural production. Moreover, by tracing the figure of the "queer South African," we are able to gain a broader sense of the postapartheid cultural landscape. The sudden proliferation of queer bodies on stage, on television, online, and in the streets (as in the 2012 pride parade) signaled a departure from apartheid's culture of suppression and sexual puritanism, creating space for new narratives of diversity and openness, as well as anxiety.

The successes and gains of the LGBT movement in the first postapartheid decade had a paradoxically stultifying effect on the movement as a whole. Broad-based associations such as the National Coalition for Gay and Lesbian Equality and the Joint Working Group (formed to lobby for the 1996 Constitutional Equality Clause and 2006 same-sex marriage, respectively) shuttered, succumbing to internal dissent that had long been suppressed for the greater good of a united front. The "battle" for LGBT rights seemingly won, divisions within the movement became more apparent than ever, exposing the fact that legal rights were insufficient when those rights were not respected. For instance, those LGBT people among the twelve million South Africans classified as living in extreme poverty did not benefit from the boom in LGBT tourism following the 2008 recession. Strategically capitalizing on South Africa's natural beauty, vaunted constitution, and favorable dollar-to-rand exchange rate, private industry—from safaris to escort services—profited off the dual valence of the rainbow as signifier for both gay and nonracial imaginaries.[28] Thus, as US-Desi spoken-word performer Alok Vaid-Menon shrewdly observed, South Africa's rainbow homonationalism, pretty as it might be, might be viewed as the refraction of the white light of global capital.[29]

Bridging Queer Africa through Performance: Methodologies

In a terrain so overdetermined by structural inequality, attention to individual agency and action—both past and present—becomes particularly significant. *Prismatic Performances* intentionally approaches its case studies from an interdisciplinary orientation, assembling its argument through counterpunctual juxtaposition of key terms and embodiments. In close ethnographic engagement with readings of cultural production, I highlight how everyday life is experienced both alongside and through the consumption of popular media. While not primarily a historiographic project, the book argues that the past is intimately intertwined with the present, liable at any point to shift from backdrop to foreground. Spaces and publics, shaped by apartheid's racialized architecture and surveilled by postapartheid privatized security, are ghosted with national histories and intimate memories, creating, at times, palpable friction.

I was particularly struck by the rich multiplicity of this space walking across the iconic Nelson Mandela bridge in downtown Johannesburg during a July 2013 visit. Pausing in what was a riotous conversation with activist and Chosen FEW soccer player Manika, who plays a central role in chapter 2, I glanced down at the train tracks below. I suddenly realized that this was the same location where, over a decade before, performance artist Steven Cohen, the subject of chapter 1, had staged his iconic *Chandelier* intervention in a squatter camp, wearing the titular light-piece to illuminate gross wealth inequality. Cohen, who had previously used his "monster camp" to draw out white discomfort with queer embodiment, found himself upstaged by a much larger drama when a privatized security company arrived to dismantle this longtime informal community. Cohen was ignored and his homeless coperformers swept away to clear the space to construct the bridge on which I then stood, whose rainbow-lit spires reflected the nation's aspirations so magnificently. Retrospectively, Cohen's 2001 performance, as captured on film, serves to bridge past and future: its mechanized violence mediating between the legacy of apartheid-era forced removals and the coming decades of further displacement under postapartheid "urban renewal" projects. By 2013, the bridge provided an attractive pathway for foot traffic between the gentrifying inner-city neighborhoods of Braamfontein and Newtown.

As we continued walking, we returned to discussing our plans to attend an all-night house party in her neighborhood, where lesbians and gay men could drink and dance in relative safety. Though I had met Manika three years earlier, through her involvement with the Chosen FEW soccer team, I later realized that I had first encountered her image in 2008, as part of Zanele Muholi's *Faces and Phases* photography project (subject of chapter 3). Manika had also been an extra on the SABC 1 drama *Society*, which, next to the Johannesburg-based soap opera *Generations* (subject of chapter 4), was one of the few shows to have centrally featured gay characters. That Saturday morning, as Manika and I crossed over Bree Street, I could hear *Generations*' synth-y Afropop theme song echoing in the breeze, heralding the omnibus reruns of the previous week's episodes. The familiar refrain was accompanied by local Kwaito, American hip-hop, and gospel wafting out of the cramped "hair saloons" lining the Bree Street taxi rank, where we caught our minibus *koombi* taxi to head back to her home in the East Rand township of Vosloorus.

Capturing the interanimation of history, emotion, and location—geographical, political, and proximal—is crucial to understanding the investments that certain bodies have in certain spaces, and how identities are imagined within and through movement in space. Manika's involvement in Johannesburg's queer cultural life was not unusual, where queer activism, media, and sociality create a dense fabric of support. Queer worlds are small, and public queer stages smaller. She was also one of the One in Nine protesters attacked by white gay men at the 2012 Joburg Pride parade. These overlaps, which create the texture of queer worlds, would be lost if I took a more traditional, disciplinary route: only considering theatrical performance, everyday performance, or popular culture, for instance. Instead, I draw attention to how each site serves as a meeting point of a number of different narratives, histories, and affects during a particularly turbulent period of time in South Africa's history. Johannesburg, known variously as Joburg, eGoli, and Jozi, serves as a backdrop to much of the action in this book; looming large in the national imaginary, the metropolis's shifting, transitory populations and its repurposed material infrastructure make the city and its surrounds a stage for contestation and reinvention.

In exploring the collision of the politically and affectively charged terms "queer," "Africa," and "performance" in early twenty-first-century South Africa, this book enters into dialogue with the interdisciplinary field of queer African studies. Emerging in response to queer theory's largely unmarked Western orientation and African scholarship's largely unmarked heteronormativity, this discipline attends to the historical and contemporary erasure of queer African experiences. Its scholarship is diverse in both method and archive, united by a granular analysis of African narratives, texts, and histories that might be called queer. The field unapologetically positions itself as both a scholarly and political project, insisting that how we speak about African sexualities—in what languages, in which archives, through what repertoires—matters. This book takes the *matter* of queer African studies to its heart, arguing that performance studies—with its focus on embodiment, bridging different ways of knowing, and audience reception—is a potent, underutilized methodological contribution to the field.

While the disciplinary contours of queer African studies continue to evolve, its most substantive scholarly interventions have thus far emerged from disciplines with strong traditions in archival, ethnographic, and discursive analysis. Colonial archives have provided historians and anthropologists rich ground for strategic excavation. Beyond seeking out absent queer narratives,[30] scholars have positioned these archives as historically grounded inverted mirrors, challenging popular discourse about the alleged "un-Africanness" of same-gender desire. Through this framing, homo*phobia*, inherited from sodomy laws and missionary texts, emerges as the colonial import, rather than homosexuality.[31] Indeed, scholars argue that the colonial contact zone could itself be productively read as queer if run through the refractive matrix of its racialized desires and intimacies.[32] These excavations of queer pasts are complemented by a number of closely observed ethnographies that document queer presence in the present tense.[33] The variety of postapartheid queer narratives documented—ranging from beauty pageants,[34] to urban township gender constructions,[35] to members of mostly white ex-gay ministry and black gay and lesbian churches[36]—provides the rich theoretical underpinning for this study's understanding of how location and context shape discrete, culturally situated manifestations of desire and identity. In reading postapartheid queer representations and national narratives through the prism of performance, this book contributes a much-needed embodied dimension to a field that has previously primarily addressed this intersection in literature.[37]

Individual scholars have long written about sexuality in Africa in innovative ways.[38] Only recently, however, has this scholarship reached such a critical mass as to form its own discrete field and canon.[39] While queer African studies' organic and interdisciplinary development has resulted in rich conversations across a variety of locations and registers, its differing vocabularies have created moments of ideological and discursive tension. This book proposes that some of these tensions can be bridged—or at least productively engaged—through a more sustained analysis of the performing body and its varied audiences.

One of the most contentious methodological debates involves the application of Western-based theory in non-Western contexts, which almost all scholars discussed here acknowledge as a site of ambivalence. "Queer theory" has become a particular sticking point for certain scholars, who view it as standing in for all that is disembodied and imported. In *Heterosexual Africa?* (2008) Marc Epprecht makes impassioned argument against the continued use of "queer theory" in general and the word "queer" in particular when discussing African sexualities. Noting that "queer" is part of a long history of Western theory imperfectly mapped onto African contexts, Epprecht argues that any theorization of African sexualities not gained through significant time spent in Africa alongside African collaborators is inherently flawed: "The gap between queer theory as stated and queer theory as practiced, in short, deeply compromises the project."[40] Yet, as Kenyan scholar Keguro Macharia points out, such perspectives deny African subjects entry into contemporary debates a priori, leaving them "fixed in anthropological time," as objects rather than actors. How, Macharia wonders, "might one describe the encounter between 'queer' and 'Africa' without the weight of anthropology as gaze, as frame, as method, as affect, as expectation, as pleasure?"[41]

Prismatic Performances takes up this provocation, arguing that performance studies can be a particularly productive tool for navigating and deconstructing the anthropological gaze that has for so long been the dominant framework for documenting African lives and sexualities. It posits that the space of imperfect translation between queer theory and practice—symbolic discourse and material embodiment—put forth by Epprecht as a failure, can equally be viewed as a productive space of charged potentiality. Though Epprecht is right to question the imperfect application of Western theoretical paradigms, consigning "theory" (conceptual thought) to the West and, implicitly, "practice" (embodied action) to Africans poses the danger of reinvoking enlightenment binaries. This division creates a gap that does not need to exist and ignores the ways that "queer theory" is itself a flexible conceptual tool, one that can be used to deconstruct and critique structures of knowledge and power. When queer theory is put into dialogue with queer practice(s), queer practices themselves become the locus of new queer theories. Where queer subjects put their rights into action—literally, their bodies on the line, in the case of the One in Nine protesters—they engage and make visible the norms governing postapartheid space: they put theory into practice.

Though "queer" may not have been taken up as broadly as a self-descriptor in African contexts as it has been in the West, it *has* been adopted strategically by a number of activist organizations and by African scholars across the continent. Ugandan feminist scholar Sylvia Tamale, editor of the capacious, African-authored *African Sexualities: A Reader* (2011), persuasively argues that many theories deriving from the West can be a useful starting point for revision and reimagination. Rather than view the relationship between theory and practice as an insurmountable gap, Tamale views it as a "circuitous, undulating process."[42] Here methodology itself, far from being static, can be "a political process, a 'space' in which complex issues of context, voice, ethics, and ideological depth are played out. . . . It is part and parcel of theory-building and transformative change."[43] However, as Ugandan scholar and activist Stella Nyanzi notes, this space cannot solely be the preserve of Western theorists. Particularly in contexts where queerness is viewed as a neocolonial import, "Euphemisms, metaphors, similes, proverbs, and riddles must be re-read queerly, alongside gestures, silences, erasures and invisiblization."[44] Rather than obfuscating texts and imported academic genealogies, Nyanzi argues, scholarship on queer Africa needs to reimagine oral and nonverbal repertoires, drawing out the (culturally specific) "queerness" that has always been present.

Both Tamale's insistence on the inseparability of experience and its theorization and Nyanzi's evocation of queer Africa's gestural repertoire, importantly, center the live body as a crucial site of discursive intervention. Their words uncannily echo performance theorist Dwight Conquergood's description of how performance "struggles to open the space between analysis and action, and to pull the pin on the binary opposition between theory and practice," revealing them to be interrelated and coconstitutive. Conquergood cites the "promiscuous traffic between different ways of knowing [as] carr[ying] the most radical promise of performance studies research."[45] While South African queerness has been theorized across a number of disciplinary and methodological positions, very few have focused on the meanings of the queer South African body in space. None have concentrated on how this body mediates between the discursive understanding of imagined categories (such as "homosexual" and "African"), the material enactment of those bodies, and their reception within varied interpretive communities.[46]

Throughout *Prismatic Performances*, I engage academic theory, analyze embodied practice, and document theory-in-practice, using the latter to illuminate the former and to make an intervention into studies of African queerness and queerness more generally. My analysis of the Chosen FEW, a soccer team and activist organization for black lesbians in and around Johannesburg, for instance, explicitly addresses the gaps between differing expectations of "Africanness" in their varied communities. Rather than drawing exclusively on the work of queer and performance theorists to analyze the players' lived experiences, I pose their self-understandings and languages as innovative ways of doing theory, and pose their particular subjunctive relation toward futurity as an African intervention into recent theory on queer utopias. Indeed, this fluidity is one of the most valuable contributions of performance studies as a methodology: an ability to bridge different ways of knowing and to view knowledge and culture as contingent. Following Tamale, they are "undulating processes."

Mapping the Postapartheid Queer Landscape

In *Prismatic Performances* I contend that queer embodiments, because of their ambiguous relation to the nation-state, serve as unstable and prismatic lenses on the postapartheid moment. In one sense, legal incorporation into the body politic allowed certain (often white, cisgender, middle and upper class) queer bodies access to citizenship that had previously been proper to white reproductive heterosexuals: basking in the light of white-controlled neoliberal capitalism in multicultural, yet class-segregated spaces such as Rosebank. Those whose bodies did not fit the brand of recalibrated, cosmopolitan citizenship that Joseph Massad has termed the "Gay International"—those queers and gender nonconforming people who fell in the rainbow's metaphorical shadow—were kept out via a broad system of privatized policing.[47] Yet those queer "others" whose presence actively disrupts the pageantry of a unified postapartheid identity, as One in Nine's intervention into Joburg Pride highlights, facilitate a mode of seeing differently.

The fractures and refractions, jarring against the appeal of the rainbow success story, make visible not only the fragmentations, but also reflect the possibility for more expansive geographies of both queerness and Africanness. As South African queer theorists Zethu Matebeni and Jabu Pereira have argued, taken together, queer African cultural production, theorization, and community hold the potential to transform the site of cultural alienation ("un-Africanness") into one of cultural belonging. Queering Afrika (their spelling) can thus be a radically decolonial act of imagination and reterritorialization, "cut[ting] across the rigid borders and boundaries that have for so many years made us feel disconnected and fractured."[48] The performances charted in this book complicate the binary coming-out narrative imported from the West and circumvent the limited right-based framework of the South African constitution. They unsettle national narratives in order to reconfigure them and reveal divided spaces in order to reclaim them.

Having now laid out the prismatic as an analytic, the following chapter transports us to an earlier moment of possibility—the mid-1990s interregnum period—outlining two white drag performers' strategic use of gender subversion to mark the political transition from white minority rule to a nonracial democracy during Mandela's presidency. At a time when apartheid had been abandoned but the conceptual borders of the New South Africa had yet to fully take shape, satirist Pieter-Dirk Uys and performance artist Steven Cohen each used drag to reflect and refract the affective excess and ontological insecurity of the first decade of the New South Africa. Both artists attempted to transform South African whiteness into a queer sort of "Africanness," embracing aesthetics of simultaneity and critique that previewed a possible revision of racial, gendered, and cultural signs. Though the imperfect transition to democracy inevitably foreclosed the efficacy of these transformational gestures, Uys's and Cohen's failures, as much as their successes, highlight the complexities of performing the racialized body.

Chapter 2 charts the everyday performances of members of Johannesburg's Chosen FEW soccer team. As an all-black, out lesbian soccer team on a continent noted for its homophobia, the Chosen FEW experienced a brief brush with international fame during the 2010 FIFA World Cup, where their stories—variously casting them as victims and victors—were mobilized by journalists to comment on the state of the by-then-flagging Rainbow Nation. While 2010 marked a brief national return to Rainbow optimism, the games failed to provide the economic panacea that many had hoped. This chapter, drawn from five years of ethnographic fieldwork, explores the players' lives in the immediate aftermath of their time in the limelight. It contends that their daily performances of complex, out black lesbian subjectivity provide a far more nuanced engagement with post-apartheid contradictions than the pat narratives into which they were initially drafted during the national spectacle. By utilizing the subjunctive framework of acting "as if" (as if their constitutional rights were protected), the players were able to latch onto queer's utopian possibilities. Yet, unlike utopia, their quotidian performances in hostile environments were, of necessity, pragmatic, maintained through a series of what I term *subjunctive performatives*.

I then move from the quotidian performances of a single group of black lesbians to consider the broader ethics of representing and witnessing sexual violence through art and performance. Chapter 3 takes as its focus the popular and artistic representations of a phenomenon popularly known as *Corrective* or *Curative Rape*—where men specifically target lesbians for rape to "correct" them "back" to heterosexuality. Noting how protecting lesbians from being correctively raped by black South African men has become something of a cause célèbre in the West, I outline the aesthetic strategies employed by two black queer artists to represent sexual trauma in a way that avoids prurience and neither trivializes nor retraumatizes survivors. The ongoing bodies of work by photographer Zanele Muholi and choreographer Mamela Nyamza draw attention to their subjects' always-already-vexed relationship to visibility, marked either invisible (un-African) or hypervisible (in their assault). Their work engages an *aesthetic of displacement* to performatively displace spectators' focus from the violated bodies onto their own complex and ambivalent desire to view the violation.

The book's final chapter analyzes the impact of proliferating virtual spaces during this period, arguing that they create new possibilities for deliberation on the nature of queer African identity. A virtual ethnography of the online response to a gay storyline on the wildly popular South African soap opera *Generations*, chapter 4 traces how soap operas and their virtual fandoms—each requiring a high investment of time and emotion—can create space to transgress bodily, cultural, and national boundaries. It focuses on *Gensblog*, an online message board that, at its height, hosted a community of hundreds of geographically dispersed black middle-class bloggers across the African continent who daily logged on to discuss their South African favorite "soapie." The participants' playful performative spectatorship was thrown into crisis when confronted with the reality of a love story between two black South African men in what was then the country's most visible and aspirational space celebrating black South African success. I posit *Gensblog* users' shifting responses to the storyline over several years as a revealing microcosm for a larger national cultural crisis that the storyline triggered. Far from being frivolous or uncritical, the serialized emotionality of the soap opera genre, coupled with viewers' investment in their online space, moved an initially resistant audience to confront their homophobia and shift their perceptions toward a more inclusive definition of Africanness.

Prismatic Performances concludes by returning to its beginning. I consider the long-term impact of One in Nine's protest, the resulting collapse of Joburg Pride, and the emergence of a new grassroots organization, People's Pride, as previewing future queer social movements. This pride celebration, first organized in 2013 by radical queer and antiracist activists, retraced the route of the first pride parade in the inner city and embraced a number of overlapping, seemingly contradictory affects and agendas. These queer enactments, breaking the spatial norms of the inner city, not only made those norms visible but, with their presence, reshaped its possible futures. While Nelson Mandela's death in December of that year signaled the end of a particular postapartheid Rainbow moment, I close by briefly tracing recent reinvigoration of queer activism. Prismatic performances, in fracturing spatial and temporal norms, refract in ways that are not always predictable, and—as the postapartheid landscape continues to shift and evolve—extend outward to create new acts and audiences.

While its title indexes the Rainbow Nation as a space of fragmentation—an inadequate aspirational identity, fractured from its inception—*Prismatic Performances* views this space of broken dreams as simultaneously one of reanimation and imagination. The performances I chart are not meant to be representative—either of queer South Africa or South African performance generally—but are rather rich cross-sections of contested terrain: glimpses into how queer performances weave, unravel, and transform the fabric of the postapartheid physical and imaginary landscape.

ONE

A Queer Transition

Prismatic Whiteness in Postapartheid Drag Performance

In November 1994, just six months after he had been elected president of South Africa's first democratic, nonracial government, Nelson Mandela appeared on a talk show hosted by a drag queen. Evita Beduidenhout, an Afrikaans matron and satirist Pieter-Dirk Uys's most famous persona, hosted the politically themed *Evita's Funigalore.* As his alter ego Evita, Uys vacillated between flirting with the president and posing hard-hitting questions. Mandela acted genial and relaxed, discussing his new government's policies, complimenting his hostess, and flirting right back: "Ah Evita, my dear, you look so beautiful!"[1] A satirical drag performer might seem to be an odd interlocutor for a president overseeing one of the most highly anticipated transfers of power in recent history, yet Mandela viewed Evita as a tactical intermediary between his ANC government and the cable channel MNet's primarily white audience.[2] The elections had passed the previous April without the feared race war between white and black. Mandela had painted a rosy vision of the Beloved Country in his inauguration speech, invoking a postapartheid "rainbow nation, at peace with itself and the world."[3] Yet lingering factional ethnic violence between Xhosa, Zulu, and white Afrikaner groups suggested that the voting box alone could not overcome forty-six years of the enforced divisions of apartheid and over three hundred years of colonial rule. The new government's legitimacy remained tenuous, particularly among the white minority that had been indoctrinated to believe that their new leaders were terrorists. Mandela conscripted Evita, a familiar figure from years of Uys's satirical revues and television specials, into the new national narrative of the "Rainbow Nation."

Though initially conceived by Uys during the 1980s' state of emergency

Fig, 2. Evita/Uys and Nelson Mandela at former president F. W. de Klerk's birthday party, 2006. The photograph, signed by Mandela, reads: "To Evita, Best wishes to a wonderful lady." Original photo by Eric Miller, courtesy of Pieter-Dirk Uys.

as a satirical reflection of white privilege and complicity, Evita played a participatory role in the transition to democracy and the earliest years of the postapartheid dispensation. During the second presidential election in 1999, Uys-as-Evita led a nationwide get-out-the-vote campaign on the streets and in the halls of parliament. He later commented in his memoir on the incongruity that Evita—an invented, satirical character—received an official parliamentary send-off from those who were shaping the realities of postapartheid life: "Here I was in Parliament, by invitation, and in drag! . . . the nation watched in amazement as *Tannie* [Auntie] Evita commanded the attention of those who ruled, managing to dissolve them into hysterics."[4] This incongruity—and the frisson between drag transformation and transformational politics—made Evita Bezuidenhout a singular figure in the postapartheid public sphere.

Yet in the face of unprecedented political and cultural openness, not all artists were so optimistic about the future of whiteness in South Africa. Performance artist Steven Cohen used drag to explore whiteness's unassimilatability and strangeness within the South African landscape. As Evita took to parliament in her get-out-the-vote campaign, Cohen, a performer known for shocking guerrilla interventions, arrived at his local voting station—in a primarily black neighborhood—wearing whiteface makeup, a short black corset, a crown of feathers, a Star of David glued to his forehead, and boots with meter-long gemsbok horns for stilettos.[5] Unable to walk in his "heels," Cohen crawled on all fours, pulling himself along the pavement, much to the bemusement of those waiting in line with him. Cohen's intervention concerned the body's limitations, as he performed gymnastic feats in ten-inch heels, with trussed testicles and a variety of butt plugs. Where Uys used drag to engage audiences critically through humor, Cohen's work—judging by the shocked bystander reactions in his filmed interventions—was alien in whatever landscape he inhabited. His self-proclaimed "monster drag" touched something unspoken and taboo about the values given to postapartheid bodies, and the darker shadows that haunted the narrative of the Rainbow Nation.

This chapter analyzes performances by these two artists during the long decade bisected by South Africa's political transition, from roughly 1990 to 2001, arguing that drag and gender subversion allowed for what I am calling a *prismatic* deconstruction of white identity in the context of political transformation. Race's inescapable primacy in the South African imagination at that time made for extremely charged conversational ground in public discourse. By contrast, queerness and gender subversion, while subject to prosecution under the apartheid era's Immorality Act, were arguably far less visible vectors of difference during apartheid. They were, however, central to the country's postapartheid self-fashioning, as South Africa became the first country in the world to explicitly include sexual orientation as a protected category in its 1996 constitution's bill of rights. As a phenomenon only emerging broadly in the national consciousness in the 1990s, queerness was explicitly aligned with the new Rainbow Nation paradigm and therefore uniquely positioned to mediate between and across racial divides when made visible through strategic performances in the postapartheid era. In the context of a country rapidly transforming, Uys's and Cohen's drag performances made space for audiences to engage with the history and future of whiteness and, particularly, white masculinity. Where racial difference had been constructed as monolithic and impenetrable during the apartheid regime, these artists used the prism of drag to facilitate the process of seeing race differently. Through a process of categorical ambiguity and affective displacement, Uys and Cohen each used drag to open up a space for the whites who had formerly been classified as "European" to claim a queer form of Africanness.

As outlined in the Introduction, my evocation of the prism—a three-dimensional geode that creates a rainbow by refracting and deconstructing light into its composite parts—plays on both South Africa's metanarrative as the Rainbow Nation, united in its diversity, and the rainbow as the global symbol for gay rights and visibility. Where a prism separates light into its composite parts to create the one-dimensional rainbow image, a prismatic *performance* reflects and refracts the emotional investments projected onto it by its audiences. My analysis here draws both implicitly and explicitly upon the foundational work of scholars of drag and gender performance. Marjorie Garber's conception of the cross-dresser or transvestite onstage as indicative of a societal "crisis of categories,"[6] for instance, has obvious resonance with the period of South Africa's political transition broadly referred to as the interregnum. Yet in her focus on the figure of "The Transvestite"—primarily in Euro-American context—Garber's argument is unable to fully capture the cultural specificity and range of meanings that emerged in the postapartheid context. Moreover, as Laurence Senelick has commented in his critique of Garber, the rhetoric of crisis (which views the cross-dressing performer as a mere reflection of current cultural anxieties) misses the ways in which performance itself shapes that culture and produces something new. Those aspects of gender performance "observed in life," Senelick notes, "become refracted through the theatrical presentation: if the stage is a mirror, it is a funhouse mirror, magnifying, distorting, and ultimately sending out an image in which the shock of recognition is promoted by an alienation effect."[7] This space, between societal reflection and Brechtian refraction, becomes the staging space for what I am calling the prismatic, an aesthetic that privileges simultaneity and contradiction (of both/and) over categorization and division (of either/or). The exact impact of these performances is dependent on the affective triangulation between performing body, space, and audience.[8]

Performance functions prismatically when white audiences watch as the former black "terrorist" Nelson Mandela embraces a white woman—triggering anxieties of cultural and sexual miscegenation—who, on second glance, is a man in drag. The ambiguity of Uys's drag performance—the moment of (mis)recognition, caught between genders, between "reality" and "play"—may disorient his audiences; their confusion about Uys's gender ambiguity would then force them to reorient their conception of racial difference and proximity, the two pillars of apartheid. This reorientation through humor and camp allowed audiences to view the time-space of post-1994 South Africa as a space for reconstituting fixed identities, outside of the bounds of the previous regime. Steven Cohen's dragging himself through the dirt to vote alongside those who had formerly been considered less than fully human performs a similar intervention, presenting a white masculinity defined by its otherness in relation to the newly elected majority. In their vulnerability and strangeness, Cohen's performances suggest that the white body could be transformed into a beast both monstrous and, in its degradation, potentially beautiful.

Uys's and Cohen's strategic performances of whiteness reject the oppressive norms of South African white masculinity while still claiming allegiance to a South African identity, of which whiteness is just one queer form. This prismatic process—of avowal refracted through disavowal—is key to José Muñoz's theory of disidentification.[9] My analysis resists any totalizing theory of drag that would frame these performances as inherently reflective or deconstructive of the culture in which they were created. Rather, I draw on this fertile theoretical ground from the location of the particular racial geometry of transition-era South Africa, attentive to the ways in which white masculinity was constructed alongside and against other historical configurations of race and gender.

Here I follow scholarship in critical race theory in conceptualizing whiteness as a historical construct used to justify imperial conquest and domination and aided by collusion of medical, judicial, and religious institutions.[10] Whiteness in South Africa, despite the best efforts of apartheid architects to construct a monolithic vision of the race, was deeply divided on cultural, linguistic, and religious fronts between multiple groups. The *boer* (farmer) Afrikaners descended from employees of the Dutch East India Company who arrived at the Cape of Good Hope in the 1600s; they intermixed with the indigenous Khoi/San inhabitants of the Cape, before migrating inland to escape the influence of the British, who in 1820 imported four thousand citizens to settle the interior of its newly minted colony. These settlers then served as a buffer between the Cape and the Zulu tribes who resisted colonial insurgence. Complicating this narrative further, over thirty thousand Lithuanian Jews immigrated to South Africa during the late nineteenth-century pogroms and found success in the gold and diamond industries. South Africa, unique in the world, offered Jews full benefits of whiteness, which allowed them to prosper off of black labor in the mineral industry. During apartheid these differences within whiteness and lingering resentments from the Anglo-Boer War (1899–1902) were largely contained by the government's use of fear tactics, the supposed looming *swaart gevaar* (black threat). Much as Uys and Cohen used queerness and gender subversion to critique race at the cusp of democracy, they also drew on their Judaism and its complex histories as both victim and beneficiary, to illuminate the fractures within any unitary concept of whiteness.[11]

In what follows, I analyze the paradoxes of whiteness revealed in these fractures as they are negotiated by each artist and chart the different performative tactics used by each to reenvision whiteness and Africanness through the prism of drag.[12]

Pieter-Dirk Uys and/as Evita Bezuidenhout: The Most Famous White Woman in Africa

Evita Bezuidenhout was born out of necessity. Following the 1976 student uprising in Soweto, the National Party censored all reports of the violence and resistance that increasingly gripped the country. In 1978, an editor for *Sunday Express* asked Uys to write a weekly column. Faced with the prospect of having to write something trivial or be banned, the playwright decided to use the format of a society insider's gossip column in order to escape attention. He juxtaposed Evita's triviality with the violent reality that crept under the surface of her society life. Evita Bezuidenhout first appeared as a nameless wife of a National Party member of parliament, writing about political scandals and rumors. She became so popular among readers that she earned the nickname "The Evita of Pretoria." In 1981, Uys embodied her in his one-man revue *Adapt or Dye*. Over the next decade, through a number of performances, Uys developed a labyrinthine Bezuidenhout family mythology.

In 1990, the year of Mandela's release from prison, Uys began to reconfigure Evita from a relatively one-dimensional depiction of white ignorance to a more fully developed woman struggling with a rapidly changing world. In his exhaustive biography of Evita, *A Part Hate, a Part Love,* Uys revisits much of the material of his earlier revues to undermine apartheid's official history, using Evita as a touchstone to highlight all of the inconvenient parts of history that white South Africa had not been completely able to overwrite. Evita Bezuidenhout, like her Argentinian counterpart Eva Peron, started her career in the local film industry before marrying a government official. When her MP husband suffered several strokes, she took over his political career to become the self-proclaimed "most famous white woman in Africa." As the South African ambassador to the independent black homeland Bapetikosweti, a fictionalized Bantustan,[13] Evita became an overseer of apartheid's ultimate goal of a South Africa without blacks. Yet as she held court at her mansion, the aptly titled Blanche-Noir situated on the dividing line between South Africa and Bapetikosweti, her emotional fault lines began to widen as the apartheid dream exploded into flames around her.

The New South Africa would be defined by grand, space-clearing legislation, meant to serve, in the words of Constitutional Court chief justice Albie Sachs, as "radical rupture from a past based on intolerance and exclusion," in hopes of facilitating an equal and integrated society.[14] Evita's breakdown on the fault line between Cloud Cuckooland and the rapidly approaching end of apartheid paralleled this dramatic, traumatic rupture for the sake of national unity. Yet Evita's "radical rupture" came not with a political bang but with a personal whimper, when her daughter announced her plans to marry Evita's black gardener's son. Evita found herself unable to justify her prejudices in the face of her daughter's happiness. Her house, like apartheid during the 1980s, became a self-inflicted prison without hope for escape.

In the "found" pages of her diary, Uys dramatizes a woman in the midst of her own transition and identity crisis. Trapped in a state of indeterminacy between an impossible past and an unknown future, Evita struggles to articulate the ever-fracturing aspects of her identity as an Afrikaner and a mother. The entries begin with anger and accusations and trail off into elliptical phrases. For example:

> Friday 22 July
>
> I'm sorry I'm not white. Damn it, I'm working hard to stay white and no one is going to take that away from me! It's some time

> later . . . I think . . . God I'm so tired . . . I read this diary . . . something is wrong with me . . . I think I must be going mad . . . I am sick . . . Help me . . . am I mad?[15]

Evita's breakdown is triggered by what could be called a racial "category crisis," spurred by the possibility of not only broken apartheid laws, but of having a Coloured (mixed race) grandchild. Mixed-race bodies always held a destabilizing role in apartheid South African society. They were instrumentalized by the apartheid government as a unique racial category and a "buffer" of sorts between other subjugated populations of color, the "Indians" and "Africans"; yet the very existence of a large Coloured population revealed the lie about the purity and incommensurability of the races. Faced with this personal crisis of racial definition, Evita realizes that she is not white and cannot be white when "whiteness" means denying the humanity of her family members. This dilemma was likely familiar to many of Uys's white audiences in the late 1980s and early 1990s. Like Evita, they did not know how to be white without the framing context of apartheid. Anthropologist Melissa Steyn's work on postapartheid whiteness suggests that while the end of apartheid wrought a multiplicity of responses from white individuals—ranging from racist defensiveness to enthusiastic embrace of ethnocentric "Africanness"—the responses of her subjects were linked by one common theme: material, ideological, and profound loss.[16] Much of Uys's performance in Evita's biography addresses these losses by undermining the foundational mythologies of apartheid, leading the readers toward the climax of her eventual crisis.

Though Evita's antics were often ridiculous, her sense of profound psychological stress is treated seriously, in part because they mirrored Uys's own youthful experience of cross-racial intimacy at the height of apartheid, cruising the rocks at the "in-between zone" on segregated beaches for casual sex. These brief affairs led to deeper connections, where he "started feeling less white, and more real," realizing "if being human meant finding your own way and following your inner instinct, then being naked on that beach with confidence may have been the first step to being naked in the world with commitment! Stripped of all the deceit and disguise that comes with fear."[17]

Uys's philosophy, both in life and in performance, is that to be African is to not be white or black (or Coloured), but rather to be human. Being human requires a radical humility that doesn't hide behind so-called color-blind nonracialism, but demands an engagement with the psychic and material remnants of a colonial, racist society. As Richard Dyer notes, whiteness's unexamined claim to universality is imbricated in power dynamics: "There is no more powerful position than that of being 'just' human. The claim to power is the claim to speak for the commonality of humanity."[18] South African cultural critic Njabulo Ndebele centers the body as both the site of violation and, conversely, the site of reintegration and the development of a culture of rootedness. Ndebele argues that only by repudiating the "global sanctity of the white body" can white South Africans claim an African identity: "Putting itself at risk, it will have to declare that it is home now, sharing in the vulnerability of other compatriot bodies. South African whiteness will declare that its dignity is inseparable from the dignity of black bodies."[19] Through this process, Ndebele argues, white South Africans can earn cultural citizenship. This process of self-reflection/refraction through the Other was central to the postapartheid popularity of *ubuntu*, a Nguni traditional philosophy popularized by Archbishop Desmond Tutu.[20]

Yet even as Uys and Evita became devotees of the Rainbow Nation, the duality of their performance always critiqued the difficulty or impossibility of a full transformation. The gap between Evita's sincerity and Uys's satire—and between Uys's philosophy of being "naked with confidence," stripped of disguise, and his performance's *use* of disguise as a method of critique—confronts the audience with a productive, multifaceted paradox. Rather than a dangerous humanism, with the authority to claim universality, Uys's work confronts the naked human body with the deceits and histories in which it cloaks itself. The ability to be "fully human" has to be earned; layers of cultural baggage must first be acknowledged before they are stripped away. Uys's satire demonstrates white baggage for what it is: armor, dividing lines, barred windows, and electric fences of fear and privilege. It signals, in the person of Evita, its *potential* for change, adaptation, and transformation.

Throughout the early and mid-1990s, Uys primarily directed his cabarets at white audiences. He aimed to drag these audiences—quite literally—through their fear and ambivalence into the postapartheid era. Though his cabaret shows included Evita, she usually arrived to begin the second act and never stayed long. While Evita remained the principal attraction, these shows—with three- to five-minute skits—provided a larger commentary on the many of faces of whiteness in South Africa, providing ample opportunity for audience (dis)identification. Where the apartheid government had stifled dissent and put forth a unified white community, Uys's skits modeled the diversity that had always been *within* whiteness. His 1992 performance at the Baxter Theatre in Cape Town, for instance, presented a number of white archetypes, running the gamut of white characters from two well-meaning farmers trying to mate their pigs, to an Afrikaans girl who—realizing she's too white to be Miss South Africa—decides to run for an international Miss Scarlett O'Hara contest.

Though he occasionally portrayed Winnie Mandela or Desmond Tutu, Uys mainly focused on his white figures and, in particular, white men. The evening's most strikingly serious skit involved a torturer encountering a man he had tortured (both white) during a Madonna concert. While their interaction began with pleasantries, the torturer increasingly taunted his victim with their shared history and his own position enjoying the fruits of the new South Africa, scot-free. On the recorded video of one performance, the previously gregarious audience's laughter became progressively nervous, as the interaction between the two white men reflected the post-conflict reality. Who, they perhaps asked, might be sitting next to them in the theater? What must be forgotten in the name of reconciliation?[21]

In portraying so many different types of whiteness, Uys addresses his audience from within by deconstructing the concept of a unitary whiteness to explore whiteness's many shades and ethnicities (encompassing a variety of class, language, and political positions). Beyond gendered drag performance, Uys performs what Katrin Seig has termed ethnic drag, a form of performance that "exposes and disavows traumatic holes in the social fabric, and facilitates both historical denial and collective mourning."[22] Indeed, though most of Uys's interregnum satires attempted to draw unity from fractured histories, they remained rooted in mourning the losses experienced in apartheid, both of shared humanity and of past privilege. Rather than dwell in the melancholia of the past, his performances used humor to move his audiences through loss and to a hopeful vision of the future. Following her epiphany, Evita evolved with the times, becoming a public face for white change and adaptation. Unemployed after Bapetikosweti reincorporated into South Africa's mainland, she catered meetings between the ANC in exile and the members of the apartheid government. These interactions with former "terrorists" inspired the premise of *Funigalore* and Uys's goal of engaging a white audience with its fears. In her very public blundering, Evita modeled a new mode of being white. Beyond humanizing those who had been labeled "enemy" by the apartheid government, her approach to living in a democratic South

Africa created a pathway for whites to rehumanize a much more insidious enemy: the fear and racism in themselves.

Uys also notably used Evita to shift the signifying power of whiteness for nonwhites. Evita's sincere desire to participate in the new postapartheid government's project of nation-building took her (and him) away from traditional, theatrical venues, and into more public and populist spheres. The success of *Funigalore* led to a number of other television appearances and made her face familiar to a variety of audiences. In her 1999 "get-out-the-vote" *indaba*,[23] Evita underscored the importance of public engagement in democracy at diverse venues. Uys's presence in townships—spaces where the majority of white South Africans rarely went—was cause enough for disruption; his presence in those historically divided spaces as Evita created a liminal zone that blurred the lines between the day-to-day experiential negotiations of power in postapartheid South Africa and theatrical performance. By creating a space that encouraged nonwhite audiences to play along and laugh at their (previous) oppressors, Uys urged spectators to imagine new ways of engaging with democracy and making it their own. People who might otherwise not listen to either Uys as a well-meaning satirist or Evita as a "real" recovering-Afrikaner Nationalist matron, were—judging by his large and enthusiastic township audiences—willing to listen because the satire provided a space for them to critique white privilege.

In order for Uys's performances to be effective, the audience needed to be "in on the joke," able to recognize the man underneath the woman. When s/he was (mis)recognized, s/he seemed to represent all that was bad about the old regime: patronizing whites bossing blacks around. Uys recounts one such instance from an *indaba* in Mamelodi Township:

> I notice a black woman in the middle block listening to Evita's chat with a frown. She is not impressed by this loud Afrikaans woman being so racist, so superior and so warmly received by other black people. What is wrong here? She obviously doesn't know the secret! Eventually her companion laughingly whispers in her ear. Evita's critic dissolves into chuckles and becomes a fan. Once they know that this woman is actually a man, Evita can say anything![24]

Once the premise of his performance as Evita was understood, and the tone set, Uys worked hard to ensure that "the women recognize the woman and the men forget the man."[25] Uys's incursions with Evita in the public sphere arguably challenged these strict, gendered divisions and, in the process, queered and transformed the signifying power of whiteness.

Evita's ability to transgress numerous postapartheid spaces destabilized the naturalness of racial and gender categories, requiring of her audiences a suspension of belief, a leap of faith, and a willingness to play and laugh at one's self and one's Others.

In interviews, Uys frequently refers to Evita as his clown, noting that she resonated with audiences because of her familiarity as well as her outlandishness: "In the old days when the world was normal, the clown had to have purple hair and a green nose. And the world is now totally crazy, so the clown has to be totally real. What is happening is not original, it is absurd."[26] With "Reality [as] her purple hair and Familiarity [as] her large red nose,"[27] much like Shakespeare's fool, Evita assumed the role of the jester as truth-teller who can skewer holy cows and kings with relative impunity. Clowns have historically operated in the realm of the satirical, overplaying the social hierarchies, only to reveal their absurdity. Evita's gender performance—her immaculately coiffed hair and makeup, and Uys's total commitment to making her real, both on stage and in public spaces—is part of his critique, creating a vivid, real person with a history whose supposed gentility and believability only underscores the banality of apartheid's evil. During apartheid, Uys played Evita as the ultimate insider, operating within and against the theater industry where he produced his revues. Evita's current, postapartheid incursions into the public sphere are more complex. She critiques the government from an ostensibly disempowered, minority position. Yet she also operates with a certain amount of authority; as a reformed insider from the previous regime, she has the perspective to draw uncomfortable parallels between the old regime's tactics and the new regime's avoidance, particularly around issues of HIV/AIDS and censorship.

In a postapartheid space, Uys's white face serves as the clown's whiteface; Evita, as a character, wears no mask. She reveals the best intentions and the worst ignorance of all white South Africans. Her desire to change and to participate in the system is utterly sincere. This sincerity, the desire to be the *gogo* (grandmother) of the nation, places her as an unlikely guardian of (im)morality. She is a relic from the past, reinvented, but with a survivor's memory. She has the authority (both of her "past" and of her invented nature) to make uncomfortable comparisons, a position that very few people (white or black, real or fictitious) occupy. By playing this role, Evita Bezuidenhout—fictional character or not—models a whiteness that is rooted in its complicity in South Africa's past and, therefore, even more engaged in its present.

Despite his use of drag, Uys is unimpressed with being pinned down as a "gay performer." Though he acknowledges that his identities are numerous, Uys's priority as a white, middle-aged, gay man has always been to subsume those identity positions under the larger category of shared humanity. When I met with him in 2008 in a café near his home in the Western Cape town of Darling and asked him what role his queerness plays in his work, he responded fervently, expressing frustration with what he sees as an unnecessarily confrontational approach taken by early years of South Africa's (recently unbanned) gay rights movement:

> For me gay rights and human rights are the same thing, not something specific. Noel Coward always said, "Don't make too much noise and frighten the horses. Do whatever you want to do, but don't frighten the horses." And I believe it: don't frighten the horses. Don't confront people with children and make them frightened by being the bogeyman by saying, "I'm going to take your child's trousers off and suck his penis!" No! I would be the first person to say, "Fuck off, you don't say that sort of thing."[28]

Now well into their seventies, Evita Bezuidenhout and Pieter-Dirk Uys continue to inhabit a number of (often seemingly contradictory) social spaces in South Africa's public sphere. Evita and Uys highlight and attempt to bridge the country's raced, gendered, and classed divisions. He is the gay-Boer-Jew who makes a career of inhabiting others' subjectivities. She is the staunchly heterosexual *Boeremeisie*,[29] once the darling of the National Party and now with three black grandchildren. By holding South Africa's varied identities and histories close to—and against—his skin, Uys's prismatic performances not only reflect the continued divisions, but also make space for a new national identity and a new model of whiteness. As Uys puts on his Evita "clown," he encourages his audiences to laugh at the absurdity of their everyday surroundings, to participate actively in the continuing transformations, and to strip themselves bare of the fear that prevents them from encountering each other as "fully human."

Steven Cohen: Monstrous Drag

If Pieter-Dirk Uys bases his drag work on "not scaring the horses" with unnecessarily confrontational approaches, Steven Cohen would be more likely to take as his performance motto "Fuck the horses!" In fact, Cohen carried a banner in the 1996 Joburg Pride march, wearing his trademark latex fetish heels: "GIVE US YOUR CHILDREN—WHAT WE CAN'T FUCK WE EAT." This sign's playful take on heterosexual fears about the outcome of queer visibility and pride may have contributed to a PR nightmare for a pride committee much more interested in assimilation than confrontation, but it is typical of Cohen's message: you think we are monstrous? We will be fabulous monstrosities and claim the marginal role you give us, in a tactical space to show you your own fears. By breaking his white, queer body down to its innermost parts and most primal desires—its need to copulate, eat, and defecate—Cohen used guerrilla tactics to expose both the hypocrisies of contemporary white society and the stratified spaces of postapartheid South Africa, revealing the margins of belonging and acceptance.

Cohen shares a number of background similarities with Uys: both were born in middle-class/upper-middle-class white families, close to urban centers; both were raised by Jewish parents who benefited from the apartheid's state's complete acceptance of Jewish identity into the privileges of white South Africa;[30] both suffered loss and alienation in their childhood (Uys's mother committed suicide and Cohen's mother was an absentee alcoholic); both discovered that they were attracted to men at an early age. Importantly, Cohen's work would likely not have existed without Uys and other apartheid-era theater practitioners' tireless campaigning against any form of censorship in the new dispensation.

Yet these superficial similarities make their differences even more visible. Where identity has always been important to Uys's satirical performances, it has not been his individual one. For Uys, the body is a vehicle, a medium for the message that must be forgotten in order to be effective. Steven Cohen's living art is pointedly and explicitly focused on the limitations of his individual body. Even when he developed personae, as he did in the middle to late 1990s with the characters of Ugly Girl, Faggot, Jew, and Dog, the drag is never complete and always highlights the specificity of his "queer-jew-white" body under his costumes, simultaneously owning and exaggerating the stereotypes that he performs.

Unlike Uys's performances of Evita, which depend on the audience's ability to "forget the man" and play along, Cohen's drag is always excessive, drawing attention to the incompleteness and inadequacy of performance. His work stretches the boundaries of drag and, moreover, binary thinking itself. Morwenna Bosch has noted that his performance "is subversively extreme in the sense that he does not merely 'act out' female/feminine, but performs a distinctly queer/ed drag act. He is a strange creature and yet he is human, he is a woman but he is also a man—the binary structures that construct gendered subjectivity are threatened and rendered semiotically collapsible."[31] Cohen's penis, rather than being tucked away as it is by most drag queens interested in female authenticity, is usually highlighted in the performance by being either trussed or decorated. He often uses animal prosthetics, such as giraffe leg extensions and turkey neck codpieces, to perform a sort of a sort of cross-species blurring, giving the impression of a physically unstable monstrosity that resists categorization.

Cohen uses a camp aesthetic to overperform his identities and to highlight the ways these identities are already bracketed in the larger society.[32] The characters that he performed throughout the 1990s animated the worst fears and stereotypes attached to each identity. With her overplayed femininity, his character Ugly Girl is the closest to a traditional drag queen; yet her bloody thighs highlight those messier aspects of female identity that are erased in normative gender performance, as well as the lurking threat of sexual violence. Jew, a figure on crutches wearing a gas mask, is always marked by the Star of David (variously located on his penis or forehead). The mask, with its mouthpiece hanging loose like an elephant's trunk, perhaps comments on the ways in which the humanity of Jews is always seen as suspect; the crutches suggest the wounds of history. Finally, Faggot comments on society's perception of homosexuals as frivolous pleasure-seekers. Coasting through his intervention sites on his roller skates and penetrated by a dildo with a sparkler attached, Cohen's Faggot is literally flaming.

These figures' over-the-top ornamentation serve to draw attention to how his individual body and its many identities are predetermined. His body becomes a multifaceted—literally many faced—prism through which he deconstructs the stereotypes projected on to him, accentuating and overperforming their ridiculousness. These personae also comment on and perform the diversity of whiteness in South Africa, making strange and visible—in a Brechtian sense—the socially fractured postapartheid white body and the spaces it inhabits. They open up questions of the "strangeness" of the South African body and its very construction.

When he performs in either a gallery or a theater, Cohen's particular brand of performance art troubles the line between each medium, never fitting comfortably in either.[33] In the gallery space, his queer(ed) body's presence among the (primarily female) nudes poses questions about which bodies are artful and which obscene. His performance of *Taste* had him consume a liquid from his anus to the song "L'Chaim" ("To Life!") from the musical *Fiddler on the Roof*. The performance confronted his audience (many of whom walked out in disgust) with questions of which rituals are appropriate for public consumption. Simultaneously, his early guerrilla interventions intruded on the privatized spaces of the supposedly open New South Africa, demonstrating the limits of tolerance. Cohen's intervention as bloody-thighed Ugly Girl in *Virgin Penetrated* at Johannesburg's Killarney Mall's bridal show, for example, reveals the extent to which these "multicultural" spaces—supposedly free, transparent, and public—are in fact policed by raced, classed, gendered norms. Even individuals with the financial and racial privilege to purchase a ticket to the fashion show are not able to participate if their fashion critiques—as Cohen's did, quite literally—the very lifeblood of consumer capitalism.

Perhaps the most crucial difference between Uys and Cohen's dragging of postapartheid whiteness is their attitude toward the loss of whiteness's privileges and the means necessary for whites to renounce its "global sanctity." Where Uys's work is invested in the process of turning white mourning into productive participation in a nonracial democracy ("becoming less white and more real"),[34] Cohen's work dwells in the realm of the melancholic and the more oblique bodily architecture of whiteness. If mourning is a process through which individuals grieve and eventually accept and integrate a loss, in melancholia, the loss is not always clear and is often in fact the transference of feelings toward the loved object onto the self. Indeed, Cohen's provocative interventions' fixation on the consumption and public debasement of his (white) self echo Freud's conception of melancholy as a theatrical internalization of the lost love object into the ego, to the point that it becomes "cannibalistic."[35]

Scholarship on Cohen has generally focused either on his performance of Jewishness[36] or on his use of abjection to challenge the presumably stable borders between life/art, male/female, white/black, self/other, and so on.[37] Scant focus has been given to the ways in which Cohen's public performances—and their critical efficacy—depend on his interaction with his audience(s). Cohen's art is, crucially, about coperformance: the meanings of his "whiteness," "queerness," and "Jewishness" are dependent on interactive juxtapositions with their supposed opposites, across a South African landscape. The juxtaposition of his white body with black "African" spaces—such as the urban streets, taxi ranks, and squatter camps—highlights both its vulnerability and its authority, by revealing it at its least in control, least at home, and where it is most strange. The intrusion of his

Fig. 3. Steven Cohen and onlooker in *Chandelier* (2001). Photo courtesy of Michael Stevenson Gallery, Cape Town/Johannesburg

art in situations with people going about their daily lives enlists them as both audience and coperformers. During these encounters, he highlights his body's strangeness—its abjection—but also its privileged place in the history of South Africa and its accustomed distance from the majority of South African citizens. Crucially, by taking his living art outside of the spaces where it is intelligible as such, Cohen's interventions draw attention to the role and relevance of art in a stratified society.

The multifaceted orientation of Cohen's work is nowhere more apparent—or, indeed, more literally prismatic—than in his most famous and controversial intervention, *Chandelier* (2001). In the performance, Cohen arrived at a squatter camp near Newtown, Johannesburg, wearing a heavy corset chandelier, its lights powered by battery. This intervention was different from many of Cohen's previous interactions in that the rules of the space were less clear-cut and Cohen himself was less active/interactive than he had been previously (in part because of the difficulty of his costume). Less focused on instigation and interaction than his earlier pieces, Cohen used *Chandelier* to draw attention to the politics of space and witnessing. Though initially a study in juxtaposition between the reality of life in Johannesburg and the dreams of riches promised in its Zulu name *Egoli* (place of gold), *Chandelier* quickly spun out of Cohen's control. Workers from a private security and demolition company, the Red Ants, began destroying the makeshift homes of those around him in order to clear the way for the rainbow-lit spires of the future Nelson Mandela Bridge.[38] Cohen—his chandelier tinkling as he stepped around piles of rubbish and over the rusted train rails—became a lightning rod for the recently displaced who, unable to interact with the men tearing their houses apart, started using Cohen as a stage onto which to project their emotions. The final document, a sixteen-minute film edited from several hours of footage, captures moments of brutality, tenderness, empathy, and grief.

In the video, Cohen's face remains placid as he walks among the makeshift community. Men and women gather around to stare. Cohen does not outwardly react to the people around him, despite their efforts to engage. More aestheticized than his other performances, his *Chandelier* is reminiscent of an art deco tableau vivant. His silent presence in chaos, a specter of detached glittering beauty in the midst of squalor, created an image that he admitted was "half beautifully imagined, half horribly real."[39] Cohen's beautiful abjection encouraged a number of reactions from those around him. One woman, her face caked white with clay meant to deflect the day's heat, crooned that he was an angel. A man in a red hat approached him with a *knobkerrie* (traditional stick-fighting weapon) and yelled at Cohen to "*Hamba*!" (Go!). Direct physical confrontation was diverted by an older woman. Cohen was increasingly surrounded by *gogos* (grandmothers) in *doek* headscarves, who circled protectively around him. In one of the few moments of reciprocated interaction, one elderly woman offered him her hand to shake in the traditional African way.[40] He kissed her hand, and she kissed his in return.

One older, obviously drunk man in a construction worker's outfit delighted in Cohen's appearance. Laughing, he gave Cohen an odd parody of a lap dance. Cohen seemed unsure how to respond to this aggressive sexuality. The man left and returned with a copy of *Hustler*, and enthusiastically showed Cohen images of naked white women with their legs spread. Relating Cohen's artful nakedness to images of pornography, he took Cohen's hand and, in an unlikely dance, happily posed for Cohen's cameraman with his addition to the art.

The soundtrack became increasingly chaotic. The shouts of the Red Ants as their crowbars rang out across the emptying lot clashed with the tinkling of Cohen's crystal, the rhythmic clapping of bystanders. At one point, someone sang the national anthem "Nkosi Sikelel'iAfrika." Cohen continued to strike dramatic poses. As the sun began to set, the Red Ants finished their demolition. The chandelier lit up, providing artificial illumination through the smoke of cooking fires. The displaced people dispersed. Striking a few more poses, Cohen left the former squatter camp and called it a night.

Shortly after its initial performance, Cohen reflected upon the staging of the piece:

> Our rough footage record is a strange visual; a white man in high heels wearing an illuminated chandelier tutu and improvising movement amidst a community of black squatters who's [*sic*] shacks are being destroyed by the city council workers, in their own ballet of violence is very South African. . . . It was hard for me to set myself up as, in part, a privileged white luxuriating among the despair of our lowest class citizens—Nero fiddling while Rome burns. . . . I felt displaced (hectic in heels and strange place to be near-naked)—and in a sort-of unreal and slow-motion-type-paralysis I am more used to experiencing in my nightmares than on a Thursday afternoon in the real world.[41]

Chandelier was a turning point in Cohen's work. Previously, he had interrogated the social norms that structure public space, with his body as the abject other. *Chandelier* forced him to acknowledge that his white queer body will always be privileged and carry the wealth of its history. As he wandered through the wreckage of the New South Africa in his "hectic" heels, he bore witness to the passing of a national dream and enacted the precarity of his own relation to the nation. In his chalk-whitened body and its crystal glamour, he momentarily took on the coperformer role in a drama much larger than one of his making. Yet, among the violence and displacement of this history, he was also detached from those among whom he walked. For each moment that he made a connection—the hand-kiss, the playful coperformance with the drunken man—he was unable or unwilling to cross the line toward a shared humanity. Though he witnessed the destruction of people's lives, his white body was also the cause of it. Cohen was aware of the numerous, contradictory meanings of his performance, as well as his shifting positions as perpetrator and victim, depending on the framing:

> My body language, in the context of the chandelier work, had a radical range of meanings. In the footage, if I lift my arms commandingly, I appear to be directing the destruction. If I raise my eyes and palms to God, it is as if I am also suffering, when I kneel in the dirt, it reads as a prayer for peace on earth.[42]

Unlike Uys's incursions as Evita into township spaces during her election *indaba*—which were about crossing bridges and developing shared humanity—Cohen's white queer body, powdered and hairless, is a thing of monstrous beauty and multiple meanings. His performance cracks open any surety about whiteness and about humanness. By highlighting the strangeness of the white body, and breaking it down to its fragmented identity positions, Cohen's interventions into public spaces make hypervisible the legacy of whiteness and comment on the distance between both individual and social bodies.

Performing the Rainbow's Fragments, Twenty Years On

In the earliest years of South Africa's democracy, the drag performances of both Pieter-Dirk Uys and Steven Cohen crossed space and media to comment on the boundaries of the nation and to question what white South African citizenship might mean. Performing during a time where laws and identities were being reconstituted in the public sphere, Cohen and Uys, in vastly different ways, used drag and gender subversion to performatively engage a variety of publics to rethink the possible role of whiteness in a now supposedly nonracial South Africa. The disorientation that followed upon the heels of the transition—particularly around what a truly equal, multicultural nation would look like—was in part addressed by appeals to a quasi-utopian Rainbow Nation, its people linked through *ubuntu* by figures like Mandela and Tutu.

These South African drag performers took the public's disorientation, prejudices, and fear, ran them through the prism of history, and revealed to their audiences that the mirror was deeply fractured along raced and gendered lines. Yet these lines allowed for unexpected moments of attachment and disidentification between their queered versions of African whiteness and their audiences. Beyond making ambiguities and contradictions of the postapartheid era visible through the appealing smokescreen of the Rainbow Nation, Uys and Cohen made these contradictions *palpable*—that is, able to be felt, experienced, and acted upon by their various spectators.

Rupture, fracture, and contradiction lay under the surface of these new national narratives and, as the years passed, the continuing legacies of apartheid and colonialism became more apparent, albeit on the grounds of class in addition to race. The roles of queer white performers also changed, as new affirmative action policies such as Black Economic Empowerment created a wealthy black elite and white voices became less audible in public discourse.[43] This shift was noticeable by 2001, when Cohen performed *Chandelier*: while whites may possess the wealth—in gold and diamonds—from South Africa's colonial and apartheid history, they were no longer entirely setting the agenda nor were they the sole beneficiaries of the country's wealth. The new actors, upstaging the old, were those who capitalized on the increasing inequity between the country's richest and its poorest, taking advantage of the opportunities for investment in the world's newest democracy.

Cohen's relative immobility is striking in contrast to impersonal, brutal efficiency of the all-black Red Ants whose "ballet of violence" was sanctioned to change the landscape overnight. The space is now home to the LED-lit rainbow spires of Nelson Mandela Bridge, in homage to the people's hero, connecting Braamfontein and Newtown, two key neighborhoods in a gentrifying Johannesburg. Any squatters are immediately chased away, their possessions confiscated by the Johannesburg Metropolitan Police. In the meantime, the arts have flourished under these conditions. Beyond the Market Theatre, known as an incubator to struggle theater and where Uys put on some of his earliest cabarets, the city is home to an increasing number of "lifestyle communities." These communities, such as the inner-city Maboneng Precinct, offer boutique shopping, art galleries, cinemas, restaurants, as well as office and residential spaces for an interracial, globally mobile "creative class." While publicity materials frame these communities as harnessing culture for inner-city regeneration, many have critiqued the displacement and policing of those who can't afford its craft beers and stunning views as being a new form of exemplary economic apartheid.[44] Where privilege had once been clearly legislated and partitioned on the basis of race, it is now increasingly experienced through the supposedly nonracial prism of class.

As much as Uys's and Cohen's prismatic, transition-era performances were dependent on the spatial relationship between the bodies of performer and audience, their temporality was also a crucial vector in their efficacy. While Uys has remained a key figure in South African theater, his relation to the state became increasingly antagonistic and distant in the new millennium, as the ANC government drifted away from progressive politics and was plagued by the AIDS denialism and corruption of the Mbeki and Zuma governments. Evita's critique had once "worked" because she was acknowledged by and incorporated into new government's performative nationhood. No longer possessing the ear of the powerful, Uys has more recently channeled his satirical energy into writing South African adaptations of Shakespearean plays such as *MacBeki* and *The Merry Wives of Zuma*.

Uys still performs as Evita in multiple shows weekly, from his home stage in the Western Cape town of Darling and via the internet in his new web series *Evita's Free Speech*. His largest project, however, continues to be his HIV/AIDS education work, which has reached over two million schoolchildren since he began touring in 2000. The 2015 National Arts Festival recently celebrated his legacy (and seventieth birthday) with "A Season of Pieter-Dirk Uys," a program that featured Uys in three solo performances, a premiere of his new play *African Times*, and screenings of three of his apartheid-era revues. Yet this legacy has increasingly come under critique from a new generation of performers and critics who see his prominence as eclipsing other, nonwhite voices. Several reviewers from the festival newspaper *Cue*, while acknowledging his talent, questioned his continuing prominence, with one commenting that "people go to see Pieter-Dirk Uys for the same probable reason they go to see the pyramids and the Parthenon: they have been there a very long time; and everyone else is going. And, like those other venerable ruins, you know what to expect, and you know you are seeing history."[45]

Aside from brief returns to South Africa with his controversial performance piece *The Cradle of Human Kind* (2012) and his grief-fueled eulogy to his partner Elu *Put Your Heart under Your Feet . . . and Walk* (2018), Cohen has largely stopped making South African–specific work.[46] Permanently relocating to France in the early 2000s, he has found great success focusing on his Jewish identity in a European context. He received international publicity for his 2014 arrest on charges of exhibitionism for his intervention *Cock/Coq*, where he promenaded in front of the Eiffel Tower in feathers with a live chicken attached to his penis. He still occasionally revives *Chandelier*—most recently as part of Toronto's 2015 Spotlight: South Africa Festival—first performing the piece's gestural elements for a paying audience and then screening the 2001 footage. The rolling credits conclude with a glib projection, perhaps Cohen's acknowledgment of the incongruence between the original enactment and its repackaging for foreign theatergoers (who project their own desires for a glimpse at South African authenticity onto his dangling crystals): "SPECIAL THANKS TO THE HOMELESS OF NEWTOWN, JOHANNESBURG."[47]

If Uys's and Cohen's earlier work had captured the particular hopes and fears of a newly democratic country, their recent interventions arguably no longer reflect and refract the concerns of what could be termed the postrainbow era: a present defined by its widespread skepticism toward both the rainbow narrative and the potential for a white transformation when that population has grown increasingly dismissive of black pain.[48] As articulated by the *Cue* reporter, these artists are forever linked to the particular, now-historical time in which they came to voice, leaving them the "venerable ruins" of the Mandela moment.

Even as the contemporary relevance of Uys and Cohen is questioned, however, their influence can be seen in an emergent generation of young black artists whose performance practice addresses contemporary racial politics through the prism of drag. Performance artist Athi-Patra Ruga is perhaps the most direct descendant in this lineage, particularly in his engagement with and rearticulation of whiteness. In the public interventions comprising his *Future White Women of Azania* series (2010 to 2016, featured on this book's cover), Ruga curated a highly stylized alternative vision of southern Africa in the near future. At the center of what he termed Azania stands the iconic figure of its titular ruler, the Versatile Queen Ivy

Fig. 4. Athi-Patra Ruga in multicolored balloons as *The Future White Woman of Azania* (2010). Performed as part of the *Making Way* exhibition in collaboration with Mikhael Subotzky at the 2010 National Arts Festival, Grahamstown (now Makanda), South Africa. Photo: Ruth Simbao.

of Azania: Ruga, adorned in high heels and cushioned by a rainbow cloud of balloons. This site-specific drag project is clearly influenced by Cohen's interventions; like Uys, his work is invested in queering iconic national homelands and mythologies—in this case Azania, the country imagined but never realized by black nationalists of the Pan Africanist Congress during the antiapartheid struggle.

Yet where Uys and Cohen perform a historicized, racialized whiteness, Ruga sees whiteness in his work as less about race or color than about a particular investment in privilege and the status quo. Ruga has commented that Queen Ivy, the titular white woman, is "a character whose identity is all air."[49] Adorned by 250 rainbow-colored balloons filled with paint and tinsel, she teeters in high heels and hot pink stockings through city streets, dusty townships, and rural roads, her balloons popping as she encounters surfaces and people. Whiteness here is not literal, but a metaphor for the larger Rainbow (balloon) Nation mythology, a body full of color and (hot) air. When deflated through performance, the popping balloons reveal the violent truth at the center of the image: the labor of a black man covered in paint that, colors running together, resembles blood. Ruga's performances use the prism of kitsch, camp, and gender play to critique the Rainbow Nation's violent history and the black majority's unreconciled present. Yet he views this process as not merely deconstructive, but transformative, commenting that in his work "you start bleeding to become something else."[50]

As white "transition era" performers such as Cohen and Uys have become less visible in an increasingly fractured postapartheid landscape, Ruga—joined by other emergent black gender-queering performers such as musician Umlilo and art duo FAKA—follows in their stead to critique contemporary politics via gender performance. By enacting alternative versions of postapartheid nationhood that depart from empty multiculturalism, Ruga's work suggests that while the Rainbow Nation narrative may be passé, another space—an imagined future that he calls Azania—can be brought into being through the animation of the nation's fragments by glitter, color, and a pair of pumps. Yet the utopic aspects of Ruga's performances rub ambivalently and messily against contemporary postapartheid realities.[51] The next chapter moves from aestheticized and theatrical performances to lived realities, analyzing the self-images and the sustaining, subjunctive—rather than utopic—orientations developed by a group of lesbian activists and soccer players.

TWO

Living in the As-If

Queering Ikultcha *with the Chosen FEW Soccer Team*

No Lesbians in Vosloorus

I first met members of the Chosen FEW lesbian soccer team at an early-morning protest in October 2010. Preceding One in Nine's intervention in the Joburg Pride parade by two years, twelve lesbians had been arrested and harassed in their homes during a pride-related house party in the Johannesburg-area township of Vosloorus. Local police had barged into the party, maced all of the guests, and dragged them to the police station. The officers shouted homophobic slurs, threatened onlookers with knives, and questioned the gender of the women involved, all the while stating, categorically, that there were "no lesbians in Vosloorus."

By the time I arrived at the police station with an activist friend who wanted to document the protests, local lesbians seemed prepared to counter the officers' assertion. A group of young black women from Vosloorus and other townships in the Ekhureleni Municipality gathered in the dusty parking lot of the police station, as more arrived on the ubiquitous *koombi* minibus taxis. They were clad in the One in Nine Campaign's purple T-shirts, covered in slogans such as "Stop the War on Women's Bodies," "Sexual Violence = Silence," and simply: "Lesbian." Some had been at the party and some had heard about the arrests from friends. As I stood off to the side, they began to dance in a circle, clapping and singing in unison to the bemusement of police officers who had come out to watch.

One of those leading the chant—a powerfully built woman with multiple piercings, skinny jeans, a bleached frohawk fade (the height of township style)—introduced herself to me as Manika and mentioned that she represented the black lesbian NGO Forum for Empowerment of Women

(FEW) and the Chosen FEW soccer team at the protest. While it might seem odd that soccer players would double as political activists, their role as visible, out lesbians within their communities had already placed them in the spotlight. The Chosen FEW was founded in 2004 as part of an outreach initiative by FEW with the goal of educating a generation of young black lesbians on their rights and empowering them through sport. The team members were drawn from the numerous townships surrounding Johannesburg. Notably, in the nine months in 2010 and 2011 that I spent working, hanging out, and protesting with the Chosen FEW, I was aware of their participating in only two soccer matches. During my time there, the players and the organization were primarily focused on political activism and combating everyday violence, homophobia, and racism.

Though soccer itself was a shared interest, defining characteristic, and organizing principle for the team, their association with Forum for Empowerment of Women placed the players of the Chosen FEW in an unusually public position as visible, vocal, and self-aware representatives of black lesbians within South Africa. Their participation in larger global gay sporting events, moreover, situated them as a face of South African "gayness" to the world. In the run-up to 2010 World Cup, the BBC, ESPN, *The New York Times*, and *The Guardian* each produced a human interest story around the team, focusing on their survival against the odds and framing their stories as metaphors for South Africa's struggles as a postcolonial state and "developing nation."

The Leadership Training Program—which brings together young feminist activists from four provinces and teaches them how to build their own NGOs—was key to providing the members of the Chosen FEW with the language to contextualize their daily struggles in a larger framework. In our discussions, the players' language often reflected the terminology of Western feminist organizing, such as "patriarchy" and "feminism." Yet they also frequently employed more culturally specific terms with potential for resignification. Manika, for instance, commented to me: "We live in a patriarchal society. We're fighting for equality, but at the end of the day, it won't work because we are oppressed by *ikultcha*."[1] This chapter argues that *ikultcha*—Zulu-ized slang for culture—is the nebulous ground on which queer Africanness continues to be negotiated. Specifically, within the context of *ikultcha*, to be African is to be aligned with heterosexual reproductivity; it also is implicitly aligned with blackness.

The embodiments of the Chosen FEW soccer players were always already circumscribed by racialized gender norms and expectations that defined black Africanness as heterosexual, linked to a conservative vision of culture. The 2011 televised debate "Is Homosexuality UnAfrican?" coproduced by the BBC and SABC, provides an instructive snapshot into how the political and personal entangle at the intersection of these two identities. Over the course of an hour, a panel of gay and lesbian Africans faced off against a number of antigay African leaders, including Ugandan parliamentarian David Bahati, author of his country's infamous 2009 "Kill the Gays" bill, then under consideration. The most revealing explanation of why homosexuality was viewed as incompatible with African identity came not from the talking heads, but from a man in the audience. Clearly nervous, South African Mandla Tshabalala introduced himself as member of the United Christian Democratic Party, before speaking with conviction: "I am an African. We believe in being remembered for eternity, so the only way to do that is through reproduction. How do I do that with another man and claim that I am an African? It can't be done!"

As articulated here, the term "African" clearly stands in for tradition, continuity, reproduction, and culture, explicitly linked to evangelical Christianity. Africanness is also, as his repetitive phrasing suggests, "a doing" as well as a being. By aligning his (presumably heterosexual) self against a presumably non-African, homosexual, nonreproductive Other, Tshabalala finds a comforting, autochthonous stability and self-definition: He is an African because he is not gay. Homosexuality, figured as all that is negative and un-African (amnesia, wickedness, with no futurity), enforces the boundaries of a positive, future-oriented heterosexual imagined nation and even forges potential pan-African solidarity. If—as Anne McClintock and Nira Yuval-Davis have persuasively argued[2]—the nation is always gendered and figured through (the control of) its iconic representations of women, lesbians haunt this affective economy as nonreproductive, failed performances of Africanness.

As I argue throughout this project, black gays and lesbians deal daily with the cultural paradox at the heart of South Africa's democracy. Their everyday lives are marked with a choice: they can remain quiet about their sexual attraction (known in local parlance as "after nines"—straight until after nine); or, despite danger, they can choose to live openly and "as if": as if the constitution were enforced, as if they were recognized as full citizens.[3] It is this projected, subjunctive orientation, I will argue, that allowed the members of the Chosen FEW—as out lesbians and as quasi-public figures—to rehearse a possible yet unattained future. This imagined future, while a response to the heteroreproductive vision of the South African nation so popular among traditionalists, is just as rooted in what might be called "traditional" African cultural repertoires as it is in global gay identities and languages. *Ikultcha* queers and pluralizes the very concept of culture used to justify homophobia and negate queer African identity.

The Chosen FEW's performances of out, subjunctive black lesbian South African identities came with very real consequences. The everyday—so often conceived of as the repetitive, the unremarkable, the banal—was for them constantly defined by their otherness and vulnerability. In order to survive and maintain coherent senses of self, the members of the Chosen FEW developed personas that operated through a prism of projection and protection. A projected, imagined acceptance of a future self (what I term the "as-if") rendered the present bearable. Yet their visibility required them to create narratives that protected their "true selves" from public consumption, resulting in hybridized and exaggerated personas. Rather than fleeing to urban centers (an economic impossibility for many), the players remained rooted in their communities, building new family structures that undermined the sense of any one traditional culture. Through these performances they claimed complex subjectivities and undermined the dominant dichotomies that frame African and lesbian as oppositional categories. Because of this pressure to perform, many of them used style and took on complicated, outgoing personas to project a front of confidence and strength, of optimism and agency. These personas became both modes of modeling an out, fearless lesbian township identity (as if safety were not an issue) and of protecting a more vulnerable "self" (from the reality that it was). Through a stylized performance of self—cultural embodiments culled from numerous sources—they negotiated the everyday world of their communities, claiming space for black South African lesbians.[4]

As a performative orientation, the "as-if" can be a useful tactic to bypass and delink binaristic thinking. Ann Pellegrini, for one, has called for "a democratic politics of 'as-if'" where "the ways in which we act . . . generate a subjunctive universe." Arguing that "the ways in which we act to produce the 'could be' and 'not yet'" could be politically productive, Pellegrini wonders if a depolarization of seemingly oppositional politicized terms (in her work, religion and secularity)—could come from a process of thinking and living in subjunctive terms, rather than current realities.[5] Though Pellegrini is purposefully vague as to what this sort of politics might look like, I would argue that the enactment of a "subjunctive universe" is and has been a necessary everyday tactic for minorities living visibly in hostile environments. Within a paradoxical situation such as South Africa's, democratic citizenship does not result in access to cultural citizenship. Many black South African lesbians are forced to choose between risking violent communal opposition or censoring themselves in order to justify their belonging. Living subjunctively, in this context, is one way they can put their constitutional rights into practice.

Much scholarship produced in the past few decades on queer temporalities (queer pasts, queer futurity, queer utopia) has argued that in order to opt out of hegemonic conceptions of "reproductive time,"[6] LGBT people have forged their own nonlinear temporalities and geographies.[7] This scholarship has opened a field of new, complex ways of analyzing the uneven terrain of identity affiliation in a time where LGBT citizens are increasingly folded into the narratives of nation.[8] These theorists note it is vitally important to consider the ways in which "queer" can operate as an analytical tool, which, in José Muñoz' words, "is not simply a being but a doing for and towards the future . . . a rejection of a here and now and an insistence on potentiality or concrete possibility of another world."[9] This orientation is particularly generative for those multiply marginalized under heteropatriarchal white supremacy. Indeed, as Tavia Nyong'o outlines in his theory of Afro-fabulation, "It is the very exception of blackness and queerness from the humanist standard that produces the possibility of imagining humanity otherwise."[10]

While I draw implicitly on the radical potential of this sort of "doing toward" and "imagining otherwise" in my analysis of the Chosen FEW, this chapter also troubles the languages and geographies in which this world has been theorized, and argues that these theories should and must be grounded in their particular cultural contexts. The vast majority of the work on queer temporalities and national identities has been written under the purview of literary, film, or cultural studies within the American and European academies, primarily about Western cultural production.

This chapter explores the generative potential of ethnography as radical research. This method, modeled by performance scholars such as Dwight Conquergood, D. Soyini Madison, and Marlon Bailey, places the situated body as the epistemological center of knowledge in context.[11] Where Lee Edelman, for instance, might critique a subjunctive perspective as embracing a dangerous futurity, "constrained to pursue the dream of a day when today and tomorrow are one,"[12] his choice to privilege the Lacanian Symbolic over the material conditions of that temporality leaves no space to evaluate alternative enactments outside of a Western framework.

I draw on recent interventions in the field of queer-of-color critique, which counter the "negative turn" in mainstream (read: white) queer theory by conceptualizing temporality through black-queer embodiments that Jafari Allen describes as "creative, promiscuous, multiple, and contradictory."[13] Yet even in its queer multiplicity, blackness in these accounts often remains implicitly aligned with African American / Afro-diasporic experiences and geographies. As South African performance scholar Mlondolozi Zondi points out, such unmarked US-centrism risks relegating Africa to "a site of folkloric tropes, aesthetic inspiration, and a past through which to trace elements of contemporary performance repertoires in the diaspora."[14] Without specific attention to geographic and cultural diversity in discourses on racialized queerness, Africa might all too easily be refracted only through a Western lens, rather than viewed as a space of creation and diversity in its own right

My reading highlights the particular stakes involved in performing "as-if" in the South African everyday, which the players I interviewed expressed matter-of-factly in terms of life and death. It traces the investment that this particular group of black South African lesbians placed in the possibility of performative citizenship, even when their constitutional rights failed to be enacted or respected in the public sphere. In order to delve into the particularities of everyday performances, I structure my argument through a close reading of the lives and self-stylings of three Chosen FEW players, supplemented with the experiences and thoughts of other members. My research draws on nine months of participant observation (September 2010–May 2011), in-depth interviews conducted with six Chosen FEW players—most in their homes—and attendance at two games, three parties, three pride celebrations, and four protests. While I remain in touch with many of my collaborators, my analysis of their performances remains tied to this time period, acknowledging the ephemerality and time-boundedness of any quotidian performance.

I make no claims that these experiences are representative of black South African lesbians; indeed, in many ways, they are distinctly unrepresentative. However, where queer black identities continue to be targeted for eradication and where ethnic, gender, racial, and class lines are both thickly drawn and often violently policed, the mobility and gusto with which the players of the Chosen FEW approached their identities allowed them to reconfigure and queer the trappings of *ikultcha*. The fluidity of *ikultcha*, as expressed in their individual and collective enactments, operated as a prismatic mode through which an ideal future can coexist with a turbulent present. Further, their desire to live "as-if" allows us to theorize beyond both queerness and performance as mere utopic endeavors. By participating in the creation of a "subjunctive universe," the Chosen FEW's repeated and politicized enactments of self, beyond merely gesturing to a different mode of being, called these new modes of being into practice.

Style, Swagga, and the Performance of Self

> Ekasi [in the township], for you to get a girl, you need to have swagga. That's the thing. Swagga. You know, something with style. When you pass girls, they're like (*sighs*) "Ayoba! [Excellent!]." At the end of the day, for you to get a girl now? Lesbian swagga.
> —"Manika"[15]

Manika is difficult to pin down in a few lines of text. Her self-confidence could be overwhelming. After I met her at the protest, she quickly became my main contact within the Chosen FEW. As she walked me through her neighborhood in Vosloorus, she was greeted by neighbors, friends, and the young men hanging out on corners with whom she had played soccer when she was younger. When interviewed about FEW's activist work, she spoke in jargon, throwing out words such as "patriarchy," "feminism," "capitalism," and "hegemony" to describe her position in the world. When off the record, she used more colloquial language to soliloquize about her girlfriends and previous conquests. She often kept her eyes on the horizon when she talked, almost as if she was talking to herself, repeating the aspects of her life that constitute her identity. Soccer. Style. Family. Girls. This, the stuff of everyday life, contrasted with moments of spectacular, politicized protest discussed earlier, where the bodies of gays and lesbians used the communal aspects of song and *toyi-toyi* dance to present a united front. Manika was a distinct individual, who used style—adornment and carriage—to produce a certain effect on those surrounding her. Her performance of self in the everyday—at turns charismatic, articulate, contradictory, and flashy—evoked and demanded a response from those with whom she interacted.

Her persona was also sexually charged, embracing a different kind of female identity than that usually seen in township women by drawing on various forms of masculine and feminine cultural signifiers. Early on she commented to me, "I think like a man, act like a lady," an "acting like" that propelled an exaggerated swagga. Manika was no lady, at least not in the terms in which "ladyhood" is generally understood in her context. Yet she demanded recognition that she was female, a "lesbian woman,"[16] acting as a different kind of lady, while suggesting that she thinks like a man. One charge often leveled at township lesbians is that they act as if they are men. Manika's insistence that she acted like a lady (but a different kind of lady), driven by a masculine mind, both unsettled and attracted those around her. Her appropriation of so-called male desire—and its location-specific enactments (with *ikasi,* urban township, swagga) she insisted on expressing through her female body—undid the presumptions of both men and women she came across.[17] This "undoing" revealed just how closely gender identity is enmeshed with sexed bodies, and the ways both are related to performances of a particular form of (heterosexual) black African identity.

The first time we met, I felt the full force of her charm: she asked me for my number and later texted me a message loaded with innuendo, telling me that she really wanted to get to know me. Though I eventually fell into the role that she termed her *inja yami* (literally: my dawg),[18] she never failed to mention that she had dated a European woman she had met at the Gay Games in Germany, and that she didn't want to be tied down to a racial or sexual type. Similarly, while her gender presentation drew upon recognizable signifiers of masculinity in her community, she rejected the gendered paradigm of butch/femme ("amabutchie/amafemme"), preferring to identify herself as a dyke. This sexual and racial fluidity, she would later explain to me, was an integral part of her "lesbian swagga," a mode of confident self-presentation that drew on a number of styles and performances to attract women and deflect homophobic insults.

Manika connected her swagga to a larger trend within youth culture, which she saw as providing space for a more expansive and inclusive sort of township identity. As she commented: "Now these men wear skinny jeans, these women wear men's clothes. They have unisex clothes now. In olden days, if you were a man you would wear a man's clothes. And a woman wears women's clothes. But nowadays things are changing."[19] Indeed, following a short distance behind them, I found it difficult to tell Manika and her straight, self-identified "metrosexual" male friend apart when we ventured to pick up beer at the local *spaza* (corner store).

He wore tight black pants and a fuchsia dress shirt; she sported a puffy black jacket and purple skinny jeans, slightly baggy to show off matching purple briefs.

Her association of her swagga style with a dyke identity (as opposed to the butch-femme model, popular with many township lesbians) suggested a strategic blending of transnational expressions of queerness and local, site-specific understandings of sexuality. As part of a larger queer mediascape, members of the Chosen FEW fashioned identities that were responsive but not reduceable to the reach of global gay cultures and medias. Unlike many lesbians (indeed, many people) within their township communities, they had traveled internationally, participating in the International Gay Games and interacting with South African activists from a number of different racial, cultural, and class backgrounds through their work with FEW.

For members of the Chosen FEW—who, unlike other lesbians from similar backgrounds, didn't have the luxury or desire to slip under the radar—the everyday performance of self became both a projection of an ideal self (an accepted lesbian South African identity) and a public persona that could be put on to shield that self from violation/negation. A "true" self could simultaneously be evoked and safeguarded, through a refractive double move of projection and protection. Manika, for one, was aware of the ways her identity functioned as a public performance, calibrated to project a certain, controllable image. Even her nickname, Manika—which, when spoken, intentionally sounds like the African American vernacular "ma nigga"—was about style and swagga, rather than a true essence. When questioned on the origins of her name, she reflected on how it had become a symbol on which she has built her persona:

> "Manika" has a history . . . "Manika" has made me to have so many friends, number one. This "Manika" name made me to be famous, I don't know why. . . . This "Manika" made me to have so maaaany girlfriends! . . . "This "Manika" name, it was given by people who saw something in me that I didn't see.[20]

The persona—to which Manika attributed a life of its own—resulted from a conscientious mixing of the stylized global hip-hop culture (for example, the African American vernacular: "what up my nigga?") with localized South African meanings. She noted that "here in South Africa, when you say 'nika-nika'[21] [sounds like "nigga-nigga"], when they call you 'nika-nika' . . . 'nika-nika' is like 'I give—you give.' If you give me respect, I give you respect back, you see?" In many township communities, the term "ma nigga" allows youth to claim affiliation to transnational hip-hop culture, and has a resonance similar to other slang street affiliations, such as "ma dawg" (*inja yam*), "ma china," or "ma gent." The term is so banal that Manika's mother often called her daughter home for dinner by standing at the gate and bellowing, "Ma niiiiiggaa!"[22]

When Manika spoke about "this Manika name," her naming story took on the aura of myth, as if the name had chosen her, something out of her control. Just as many cultures attribute meaning (and often a change of name) to a particular ritual, such as puberty or sexual maturity, Manika was given her name at a particularly formative time—when she was first discovering her attraction to women—by a group of lesbians at her school. She soon realized that this name (and the naming of her desire as "lesbian") would mark her as different from other girls in Vosloorus. Yet she also experienced a certain amount of relief knowing that she was part of a potential community of women already within her own community, those who "saw something in me I didn't see." In this paradigm-shifting moment of seeing herself refracted through a queer gaze, Manika's perception of her identity was transformed and consolidated into something new. By sharing this label with a group of older women, she suddenly encountered multiple reflections of a future self. The process of her transformation into Manika accompanied her larger sense of place in the world, and was imbued with what might be called a sort of lesbian *communitas*.[23]

This lesbian *communitas*, resulting from everyday rituals of belonging, advocacy, and education, transformed the Chosen FEW into something more than a soccer club, or even an activist organization. The soccer team became a space of support and self-awareness for its members and their friends. When I interviewed them, several players pinpointed their connection with Forum for Empowerment of Women as giving them definition, both as activists and as people. As they began to realize that they were not interested in the expected heterosexual partnerships, they found themselves without language to express their particular embodied desire (the word most associated with homosexuality is *isitabane*, which means "hermaphrodite" and is generally an insult).[24] Many spoke of finding a "true self" that their communities would prefer they hide. According to K. K.—a player from Chiawelo, Soweto—playing on other girls' teams in the township, "You have to hide your lesbianity. And I wasn't free, man. Like now, I'm free. [Because of] Chosen FEW, I know how to take off clothes.

You don't have to hide. We are free. You are a lesbian, especially, as I am around lesbians."[25]

K. K.'s focus on freedom and Manika's fixation on style and "swagga" in relation to the self are part of a larger trend within the "Born Frees," the generation born around or after the freeing of Nelson Mandela in 1990 and the negotiated settlement that led to the first democratic election in 1994. Since the end of apartheid, South Africa has developed a vibrant youth culture that fashions itself through a process of cultural bricolage: sampling and remixing itself from a number of local and global sources. Style (often synonymous with consumption) has become a tactic for youth to claim autonomy, both from their parents' generation and from a past that so often ties them to an identity of victimhood. Sarah Nuttall, who terms this conspicuous consumption "cultural accessorization," quotes one such perspective of what she calls the Y Generation: "We understand where we come from, but I am not interested in politics and about what happened in the '80s because I wasn't there. And even if I was, I live for the future."[26] This performance of contemporary self challenges a static reading of blackness, producing instead a flexible view of identity, rooted in a postapartheid ideology of diversity and the free market.

For lesbians, this focus on futurity and cultural elasticity challenges the version of African culture that is often cited as a proof against the possibility of gay African identity. Through "cultural accessorization" young queer South Africans are able to play with personas freely, trying on identities and picking and choosing their affiliations, including choosing when to be out about their sexualities. For the members of the Chosen FEW, this pressure to develop a style that was both recognizable and individual was complicated by the simultaneous allure of so-called global-gay styles. Most of the players had the piercings (labrets, eyebrows, ear cartilage), tattoos (interlocking women symbols), and accessories (studded belts, thumb rings, rainbow bracelets) that telegraph "lesbian" or "dyke" transnationally to those "in the know." They frequently attended the once-monthly lesbian party Open Closet in Johannesburg's historically gay suburb of Melville and gathered in large groups to attend events such as the annual Joburg Pride celebration.

K. K.'s earlier metaphor about her lesbian identity allowing her to take off clothes stands in productive tension with Manika's contention that "when you wear something, it demonstrates the kind of person you are," and captures what I've called the double move of projection and protection at work in their performance of black South African lesbian subjectivity. When same-gender-attracted and gender nonconforming women are interpolated into a community under the label of lesbian, they feel safe to imagine a space where they can visibly exist and thrive. However, in beginning to live this life, to claim ownership of the spaces (rather than slipping under the radar), many perform overproduced identities for the public sphere—lesbian swagga—clothed behind a gender-queering confidence and cutting-edge style. Though this style puts them at risk for not "passing," it also keeps them from feeling vulnerable and allows them to maintain a self that is relatively untouched by whatever prejudice is thrown their way. Strength against adversity is a highly respected quality, and much like Manika's name, respect begets status within one's community. The Chosen FEW's celebrity—traveling internationally to the Gay Games, guest starring on TV shows, and occasionally receiving local press—also allowed local community members to respect their fame, if not their life choices.

Choice, "Culture of Democracy," and the Closet

> *So, some [people], they're good and some they . . . go with the flow, like, "It's okay, you can do whatever you want to do with your life, we can't choose for you." Others, they just stereotype: "You need a man who can take you over and control you. You should be somebody's wife." And those stereotype people, they attack me playing soccer. "How can a woman play soccer? They need to be in the kitchen, cooking, have children, whatawhata." And I ask them, "Who told those women to be like that? They chose for themselves. I didn't like that. That's why I don't do that. That's why I chose to play soccer."*
>
> —Khambi[27]

For our interview, Khambi sat me down on the single bed that took up most of the space in her *zozo*, a one-room tin "shack" adjacent to the family's main, cinderblock house in Katlehong, a sprawling township neighboring Vosloorus. Her extremely pregnant cousin interrupted us at one point to tell us she was going into labor. Khambi rolled her eyes. It turned out to be a false alarm. She was helping her cousin through the pregnancy, accompanying her to her sonograms, and planning to raise the baby along with her girlfriend and her cousin ("I am the baby-mommy-daddy," she joked).

From the start of her interview, Khambi demonstrated a keen awareness of playing to a number of different audiences, outside of our individual interaction. When I asked Khambi to tell me about herself, she asked if I wanted the short version or the long version. When I replied I wanted to hear whatever she wanted to tell me, she paused before stating clearly (and, pointedly, to the unknown audience on the other side of my microphone):

> My name is [Khambi]. I live in Joburg, in Katlehong side. And I am an activist. And I am a soccer player. And I am a human rights defender. So I play for a soccer team called Chosen FEW. It's a lesbian team based in Braamfontein.[28]

Despite having spent time socializing with me "off the record" for several months at that point, Khambi approached this interview with an almost mechanical precision, enumerating her identity affiliations to me as she would with a stranger and highlighting those aspects that would be most intelligible to me, as a (white, American) outsider: her geographical location, from a general locatable point ("Joburg") to a specific community (a township, Katlehong side); her political position (activist), linked to her passion (soccer), which was facilitated by the Chosen FEW. This "introduction" had the pat, rehearsed quality of a sound-bite and was markedly different in tone and diction than when Khambi was telling me about her love life. There, she tended to speak in half-finished sentences, punctuated by laughter and Ndebele phrases, frequently switching verb tenses (English was her third or fourth language).

The members of the Chosen FEW received extensive media training as part of their induction into LGBT activism, and played an active role in advertising the Forum for Empowerment of Women both at home and abroad. Sociologist Ashley Currier notes that this sort of rhetorical training is commonly employed by FEW, with the goal of strategically shaping its members' vocabularies to prepare them to self-advocate for a variety of different audiences. Arguing that FEW deployed queer visibility as a fluid, "dynamic, multidirectional" process shaped by audience interaction rather emphasizing visibility as product or end goal, Currier describes the organization's politics in explicitly performative terms.[29] Khambi and other members of the Chosen FEW were acutely aware of their role as representative black South African lesbians, playing to a variety of local, national, and transnational audiences. They were continuously called upon to perform and translate, so that one aspect of their identities (such as "lesbian-ness") would be recognizable in the frame of another (such as "blackness" or "South Africanness"). To this end, throughout our hour-and-a-half-long interview, Khambi strikingly outlined her self-image through the rhetoric of "choice," both as a personal quality and as a constitutional right. Though Khambi's performance of self was more muted than Manika's—on the day I interviewed her, she wore a simple black T-shirt and a pair of mesh soccer shorts—she was equally aware of the importance of crafting her own sense of style, especially when it related to others' perceptions of her.

> I feel like wearing shorts, I wear shorts. When I feel like I can wear skirts, today I wear skirts. Tomorrow I wake up, I feel like wearing trousers, shorts, and when you see me walking with a tie, look like a butch lesbian. Tomorrow you see me wearing a dress, like "Woo!" So I consider myself as a dyke, 'cause I can dress butch, I can dress femme. So I'm in the middle of the two.[30]

Khambi's performance of self privileged her own comfort and took pleasure in confounding others' expectations. When community members came at her with a particular vision of what she should be as a woman, as in this section's epigraph, she tellingly turned the question back on the asker, reframing it in terms of choice. Playing ignorant to those who questioned her right to play soccer and her difference from other women, she gave them a deceptively simple answer: "Who told those women to be like that? They chose for themselves. I didn't like that. That's why I don't do that. That's why I chose to play soccer." Though as a self-proclaimed feminist and activist she might have argued (and, indeed, did argue at other points of the interview) that the women who cook and clean often do so under duress from the expectations of a larger culture rather than their own choice, she framed the situation as if the women chose to be like that. They did, she didn't: end of story. If her homophobic community—"those stereotype people"—argued with her logic, they were forced to acknowledge that women have a very limited choice of roles in patriarchal culture, and if they did have a choice (which they, in theory, did), they might choose differently. Through her response to her critics, Khambi undermined the assumed "naturalness" of female behavior and subtly called attention to the paradoxical relationship between women's constitutional rights and their realities.

Khambi's insistence on her right to choose her own self-representation reflects the larger role that the soccer team played as ambassadors for the

Forum for Empowerment of Women. Beyond being an adroit wordplay on the name of its host organization, the team's positioning of its players as the "Chosen FEW" (with its emphasis on the act of choosing and being the subject of choice) resonated on a number of registers. In an Austinian sense, the name performatively transformed lesbian identity from one of shame and invisibility (a few bad apples, nothing worth remarking upon) into a forceful, positive presence.[31] The players were not accidents; they were chosen. The specifics—by whom? for what?—are open to interpretation.

Choice—especially in relation to transnational queer identity—continues to be an ambiguous, slippery concept. The rhetoric of "choice," as feminist scholar Inderpal Grewal has noted, is often used to co-opt potentially radical social movements and complex identity formations into the neoliberal frameworks where "freedom" is measured in the freedom to consume.[32] Certainly, postapartheid South Africa's GEAR (Growth, Employment, and Redistribution) policies have aligned the country with free market principles, without acknowledging that these ostensibly "free" market principles end up circumscribing the options available for the majority, who have limited choices available to them. Choice thus becomes entangled with questions of access: to bodily safety, to larger queer communities, and to the legal protections promised by the constitution.

Despite Khambi's assertion of the importance of choice in a democracy, much queer organizing—including for the inclusion of "sexual orientation" in the constitution's equality clause—has argued against a framework that includes sexual identity as choice. Rather, LGBT organizing has tactically framed sexuality as predetermined, arguing for sexual identity as deserving of the same protection offered to other minoritarian groups, alongside ethnicity and disability. As noted previously, in South Africa this protection fails in its everyday enactment, often because those with normative sexual identities believe that the women are "choosing" to behave in a certain "unnatural" (and un-African) way, behavior that deserves punishment and discipline.

The rhetoric of choice coupled with the rhetoric of tradition and traditional law has been used to justify violence against queer South Africans. This is especially manifest in the phenomenon of so-called corrective or curative rape, which I address at length in the next chapter. Though the threat of sexual violence was an ever-present reality for those I interviewed, the popularity of these particular terms is problematic; by naming the act from the perspective of the male perpetrator, the terminology suggests that rape might correct a "chosen" orientation ("you just need the right man") and that semen might be able to cure the implied illness/evilness of lesbianism.

Within this hostile environment, the members of the Chosen FEW developed nuanced relationships to their communities, particularly around the issue of representation and their own relationship to the closet paradigm within a black South African context. As Marc Epprecht has argued, the construction of Africa (and Africans) as heterosexual depends not upon the erasure of same-sex activity, but the disavowal of LGBT identity because it is a Western construct, a connection that persists in the argument that homosexuality is a "colonial import" or a "white thing."[33] Notably, where some of the players I interviewed had harrowing "coming out" stories, others did not have a moment where they actively announced their sexual orientation to their parents. It was just understood, and when a girlfriend was brought home the parents treated her as such. Their gendered "difference" had been apparent and, to varying degrees, accepted throughout their lives.

Some of the players who were quick to identify themselves as "lesbians" in the public sphere (and for numerous publics) chose not to actually "come out" in their private lives. As Manika recounted: "For me I can say, *ne*, I never came out of the closet and say, 'Hey, the world, check, I'm lesbian.'"[34] Here Manika acknowledged the reach of the Western notion of "the closet" and its inadequacy in non-Western contexts. This critique, central to queer postcolonial scholarship, suggests that the performative gesture of "coming out" is not always appropriate, nor does it reflect specific, culturally intelligible performances. By embodying their difference—refusing to wear skirts, to do "girl things," and sometimes binding their breasts—Chosen FEW members performed an identity that was simultaneously oppositional and comprehensible to the norms of their communities, without overly emphasizing these performances as "lesbian." Perhaps most significantly, they were able to remain safe and connected to people whose support was important to them. By choosing when to put on and take off the "lesbian" label, Chosen FEW members were able to gain access and acceptance in spaces where these terms would alienate. For Khambi, moments of choosing to withhold and publicize her sexual identity were inextricably linked to South Africa's postapartheid culture of human rights, simultaneously personal and political.

Narrative Slippages and the Reproduction (Revision?) of Cultural Norms

> *If you are straight, you must be straight. If you are bisexual, be bisexual. It's homo, it's hetero, it's bio. You are a queen, queen of the lesbians, but you are dating men? Hell no. Hell no.*
> —K. K[35]

Even as members of the Chosen FEW drew upon individual style and communal affiliations to reproduce and promote themselves by challenging gender norms, they also occasionally took on positions that might seem paradoxical and counter to their well-rehearsed feminist stances. Lila Abu-Lughod and Saba Mahmood, both working in Egypt, have written against the tendency of some feminist scholars and academics to fall prey to the "romance of resistance," choosing to view their subject's actions as either inherently subversive or—if "problematic"—as operating under a false consciousness (the parameters of which are determined by the supposed universality of Western feminist thought).[36] Throughout my time with them, I noticed slippages between the expressed (and often rehearsed) views of the Chosen FEW as model-African-lesbian-feminists and the off-handed biases and viewpoints that would come out in less official settings. Rather than ignoring or excusing these slippages, I want to probe the gap between the "ideal self" and the "actual self" as entryway into the workings of self-sustaining narrative.[37] As they "accessorized" with different cultural values, the women tried on coping mechanisms in environments where they were required to integrate wildly divergent expectations of them into coherent senses of self. The gap or contradiction between these values often remained unresolved; other times, it could be bridged in inventive ways.

As I chatted with the players about what exactly the word "lesbian" meant to them in a South African context, their examples often reflected the gender norms of their communities. This was particularly true when the perceived gender identity did not coincide with the expected sexual orientation. Though the majority of Chosen FEW members I talked to were perfectly comfortable with (if not downright enthusiastic about) dating "straight girls," there was not as much leniency about "lesbians" or otherwise queer-identified women who dated men. In the epigraph to this section, K. K. expressed disapproval toward an acquaintance who identified as (or was perceived to be) a butch lesbian, but who sometimes slept with men. She continued:

> She was butchie like a man. But now, she had a baby. She had a baby. Because of what? Maybe she is telling herself at night, she's a lady. Morning, *emini* (noon), afternoon, she's butchie. She is a man now. Which is not right.[38]

Despite expressing respect for women of diverse sexual identities, K.K. had difficulty accepting these identities when they did not match up to gender performances she expected of them, as was the case with the butch woman ("queen of the lesbians") who slept with men. Her (most likely) unintended slip/erasure of bisexual identity (claiming, "It's homo, it's hetero, it's bio") suggested the hold that biological sex has on understandings of sex-appropriate object choice. Where K. K. might have accepted a feminine bisexual woman dating both men and women, she was less forgiving of the butch woman who slept with men, and whose gender performance and sexual orientation didn't line up. Her language and evident discomfort with this coupling (it "is not right!") unintentionally mirrored the heterosexism of those who, like Mandla Tshabalala ("It can't be done!"), believe that women—of any gender expression—should not sleep together. Perhaps K. K., who self-identified as butch, was sensitive about having her gender identity undermined by the men who dismiss lesbian sexuality. Butch lesbians are particularly targeted for "corrective rape" by those who believe they want to be men and need to have their "femaleness" shown to them. An otherwise "butchie" lesbian's willingness to sleep with men might give credence to the popular belief that visible, gender-nonnormative lesbians can be turned straight.

These contradictions suggest that even those as politically savvy as the members of the Chosen FEW had internalized biases and fears that emerged around issues of representation. Their political training as feminists did not immediately undo their socialization in a patriarchal society. Lesbians, as much as anyone, can hold unquestioned assumptions about gender roles or find some behavior or power imbalances acceptable in a female-female pairing that they would find reprehensible in a heterosexual one. One player I casually chatted with, for example, told me that she had recently broken up with her girlfriend, whom she perceived as having flirted with a man. The drunken fight that followed resulted in a physical scuffle, with the girlfriend receiving a "blue eye" and the Chosen FEW player deep scratches on her neck. Though intimate partner violence exists in all segments of society, this account throws into relief how violence against women is present between even those whose primary political goal is to stop it and empower women to escape it. Though the player felt guilty, she was annoyed that her now ex-girlfriend was taking so long to forgive her. Despite having previously mentioned the importance of "breaking the chain of violence" in heterosexual relationships, she seemed never to doubt that she should (and would) be taken back.

Thully's story was one that could be—and has been—interpreted a number of ways, for a number of different agendas. A *New York Times* video made in the run-up to the 2010 World Cup, for instance, depicted Thully walking mournfully through her township while talking about her rape and suicide attempts, as well as how she sometimes wished she were dead.[39] When we met in 2011 in the lobby of the Market Theatre (famed for fostering radical protest and antiapartheid performance), I was curious as to how open Thully would be about the trauma she had experienced. Thully was unapologetically butch, wearing men's trousers and a heavy sweater over a collared shirt the day we met. Then thirty-one, she was one of the older members of the Chosen FEW. I would see her at games or protests, but not at the more raucous postgame parties. She didn't drink and admitted to being a bit of a homebody. Quieter than many of her teammates, she smiled frequently, revealing a gap between her front teeth.

Though the interview initially started out light, Thully quickly became serious about her past and the way FEW had encouraged her to speak out about her trauma: "I just started feeling free and talking and . . . I started to be free and be open about my past. Like I can talk to anyone and tell, like, 'No, I'm one of those lesbians who survived rape.' I was raped because I was a lesbian."[40] She went on to explain how her rape at age seventeen had undone her sense of her self in the world, her place in her community, and led to a deep depression. She became pregnant and then miscarried. She then fixated on having another child and becoming a mother. After being unable to afford adoption and in vitro fertilization, she slept with a male friend, an experience that reopened the trauma of the first assault. She reflected on this period as a time when "I was not living my life. It was like having a pain inside. . . . There's something inside eating me. If I can have a baby, maybe I will be free in my life." When discussing the daughter resulting from this encounter, her face lit up: "I thought, you see: sometimes if you believe in God, things can happen the way you wish! Then I started to be happy. And I'm not afraid to say that I'm a lesbian mom and I love my babygirl!"[41]

Thully's narration of this story allowed her to process her trauma within a framework that reproduced and revised both categories "lesbian" and "mother." In order to live a life meaningful to her, Thully was able to reenact the result of her violation (an unborn child—associated by her with failure) and take control of the circumstances, so that it was reinvested with new, positive personal meaning (survival, lesbian motherhood). The baby, then, was symbolically reborn as key to her personal narrative: not in spite of her lesbian identity, but because of it. However, in order to live as an out lesbian, she would often use the baby as a way to connect to her culture and, especially, her family. Thully recounted her younger brother's acceptance of her lesbian identity as dependent on her ability to "never change and never forget about [her] baby."[42]

Though superficially Thully's story echoes that of K. K.'s much-maligned "queen of the lesbians," her simultaneous embrace of both her lesbian sexuality and motherhood reveals one person's attempt to deal with an untenable situation. In a patriarchal society that puts a high social priority on the family structure, she refused to be defined by or against her reproductive capacities. For Thully, the opportunity to have a child affirmed her identity as a lesbian and as part of her community/ies. Once again, naming becomes a subtle act of translation and self-transformation. Usually shortened to the more feminine "Thuli," the change in spelling—though not in pronunciation—provided a playful and subtle challenge to the gendering of her name. "Thuli" is a name that is often heard. "Thully" is unique: undetectable to the casual listener, but solidly present in its queerness. She did not sacrifice her "butchness" for her role as mother; in fact, it drew attention to the strength and resilience required to raise a child alone in difficult circumstances, and to the variety of roles that mothers play outside of a reproductive context.

Despite popular opinion that lesbians are reproductive dead-ends, many members of the Chosen FEW planned to have children and did not see their lesbian identity as precluding their roles as mothers, or vice versa. While traditionalists might argue that authentic "Africanness" depended on the reproduction of the heterosexual family, these women's situations demonstrated that the "African family" unit is not one thing. Impacted by the forced removals and migrant labor during apartheid, black South African families continue to bear the brunt of the HIV epidemic, endemic poverty, and a high rate of domestic abuse. The desire for stability often results in a romanticized, imagined precolonial pastoral African identity with fixed roles, an identity that is supremely affective, rooted in African belonging. By rehearsing alternatives, members of the Chosen FEW, along with other lesbians in their community, revised and redefined the preexisting models of parenting to fit their needs and priorities, without sacrificing lesbian identity.

Queering Ikultcha *and Cultural Heroes; or, Manika on the Mountain*

> *Culture . . . I can say, culture is human made. I can do my own culture. It was human made. It was made by those forefathers, the ancestors. So I can make my own culture if I want to. If I do have a family with my partner and then we adopt children, I can make my own culture, and we will just follow that culture. . . . There are some things that are going to be added, more and more and more and more.*
> —Skaaps, Chosen FEW captain[43]

Skaaps was not one to mince words. In our brief interview—a quick cigarette break on the fire escape outside FEW's offices in Johannesburg's inner city before she had to rush home to help her mother prepare for their Good Friday meal[44]—Skaaps outlined the construction of culture in opposition to homosexuality. She then decimated that logic and proposed an answer to work in conjunction with what she sees as culture's fluid character.

Her vision of culture echoes Muñoz's definition of queer: a "doing towards" the future, rather than a rootedness in a timeless past. Skaaps's assertion "I can make my own culture" is deceptive in its simplicity. Manika's use of the Zulu-ized term *ikultcha*—in between the Zulu term *isigo* and the English "culture"—enacted a similarly flexible "doing."[45] Performance enabled these queer South African women to turn *ikultcha* to their advantage. Through their tactical embodiment and critique of *ikultcha* in the everyday, they produced, reproduced, and remixed the aspects of culture that best represented themselves as complex individuals, rooted in a variety of communities.

Perhaps, then, the most effective challenge of the dictum that homosexuality is un-African comes not from the oppositional, outsider performances discussed in the previous chapter, but in how "traditional" culture and its attendant performances are seriously (and publicly) taken up by black South African lesbians who redefine the self as conduit to both the past and the future. I end this chapter with a close reading of Manika's account of her spiritual journey, which incorporated an expansive lesbian self, rooted as deeply in African cosmology as in a future-oriented, fashion-conscious youth culture. The act of recounting the self through narrative suggests possible alternatives for self-reproduction.

Though Manika was the Chosen FEW member with whom I spent the most time during my fieldwork, I did not officially interview her until my final month in South Africa. April 2011 was particularly difficult time for Johannesburg's LGBT community. The previous week, Manika's friend (and Khambi's ex-girlfriend) Thuli[46] had been found raped and murdered. Manika, members of the Chosen FEW, and other Johannesburg lesbians I talked to were shattered and increasingly afraid about the consequences of being out in the community. Thuli's death was shortly followed by the death of Noxolo, an organizer from the neighboring township of KwaThema . Manika recounted these deaths as entwined with her own everyday life: "It killed me that while I'm busy with my girlfriend, while I'm busy getting drunk, while I'm busy sleeping comfortably, Thuli's busy crying and screaming for help. That help's not coming to her. . . . What kills me is when other people went to the funeral, they were insulted about their sexuality."[47]

At the end of an hour-long interview—where she talked without pause—Manika reflected on the violent and fantastical dreams she recently had, and confessed that she was planning to make a pilgrimage to the mountains of Lesotho to find her ancestral roots:

> I need to know who I am and what I am. I need to get in touch with my ancestors. I need to know my roots. Because, me having these weird dreams—sometimes they say if you have these weird dreams, it's a message. Sometimes they say your forefathers are angry at you, or that someone, that person, needs to get in touch with you. So for me, I need to know who I am and how to get in touch with my forefathers who passed away centuries ago. I'm a Masotho person, a Sotho speaker. I'm from Mafokeng, which is Bafoka, a royal family, *uyabon'* [you see]? So I need to get in touch with my roots at the end of the day. I need to go to Maseru [Lesotho]. This is my destination in my journey.
>
> Things are hard for me because I'm still living in a dark shadow. I feel like I still have bad luck. Because if I don't get the river water, I will always have bad luck in whatever I do. So I need a light, because when I see my journey, I see nothing back. I'm going forward, but I'm going back into the earth, you know? I need to see the light, because the dreams, sometimes they're becoming a reality. My grand-

> mother once told me—she was a traditional healer—maybe this is a message that I need to go to Tlokwe [in Northwest Province]. . . . You never know, until I find out about my roots.
>
> I look to know the history of Bafokeng, *amaphoka*.[48] So if I don't know about those people, at the end of the day, nothing is going to happen. So I need to do this journey on my own. I need to do this journey on my own to find out certain things I never knew. . . . I think there's still anger and I need to find peace. So what I need, I need to get *uhlapha* [traditional Sotho blankets], I need to bathe with the river water, to take away this anger. For me, I want to see the meaning of signs of these dreams that I am having. Why is this happening to me? Why every time something happens, it becomes reality? Maybe roots here, maybe they are showing me the way. Maybe I'm using a wrong road, and there's a certain road I need to use. Because if you don't believe in your ancestors, things, they never go your way.[49]

This rather fantastic monologue, following as it did on lengthy discussions of style and politics in contemporary feminism, performed a notable shift in register and made a claim to the very ground on which lesbian and gay South Africans were supposed to have no access: the stability and continuity of a timeless, rooted "Africanness." Manika's dreams interpolated her into a larger cosmology rooted in the eternal nature of *mogologolo*, the ancestors. Her words and images—spoken with glazed eyes, as if to herself, gathering rhythm and purpose—deserve closer analysis. She began by calling on an authority larger than her own—communal knowledge (the unspecified "they")—to comment on the ancestors' use of dreams to get messages across to the modern world. Her repetition of the phrase "sometimes they say" built on this authority to justify her belief that she could only understand herself by making contact with her forefathers (an interesting gendering of her ancestors). Though some might have written her off as a township lesbian—an aberration or an anomaly—she situated herself as a product of a heritage rooted in time and space: Basotho, a Sotho speaker, her surname associating her with Bafokeng, "a royal family." She saw herself called into this lineage through the narrative of a journey, whose metaphors drew on both the mythological and the biblical. She struggled with living in the shadow and needing a light: "I'm going forward, but I'm going back into the earth. You know, I need to see the light." She sought redemption by bathing in the river water.

As Manika narrated her journey, she left the temporal context of her township life—where she sat hunched on her bed, talking to me and occasionally swigging from a beer—in search of an unknown quantity called peace. She felt she could only move forward by going back (to her roots, to the river). Through the process of "storying" herself, she took on the role of protagonist in a familiar tale. The conflict between cultural tradition and individual freedom is a staple of southern African oral performance, often joined in the body of a single protagonist, its cultural hero.[50]

Through her enunciation of a conflicted self, Manika located herself at the center of this struggle. She drew on a familiar framework to assert her desire to find a road that would be right for her and aid her in balancing the tensions that she felt between her multiple identity affiliations, her imagined community, and the freedom she hoped to find—paradoxically—in tradition. She sought to transgress the national, bodily, cultural boundaries of her life in the township, to strip down and be vulnerable to immaterial forces that guided her life. Where violent enactments of "tradition" and *ikultcha* placed her at risk on a daily basis (causing her to wear her projected persona, "this Manika name," like a shield), her self-narration allowed her to imagine immersing her naked, vulnerable, lesbian body at the source of its creation. If the lives of many South African lesbians are bisected by the contradictory lines of tradition and freedom, Manika's imagined journey becomes a prismatic space where these tensions might be united.

Rather than letting the murders frighten them back into the closet (in Manika's metaphor, "back in the earth"), members of the Chosen FEW chose to publicly perform their queer selves in the face of violent opposition: "If they [the community] are not fighting back, we will do that. . . . We can fight back. We're like soldiers."[51] Rather than guns and knives, this battle was waged through visibility in their communities, education, and, importantly, self-promotion. The members of the Chosen FEW that I interviewed seemed to take pleasure in being representative lesbians and in singing their own praises. In circumstances where they were ignored, the women of the Chosen FEW asserted their presence by celebrating themselves and each other.

To this end, their performances of self echo what Liz Gunner has termed "popular praise poetry" in Zulu and other Nguni cultures, suggesting the continuing importance of oral performance in capturing and celebrating the individual in the context of a larger tradition. According to Gunner, "Izibongo [praise poems] are an expressive form through which people can mediate diverse and sometimes conflicting parts of their experience and their identities. . . . They can provide a medium through which the individual mediates difficult, painful as well as exhilarating events and shows them to his or her community through performance."[52] Despite their original role as praise poetry to kings and great warriors, *izibongo*—and the Sotho *lithoko*—are still composed to celebrate the everyday triumphs of people going about their lives, articulating social identity. Though Manika would most likely not acknowledge the connection between her turn of phrase and traditional praise poetry, the mode through which she celebrated herself and her teammates in the everyday remixed the social role that *izibongo* continue to play in mediating complex identity positions.

After having revealed a certain amount of vulnerability in our interview, Manika concluded with characteristic swagga, enumerating her characteristics in a style that was part personal ad, part hip-hop flow, part praise poem, and part playful self-reflexivity of the personas that she slipped on and off as the situation required:

> Manika is funny, talkative, crazy (*laughs*),
> in a normal way, not in an abnormal way.
> Manika is an open-minded person.
> Manika is a go-getter.
> Manika is a person who likes people, number one: from different
> cultures, beliefs, cultures, opinions, and whatever.
> But at the end of the day,
> Manika doesn't get angry. She's always hyper.
> If she gets angry, she gets angry for two seconds and she gets
> happy again.
> That's one thing.
> Manika . . . she is loved by people.
> She's admired by people for being who she is.
> And at the end of the day,
> Manika has millions of fans.
> (*Laughs*)

This *lithoko* offers a concept of culture as both made and inherited, collective as well as personal. In her style, her focus on a self with multiple points of affiliation, and her belief in the power of myth, Manika's spoken-word prose suggested a genre of self-expression that Audre Lorde has termed biomythography.[53] An explicitly queer, female, and African-diasporic way of narrating the self, biomythography has been defined as a mode of expression that "simultaneously invokes, interrogates, and celebrates the mythic (and/or imaginative) possibilities encoded within acts of representation, providing always a polysemous cast to the 'historicity' of events being represented. Myth, dream, and history assume equal footing."[54] When Manika recounted to me her relationship to her ancestors, narrated her dreams and fears, and then slipped into a praise song, she unsettled and remixed each genre. By taking on numerous roles in her own story—hero, celebrity, pilgrim—she inhabited her own, queer conception of culture.

Conclusion: Toward a Subjunctive Cultural Citizenship

This chapter has traced how, in a context where African identity and belonging is filtered through the lens of "tradition" and reproductive futurity, a group of black lesbian activists performatively wielded culture/*ikultcha* as a prism of their own making. To imagine the subjunctive power of constitutional enactment, members of the Chosen FEW strategically combined communal/personal cosmologies of African tradition with the personas and rituals of the everyday present. By acting "as if" their rights were actualized, each woman enacted a projected "could be" via a protective "not yet." In their complex enactments of self—both individually and as a team—the Chosen FEW players inhabited multiple identities, linked by a series of subjunctive performatives. If the orientation of these performances was promissory, it is the same promise that sustains all political activism: the belief that, to borrow a lyric from the classic antiapartheid musical *Sarafina*, "Freedom is coming tomorrow."

Yet, as much of South Africa's recent history has borne out, tomorrow can be unpredictable. The present does not always live up to the utopian dreams of the past. One of the chief challenges in writing this chapter was its long gestational period. Conclusions drawn with surety over the course of a year of intensive fieldwork were inevitably complicated by the passing of time. Though I could not have known in 2010, my research coincided with the apex of the Chosen FEW's success. Just returned, when I met them, from representing the continent at the Cologne Gay Games, they were basking in the glow of international media attention in the wake of South Africa's hosting the World Cup.

It is dramaturgically tempting to end a narrative neatly and to go out on a high note; indeed, earlier drafts of this chapter concluded with the team captured in the amber of their successes. Yet I ultimately decided that it is equally important—and perhaps more honest—to acknowledge that narratives are not under the control of their tellers. The story of the Chosen FEW is also the story of how many LGBT NGOs in South Africa are beholden to the shifting patterns of international funding. When funding sources dried up in 2013, FEW was unable to finance the team's participation in the 2014 Gay Games in Cleveland.[55] This disappointment, coupled with players now in their middle to late twenties, heralded the team's denouement and eventual dissolution. By my final 2016 research trip, most of the women had moved on with their lives.

During this final trip, I met up with all but one of the women I had interviewed five years earlier, hoping to get a sense of their post–Chosen FEW lives.[56] They reported many successes: Khambi enjoyed a steady job teaching life skills at a local high school; Tumi, a bit of a notorious womanizer when I first met her, now managed an upscale burger joint outside of the township while coparenting her partner's daughter; K. K. had opened a children's daycare in her home with her girlfriend, where, despite some homophobia from local parents, enrollment was increasing steadily; Skaaps found work with the One in Nine Campaign's in-house silk screening studio, printing the distinctive slogans on the purple shirts that had drawn notice at the 2012 pride disruption. All affirmed that their activist training at FEW had given them tools to work with either established NGOs or to establish LGBT organizations within their own communities.

Their lives had also been marked with personal loss and periods of financial instability. Manika, with whom I had stayed in closest touch over the years, experienced a particularly challenging path, facing a series of setbacks beyond her control. Sidelined by a leg injury shortly after our interview, her plans for pilgrimage had been frustrated by limited mobility. The following year, her family was duped by real-estate fraud and their two-bedroom brick house with a cast iron gate and a well-tended yard had been repossessed. In 2014, Manika's mother died suddenly of a stroke. As a cook at a primarily white nursing home in a distant town, she had been the family's sole bread winner; more importantly, her ebullient presence had been a central source of support throughout Manika's life. The loss was devastating. Yet even as she reeled from these events, Manika remained resilient and pragmatic. Frustrated with government hypocrisy and the funding politics of large NGOs, she started the grassroots organization Activate Vosloo to educate and support people in her community on LGBT issues (ensuring that it could no longer be said that there were no lesbians in Vosloorus). The night I stayed in her rented one-room *zozo*, she confided that she had started attending classes again and was hoping to finally matriculate high school.

While my analysis of the performances of Chosen FEW players is specific to their roles as "representative lesbians" to their communities, their challenges and joys are shared by many young black lesbians in South Africa's urban townships living out the tension at the heart of South Africa's constitutional democracy. Where their identities locate them at nexus of de jure acceptance and de facto rejection, they tactically choose when and how to claim belonging and citizenship on local, national, and transnational stages. The enactments of subjunctive futurity I have discussed differ from the queer utopia referenced by Muñoz and from Jill Dolan's conception of the utopian performative, where the performance space allows for a collective, affective experience of potentiality.[57] Utopias, performative or otherwise, can only ever be fleetingly staged and are ultimately unattainable or unsustainable, as Dolan has acknowledged. The moment of utopia in performance does not and cannot translate into direct social action outside of its space of shared emotional communion. One cannot live in utopia. The sustained, everyday nature of what I'm calling subjunctive performatives, however—projecting the as if, protecting the not quite—is responsive to cultural context. They are individually crafted and stake a claim to the future in the present tense. By enacting the as-if—which, according to Pellegrini, is both "the becoming in time, the becoming of time"—the players of the Chosen FEW asserted their claim to *ikultcha* and to an inclusive cultural citizenship.

Indeed, by taking the utopian imperative of performance outside the space of the theater and enacting its potentiality in everyday life, the members of the Chosen FEW—through their repetitive engagement with the "world of the now"—were able to change the borders of culture and citizenship, in ways that are gradual but noticeable. As Khambi explained to me at the end of our initial interview, acceptance can be exponential: "So we're twenty in our team: we can just combine that twenty people and their families. . . . My friend and her friend and their families . . . you understand?"[58] While the team has itself dissolved, the former players have taken what they learned in its ranks and expanded outward into new, broader communities. Rather than relying primarily on a reproductive familial model, their kinships are, in Deleuzian terms, far more rhizomatic than arboreal. Linking ancestral pasts with queer proliferating presents—like Skaaps's invented culture, building onward to "more and more and more and more"—these roots stretch outward toward a future that, while unknown and likely imperfect, is of their own making.

THREE

In-Hypervisibility

Aesthetic Displacement and "Corrective" Rape

The dance begins with a burst of violence, presented to the audience without context. On a darkened stage, performer-choreographer Mamela Nyamza spends the first, excruciatingly long, five minutes of I Stand Corrected *almost entirely engulfed in a violent solo pas-de-deux with a trash can. Her feet and occasionally her hands emerge to swipe ineffectively at the air or pound into the ground, the ragged panting of her breath accentuated by the metallic chamber. Features obscured and body wracked by the violence of an attack, she is clearly in an extended fight for her life. By the time we meet her character, Zodwa, reanimated for a flashback of sorts in the next scene, we carry the knowledge of her death foretold.*

The opening moment of *I Stand Corrected*, the 2012 dance-theater collaboration between South African choreographer Mamela Nyamza and British-Nigerian playwright Mojisola Adebayo, viscerally physicalizes the experience of sexual violence. In both action and performed reenactment, the attack is rendered simultaneously deeply personal—enacted upon a living body, breath, sweat, sinew on display, pushed to its limits—and anonymous: an attack on a *type* of body, a body only visible in its violation and annihilation. The entwinement of black South African lesbian visibility and violability, recounted in detail in the narratives of the Chosen FEW players, has been starkly and publicly put on display in artistic and activist representations of "Corrective Rape," the targeting of lesbians for sexual assault and "Correction." Indeed, almost all discussions of black lesbian identity in the public sphere have inevitably been informed by the specter of this violent act. No matter how nuanced, resilient, and complex the self-presentations of the Chosen FEW players may have been, interna-

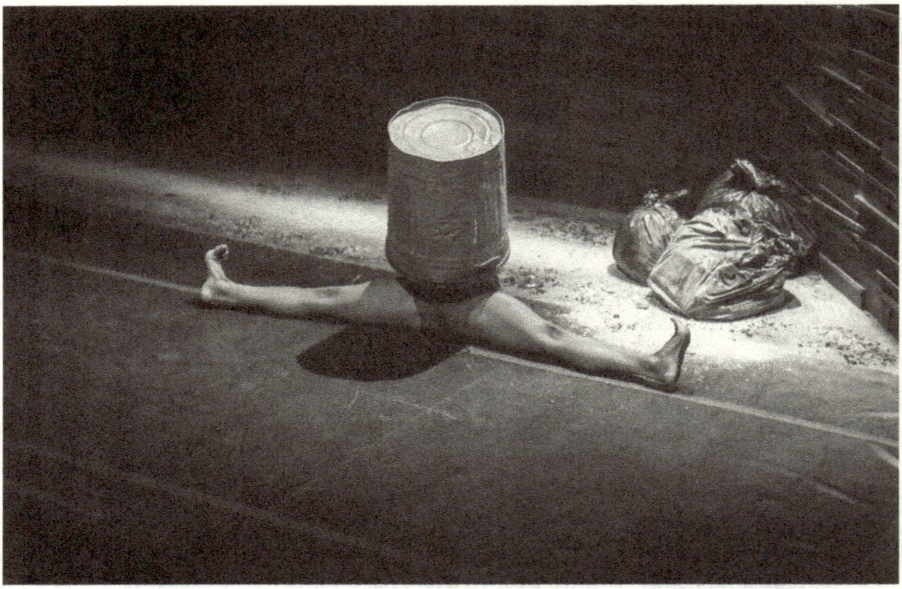

Fig. 5. Mamela Nyamza in *I Stand Corrected* (2012). Photo: Taryn Burger.

tional media coverage of the team was always already primed to present them as violated and victimized by the men in their communities. While the team members sometimes strategically played up this role to draw attention to the real problem of sexual violence against lesbians—and gain them potential sponsorship to international sporting events from sympathetic donors—they were rarely in control of the circulation or use of their images and stories.

Digested by Western audiences who view these narratives through an inherited colonial filter, even the most well-meaning media accounts on this topic continue to be colored by presumptions of African "backwardness" and the need for Western intervention. Queer Kenyan intellectual Keguro Macharia, in a trenchant critique, notes that the dependence of African LGBT NGOs on Western funding institutions has often resulted in a truncated vision of queer African humanity: individual experience and voices are "disappeared into a mass of acronyms and percentages . . . [privileging] the accumulation of injured and dead bodies over creating conditions of livability."[1] I observed this calculation firsthand conducting research for an article on Johannesburg's LGBT archive Gay and Lesbian

Memory in Action, when frustrated staffers reported that initiatives were funded on a project-by-project basis, an agenda often determined more by donor interest than their actual needs. The fact was, they disclosed, donors were less interested in funding an archive that documented LGBT life than they were funding a study about hate crimes, particularly sexual violence against lesbians.[2]

If Mandela's Rainbow Nation had been the primary postapartheid reference point for South Africa's optimistic first decade, the preponderance of articles decrying "Corrective Rape"—which peaked during and immediately following the 2010 World Cup[3]—has in many ways come to stand as a shadow metaphor for its second, reflecting outside perceptions and anxieties about the country's democratic future. Just as acceptance of queer citizens into the body politic had seemed to initially signal a progressive multiculturalism, so too has the rejection and destruction of queer bodies come to signify the violation of this pact. Performance theorist Tavia Nyong'o, writing about the flurry of online activism surrounding Uganda's controversial 2009 "Kill the Gays" bill, has cogently noted that outrage-fueled, Western-led virtual campaigns ostensibly advocating for queer Africans often reveal far more about the Western "fantasies of participation" than the lived reality of those on the ground. When Western LGBT people and their allies imagine themselves as both comrade and savior, "Activism [is converted] into a kind of informatics [where] the crucial objective is the count of signatures and the rapidity with which they can be gained and deployed."[4]

The convenience of online "slacktivism" facilitates what Nigerian author Teju Cole has termed the White Savior Industrial Complex: an imagined empathic investment across borders that draws on the rhetoric of solidarity while employing the tropes of imperialism. The targeted violence against black lesbian and gender-nonconforming South Africans is very real; as a persistent threat against queer safety it requires a well-thought-out, culturally competent response. Yet the uncritical circulation and repetition of narratives of queer African violability, whatever the agenda of the participants, performs its own rhetorical violence. Black lesbian subjectivity viewed solely through this lens risks being transformed into a hypervisible commodity: a canvas for the projection of Western desires, whether pity, outrage, or titillation. Capitalizing on the presumptive backwardness of Africa in the global economy of signs, these viral campaigns operate through shock value taglines that serve as clickbait.

This chapter posits that the loaded abstraction of Corrective Rape—as a separate phenomenon from the real, embodied experience of sexual assault—feeds into what Nyong'o reads as queer Africa's overdetermined role as a "strange attractor of global affect."[5] Drawn in by the seemingly illogical logic that sexual orientation could be changed by violent assault, the trope's allure to its Western audiences is based on scales of proximity and distance. The illogical, sexually cruel African man attracts Western wonderment, while allowing observers to distance themselves from their own culture's tendency to frame lesbian—and all women's—bodies in relation to the pleasure of heterosexual men (see, for example, the porn industry). Both familiar and exotic, Corrective Rape attracts this global affect in part because the African Other makes the Western/white self seem innocent. As Achille Mbembe has outlined, in both historical and contemporary Western imaginaries Africa plays the role of inverted mirror: a refractive "metaphor through which the West represents the origin of its own norms, develops a self-image, and integrates this image into the set of signifiers asserting what it supposes to be its identity."[6] Corrective Rape, viewed through the prism of the (neo)colonial imaginary, blurs the lines between bearing witness and consuming/perpetuating neocolonial tropes.

While lesbians are targeted for sexual violence globally, only in South Africa has this phenomenon been widely labeled as Corrective. This branding has been extremely successful in garnering international outrage, ranging from *New York Times* op-eds to a Change.Org campaign urging "South Africa: Take Action to Stop Corrective Rape."[7] Indeed, the Change.org petition, at its peak one of the website's most popular campaigns, officially declared a "Victory!" when the government established a (now largely inactive) task force in response to global pressure. In the Western rush to rescue the hypothetical black township lesbian from sexual assault—to paraphrase Gayatri Spivak, Westerners rushing to save African lesbians from African men[8]—the lived realities of women targeted because of their sexuality have been erased and flattened, viewed only through the prism of their always-imminent violation and demise.

This chapter looks at the process of looking, both the ways in which looking enacts its own violence and the aesthetic modes through which black queer South African artists have negotiated Corrective Rape's central representational paradox: how to depict the frequent, traumatic experience of targeted sexual assault without reproducing the overdetermined narratives that adhere to these particular raced and gendered bodies. Photographer Zanele Muholi's images of black lesbians, read alongside Mamela Nyamza's choreography, provide insight into how queer artists have drawn on the specific tools of their art forms to tactically re-present the embodied reality of this violence without turning the lesbian body into a hyperconsumable symbol.

Zanele Muholi's photographs of black South African lesbians in their everyday environments counter the simultaneous invisibility and hypervisibility of black lesbian existence, and have become one of the most frequently exhibited examples of South African art worldwide. Many of the top results of a Google image search for the term "black South African lesbians" are Muholi photographs. The range of websites hosting these images, from activist watchdog organizations to international news sources to queer art blogs, suggests the breadth of Muholi's influence on public discourse, providing an easily accessible visual archive for a complex cultural phenomenon. Though previously identifying as a lesbian woman, Muholi has recently come out as nonbinary—using "they/them" pronouns—demonstrating the increasingly complex, evolving intertwinement of gender identity and sexual orientation.

Mamela Nyamza, trained in ballet, has throughout her career challenged audiences' perceptions of African women. Her choreography has drawn attention to the modes through which both Western and African performance traditions discipline the black female body. Beyond staging work in Cape Town and Johannesburg, Nyamza continues to be a frequent performer on Parisian and London stages, as well as an active participant in African performance festivals such as the annual Netherlands Afrovibes and in international festivals such as Performatica. In 2018, she was appointed deputy director at Pretoria's State Theatre and has reinvigorated the country's annual Dance Umbrella performance festival.

In a visual field where the affects attached to sexual violence are already overdetermined, these artists developed an aesthetic that disrupts the process of digesting Corrective Rape by displacing both the viewers' expectations and the black lesbian subject's presumed role as abject other. If the queer African often becomes a strange attractor of affects, these artists' depictions of queer Africans are affectively refractive. In denying audiences unhindered access to view violated black lesbian bodies, their work indicts the process of looking, requiring their audiences to confront both their own desire to see the violation and the unevenness of that gaze. Utilizing what I term a prismatic *aesthetic of displacement*, Muholi and Nyamza depict sexual violence in ways that challenge the scopic regimes that have structured performances of race and gender since the colonial era.

Sexual Violence and Visibility in the Postapartheid Panorama

While Corrective Rape has come to stand for a particular category of gender-based violence, it is just one iteration in a context where sexual violence is reported to be at epidemic levels.[9] A variety of rape narratives circulate in the public sphere, rendering them simultaneously spectacular and banal. Headlines blare the most egregious cases from roadside poster boards advertising newspapers, literally blending into the daily landscape: "AIDS PASTOR RAPED ME!" and "MUM AND GOGO [granny] ROBBED, GANG RAPED, AND KILLED!" This emphasis on only the most shocking or excessive instances of rape normalizes the multitude of everyday violations to the point of invisibility: just part of the fabric of everyday life in South Africa. Feminist scholars such as Deborah Posel, writing about the phenomenon, have convincingly argued that only the most spectacular cases, such as the rape of infants, now invoke outrage, periodically arising as flashpoints for anxiety about the state of the postapartheid nation.[10]

Much of the popular media coverage of Corrective Rape has taken a similar pattern. The hypervisibility—and, often, hyperviolence—of these assaults effectively erases the daily violence suffered by both lesbians and nonlesbians, thus rendering them unexceptional and further normalizing rape culture. Helen Moffett notes the irony that the specific aspects of the constitution promising protections and parity for women and LGBT people resulted in a backlash that places these groups at even greater risk. Men who feel their patriarchal authority undermined by the law use sexual violence as a way to police gender norms, an unofficial form of extrajudicial punishment, where "if rape is believed to be deserved—if a woman is simply being 'corrected,' or 'taught a lesson'—it is somehow not considered to be a criminal activity."[11] In a context where rape has been normalized, certain women are framed as being more deserving, or "rapeable," than others. Rapists not only are rarely prosecuted, but also become icons of masculinity and protectors of Africanness.[12]

The threat of sexual assault has had the effect of rendering black lesbians both *in*visible to the general population and *hyper*visible in their violation. Corrective Rape serves as a performative act: even as it makes the black lesbian hypervisible in her un-Africanness, it erases her queerness through the act of alleged correction. In a context where rape (or threat thereof) is endemic to many South African women's experiences, rape itself becomes twisted to be a marker of "real" (i.e., gender normative, heterosexual) womanhood. For this reason, many South African feminists and LGBT activists have vociferously rejected the use of the terms "Corrective" or "Curative Rape." Noting how the term performs an erasure of the lesbian subject, they argue it linguistically affirms the position of the perpetrator who asserts that the wrong/sick lesbian might be corrected/cured.[13] The ubiquity of this term, whether circulating through lamppost headlines or internet petitions, runs the risk of paradoxically dehumanizing and erasing those most impacted. As Nicole Fleetwood notes in her work on African American women in visual culture, hypervisibility or overrepresentation of any one narrative distracts from the larger "invisibility of blacks as ethical and enfleshed subjects in various realms of polity, economies, and discourse."[14] The hypervisibility of "Corrective Rape" in the public sphere flattens all other possible narratives so that, in Melanie's Judge's analysis, "the [hypervisible] spectacle of black queer violability produces the trick of its own invisibility . . . other dimensions of queer subjectivity remain unseen within the blinding glare of spectacle."[15] Rather than focusing on sexual violation itself, this chapter takes the interplay between the body of this spectacularly hypervisible/invisible lesbian and the demanding gaze of her spectators as its central performance.

Violence is a spectacular phenomenon that binds spectators, perpetrators, and victims in a relationship of both horror and perverse delight; in both performance and reality, it gains its efficacy from the viewer's discomfort *and* inability to look away. Yet violence is also an affective, embodied reality that crosses between physical, psychic, and social geographies. In daily life during times of conflict, popular consent is strategically maintained through people implicitly turning a blind eye to violence; indeed, this is how apartheid lasted as long as it did, and South Africa's white citizens were subsequently able to claim they had no knowledge of the violence that allowed them to live in comfort.

Diana Taylor, writing about the Argentinian Dirty War, has named this particular mode of (not) seeing "percepticide," which she describes as a sort of learned blindness: "Seeing [violence] without the possibility of admitting that one is seeing . . . turns the violence on oneself. Percepticide blinds, maims, kills through the senses."[16] When people are able to live without acknowledging the suffering around them, Taylor argues, they disconnect from the humanity of others and forestall any possibility, or even desire, for action. As the rest of the chapter will demonstrate, by making these daily traumas strange—by gesturing to them obliquely, or displacing them onto symbolic objects—Muholi's and Nyamza's representations of sexual violence prick at the everyday of their audiences, gaining their attention and activating their desire to see. This desire is then turned against the viewers, who not only see the violence itself but their own relationship to it, anew.

Zanele Muholi: In/Hyper/Visibility

Since their first exhibition in 2004, Zanele Muholi's images of black lesbians have arguably been the most visible face of queer South Africa both within the country and abroad. One of the original founders of Forum for Empowerment of Women (FEW), Muholi has since become a prolific "visual activist," their photographs documenting multiplicities of lesbian—and, more recently, nonbinary—subjecthood.[17] Perhaps paradoxically, considering their averred goal of representing those who have very little representative power, Muholi has become one of the most highly visible figures in the postapartheid cultural landscape.

Muholi's renown within the local and global art world is in part due to their role in a 2010 controversy that emphasized the symbolic erasure done to black lesbian bodies under the auspices of nation-building. Lulu Xingwana, then-minister of arts and culture, attended the *Innovative Women* exhibition at Johannesburg's Constitution Hill complex, where Muholi had several photographs on display. Upon seeing Muholi's work, featuring images of nude black female couples intertwined, Xingwana walked out of the exhibition without delivering her prepared speech. When questioned on her dramatic exit, she referenced Muholi's images as a motivating factor, stating: "Our mandate is to promote social cohesion and nation building. I left the exhibition because it expressed the very opposite of this. . . . It was immoral, offensive and going against nation-building."[18] At a gallery adjacent to the Constitutional Court, where the Equality Clause had been ratified, Xingwana perceived same-gender desire as destructive of—rather than generative of—South Africa's national identity. By expressing her personal opinion that the images were "immoral" and "offensive" at an event she attended as a representative of the state, Xingwana's comments reflected an increasingly visible splintering of opinion within the ruling ANC government toward sexual diversity.

Xingwana justified her visceral reaction to Muholi's images using the limited framework through which black lesbians have been visible within the popular imaginary: the pornographic and the stereotypical. "To my mind," Xingwana's statement continued, "these were not works of arts [*sic*] but crude misrepresentations of women (both black and white) masquerading as artworks rather than engaged in questioning or interrogating—which I believe is what art is about. Those particular works of art stereotyped black women."[19] That the same few images could simultaneously misrepresent (as in go against appropriate presentations) and stereotype (draw on popular preconceived notions) of black women to Xingwana, revealed an unquestioned, essentialized black South African female body and identity whose "norm" these images deviated from and perverted. Xingwana's response paradoxically figured the lesbian as both invisible/nonexistent and hypervisible, threatening the understood boundaries of black South Africanness. Muholi's images play upon the tension between these tropes, revealing their complementarity. Their subsequent work countered the perceived spectacular "threat" of lesbianism to the nation through banal, indeed, domestic everyday images (such as women bathing, dressing, walking), countering claims that black lesbian women are "masquerading," either as art or as "real" black women.

Muholi's stated goal in their visual activism is to demonstrate the variety of black lesbian subjectivity: making their identities visible without making them spectacular. About the portrait series *Faces and Phases*, they commented,

> Individuals in this series of photographs hold different positions and play many different roles within the black lesbian community: a soccer player, actress, scholar, cultural activist, lawyer, dancer, filmmaker, human rights/gender activist. However, each time we are represented by outsiders, we are merely seen as victims of rape and homophobia. Our lives are always sensationalized, rarely understood.[20]

Muholi's belief that black queer subjectivities cannot be understood—and should not be represented—by outsiders manifested itself in a mission to document the lives and diversity of the South African black lesbian community beyond the basic narratives of victimhood previously outlined. Yet even in a series featuring quotidian images of black lesbian life that refuse to be defined by trauma, the threat of violence lurks just outside the frame, suggesting vulnerability without victimhood. Muholi's most famous bodies of work, *Only Half the Picture* (2004) and their ongoing portrait series *Faces and Phases,* dramatize the dichotomy between the invisible and the hypervisible, without suggesting any one unified lesbian experience. Rather, the images capture disjointed wounds and well-rehearsed personas, each suggesting vulnerability of lesbian experience without subjecting the individual to the violence of the curious viewer's gaze.

Only Half the Picture, Muholi's first solo exhibition, debuted at the Johannesburg Art Gallery in 2004. Its title references both the literal and the metaphorical meanings attached to the lesbian body and its boundaries. Formally, each image captures a bisected version of a black lesbian involved in her daily identity performance, leaving the rest up to the viewers' imagination, unsettling their expectations and desire for a fully captured image. *ID Crisis*, for instance, depicts a woman from top of track pants to mid-forehead; both her gaze and the viewer's gaze are drawn to her breasts, which she is in the process of binding. *Bra* similarly focuses on a woman's torso, from navel to chin. Though her bra-covered breasts mark her as clearly female, her chest is also covered in wiry dark hairs, those things that are not "supposed to" be there, undoing the easy binary of sex and gender. These two images reject the idea that lesbians (necessarily) want to be men, while upholding a space for female masculinity and self-expression outside of the viewer's frame of reference. The woman posing for *Bra* is not static; her hands, captured in motion either gesticulating or clapping, suggest agency and change. Much like the exhibition's title, Muholi's partitioned depiction of lesbian bodies and experiences suggest that any stable conceptions of black lesbian identities are, indeed, only half the picture.

A subsection of Muholi's images in *Only Half the Picture* deal with the remnants of the trauma and, particularly, homophobic hate crimes. *Hate Crime Survivor I* focuses on a woman's hands crossed in her lap, hospital bracelets hanging from thin wrists. The protective positioning of the hands—with one curving slightly open, vaginally, or like a wound—suggest the vulnerability to retraumatization experienced by many lesbian rape victims when they go to hospitals or police stations to report their rape. *Status Unknown* frames a close-up of a bare breast, with a Band-Aid crossing the nipple, simultaneously suggesting the violence of objectification, the stultifying effect of censorship, and the supposed failed reproductivity of lesbians. The series also contains photographs of Muholi's menstrual blood (on the ground, on sanitary napkins), both celebrating the essential "femaleness" of lesbian women and suggesting the sexual violence that results from men wanting to prove this femaleness.[21] In 2011 Muholi dedicated an entire exhibit to paintings created with their menstrual blood stains. *Isilumo Siyaluma (Period Pains)* turned spilled blood into complex, often beautiful shapes, resembling snowflakes or rose petals.

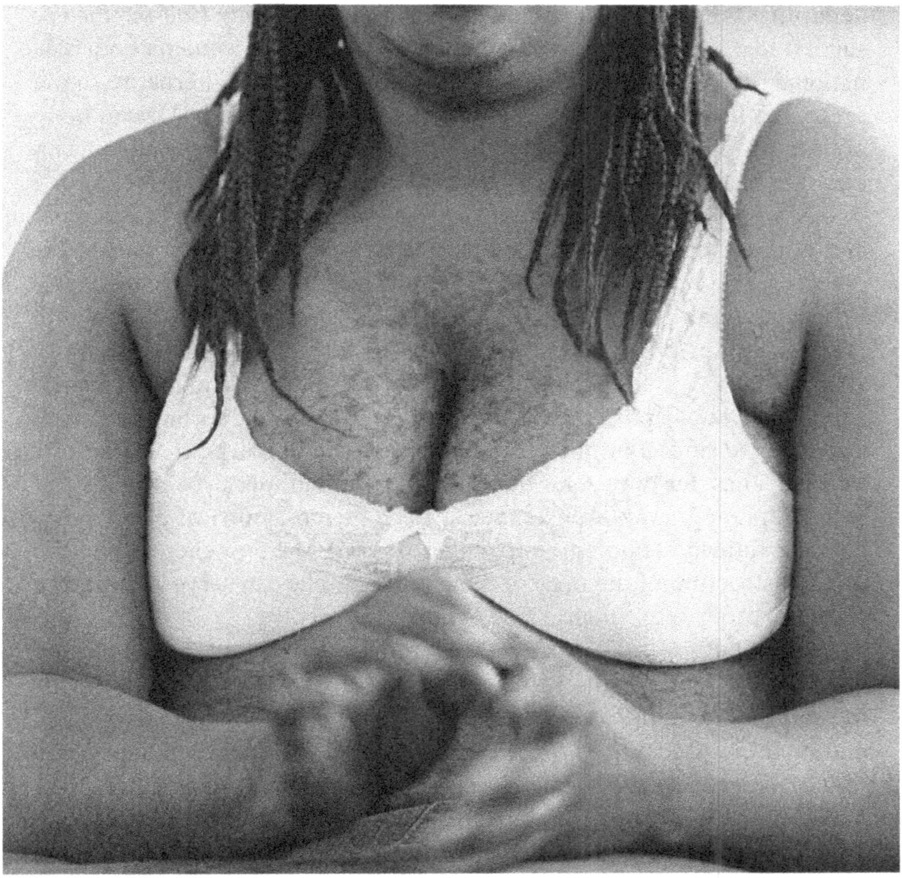

Fig. 6. Zanele Muholi, "Bra" (2003), *Only Half the Picture*. Photo courtesy of Michael Stevenson Gallery, Cape Town/Johannesburg and Yancey Richardson, New York.

The pieces' titles—*Rape* and *Murder*—however, belie the initial aesthetic appeal, just as the artistic medium simultaneously suggests and rejects a reading that would paint lesbians in terms of their vulnerability, as snowflakes and rosebuds in need of protection.

In dealing with the most visible remnants of assault while maintaining the anonymity of the participants, Muholi runs the risk of generalizing the embodied experience of individuals into a symbolic black lesbian body. Yet Muholi recognizes that the responses to this body are always already overdetermined. Indeed, the gallery book's responses to *Only Half the Picture* suggest that the viewers already implicitly understood women's bodies as national bodies. Many saw these images as a threatening alternative to the presumed heterosexuality/gender normativity of the South African body politic. The images became, according to one outraged viewer, "no longer a question of art and beauty but of discrimination—the nation cries."[22]

Such responses emanate, to a large degree, from a history of colonial and ethnographic photography that has refused selfhood to its subject-objects.[23] This is a history of which Muholi is all too aware: "[In] the early images of Sarah Baartman, black bodies and science, all those things, I think there was this kind of 'spectacling,' of exploring, of adventuring in Africa from a Western perspective."[24] The objectification and literal dissection of African—and particularly female African—bodies has been well documented and continues to haunt representational politics. Andrew Van der Vlies, for one, notes that Muholi's photographs evoke the past of colonial photography, even as they suggest the possibility of queer, postcolonial futurity: "Photography makes possible the apprehension of the divided structure of the present, how photographs can serve as evidence of and to mourning, and the idea of queer futurity."[25]

If the *Only Half the Picture* series questioned the *hyperinvisibility* of lesbian identity through segmentation and disjunction, Muholi's ongoing series *Faces and Phases* depicts black lesbian (and, increasingly, trans and nonbinary) identity *in-hypervisibility*: head-on. In an ongoing series of over two hundred portraits, Muholi documented individual black lesbians with whom they had interacted. Each person is photographed from a medium-to-close distance, from the waist or shoulders, with the face as a focal point. They look directly at the lens, usually unsmiling, returning the gaze of the viewer. Each image is titled with the participant's full name alongside the date and location where the photograph was taken.

These portraits, in their simplicity and directness, perform a corrective to singular, stereotyped notions of lesbian victimhood: the (about-to-be) raped black lesbian from the township. The durational, ongoing aspect of the project has had the revealing, unintentional effect of documenting shifts within its participants' self-presentations. Tumi, one of my collaborators from the Chosen FEW, for instance, was photographed more than once, years apart. The images reflect changes in body and style; her direct, confrontational gaze, however, remains a consistent challenge to the viewer who might pass her by, either in the streets or in the gallery.

Yet, as Muholi acknowledges in the book's introduction, several of those included in the series have since passed away. The collection, as much as it is a celebration of out lesbian presence, is thus also shadowed with the specter of (past and future) loss just outside of the frame. Kylie Thomas reads this juxtaposition as implying solidarity with the dead, creating "a community that traverses the boundary between life and death . . . This positioning which insists on the relation between the living and the dead also means that we necessarily read each portrait in the series as haunted by the possibility of violence, rape and murder."[26]

Even as *Faces and Phases* participants are clearly "situated" through their titles' triangulation of time-place-identity, their suggested proximity to homophobic violence displaces them in relation to whatever present/future context within which they might be displayed. Beyond serving as liaisons between the viewers and what might be called a particularly *hyper(in)visible* subculture, the images serve as (an) unsettling medium(s) between the living and dead. Muholi's portraits straddle the line between art, ethnography, and photojournalism, disturbing the conceits of each genre and presenting audiences with the unsettling realization that though Penny Fish might have been alive and defiant in "Vredhoek, Cape Town, in 2008," there is no guarantee that this is still the case.[27]

Even as the individual images present a more nuanced view of black South African lesbian identity than is usually depicted in the sensationalistic news media, as a whole they achieve a strange sort of uniformity that emphasizes a striking performance of butch stoicism. Flipping through the 2010 published collection, one views page after page of primarily butch women (including Manika, Tumi, Khambi, and Thully from the Chosen FEW) staring intensely at the camera, their expressions ranging from a glower to a smolder. In Muholi's choice of participants, the series runs the risk of reinforcing the preexisting image of the impassive, butch lesbian.

This particular depiction of black lesbian "hardness" seems to be an intentional, if implicit, part of the project. I observed a Muholi photo shoot of several members of the Chosen FEW outside of Johannesburg's Constitution Hill complex in December 2010. The initially playful attitudes of the players as Muholi set up the shots underwent a dramatic shift when it was time for the women's pictures to be taken. Smiles and laughs stiffened into squints and frowns as Muholi began to take pictures. They looked, by turns, serious, angry, upset, inscrutable. The overall attitude seemed to be: you don't want to mess with me. Once the pictures had been taken, however, the players invariably broke out into wide, easy smiles, calling back to their friends—who had been good naturedly teasing them—and shuffled out of the limelight to watch the next person "put on face."

While Muholi never instructed them to shift their affect, observing Muholi in action gave me insight into how intracommunity ideals are formed and solidified through representational media. Muholi's camera gave these particular black lesbians (and others involved in the larger portrait project) the opportunity to see themselves as they would like to be seen; in doing so, they all embodied a similar type, a gender performance—akin to Manika's swagga—that Muholi's photography has helped cement as a black lesbian ideal. Their bodies seemed to hold tension, the knowledge that they were committing something for posterity. Photographs are not new to these women, the majority of whom at that time had Facebook accounts and camera phones. Yet cell phone snapshots hold a different weight than images captured on high-tech camera equipment. Snapshots were meant to record and celebrate the day-to-day experiences and selves; posing for Zanele Muholi, these women seemed aware that they were creating Art and participating in a larger political project. Given the opportunity to represent themselves to a larger, unknown public, these *Faces and Phases* participants (both butch and femme) presented themselves as they would like to be seen: strong, proud, serious lesbians, *in-hypervisibility.*

In the past decade more scholarly ink has been spent on Muholi's work than that of almost any other African artist.[28] Much of it has interrogated how the photographs engage the politics of black lesbian visibility, trauma, and postapartheid space. Few, however, have explored the performative dimension of these images and how their display positions their audience's viewing experience. Yet Muholi's exhibitions increasingly use the gallery space as a stage to explore questions of (co)presence, absence, and emotion: that is, questions central to performance. Though Muholi's work had previously avoided referencing the phenomenon of Corrective Rape, *Mo(u)rning*, their 2012 exhibition at Michael Stevenson Gallery in Cape Town that coincided with the popularity of the Change.Org petition, directly and performatively addressed the violent losses suffered by the South African lesbian communities. The exhibition immediately followed the targeted theft of several hard drives from Muholi's apartment, resulting in the loss of their most recent photographs, as well as years of images, some of which had never been printed. This personal loss resulted in a performative meditation on making absence visible and the psychic toll of constant mourning on a small community. Rather than merely displaying images in the gallery, the gallery itself became the staging ground of violation and its shattering impact on the bodies and communities it affects. When visitors to the gallery passed through the space, they moved through the interstices of the politics of representation, as Muholi placed visibility and hyper(in)visibility itself on display.

The entrance greeted gallery visitors with the most visible (and crude) coverage that violence against lesbians had received within South African media: the tabloid advertisements that screamed news headlines from lampposts throughout the nation. A series of five giant, beaded reproductions presented the few times sexual violence against lesbians had received any local exposure in bold blacks, whites, and reds: "Another 'Lesbian' Raped and Murdered" (*New Age)* and "Lesbian Killed in Bush of Evil" (*Daily Voice*). By aestheticizing these attention-grabbers in bright African beadwork, Muholi critiqued the *in-hypervisibility* of these particular types of sexual assaults, while highlighting the general *hyper-invisibility* of lesbian identity when not directly under threat. By using the beadwork so important to Nguni cultures, Muholi's work rooted both lesbian existence and homophobic violence under the purview of "Africanness," while simultaneously critiquing the tabloid culture that made in-depth analysis of the violence's root causes impossible. The title of this series—*Every Bead of My Art*—played on the embodied experience of loss (felt with every beat of the heart), as well as the African artist's responsibility to represent the world around them with every bead of their art.

These reproductions were surrounded by evocative photos from sites where lesbian bodies had been found and restaged images of crime scenes (a body under a tarp, covered in leaves, legs bound). By contrasting the hypervisible sexuality and absent bodies with posted statistics of numerous murders committed against LGBT people that decade, Muholi suggested a profound incommensurability between the "facts," their public representation, and their material loss felt by survivors.

The gallery's central space was dedicated to recent images from the continuing *Faces and Phases* project. Yet this particular exhibition made visible the absent bodies and present violence that were only suggested in the images themselves, through a series of intentional gaps in the rows of portraits. On the opposite wall, a number of quotations written in marker by many different hands transcribed testimony of those who have experienced sexual violence. On either side of the testimonial wall, Muholi installed two listening stations where gallery visitors could listen to the

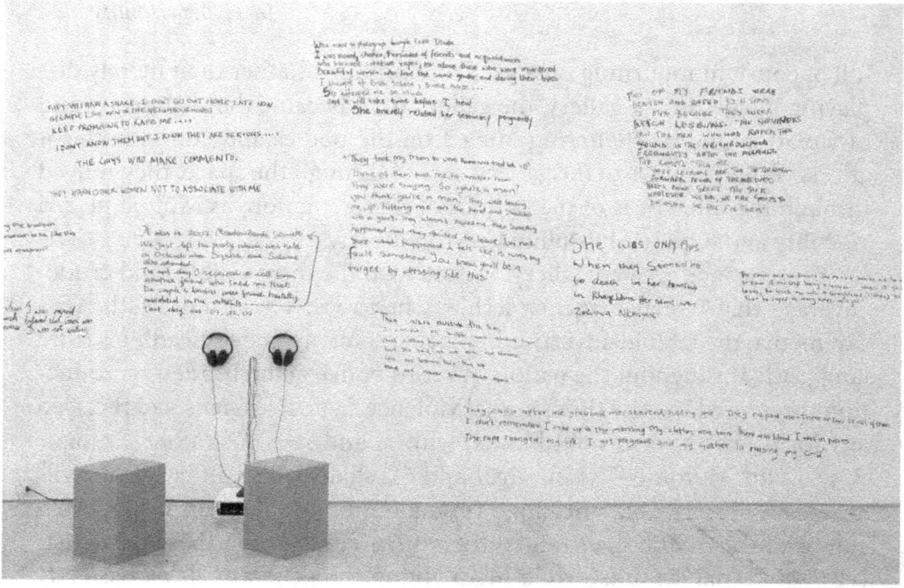

Fig. 7. Listening stations and testimony wall, Zanele Muholi's *Mo(u)rning* (2012). Photo courtesy of Stevenson, Cape Town/Johannesburg and Yancey Richardson, New York

Fig. 8. *Faces and Phases* display (with missing images), Zanele Muholi's *Mo(u) rning* (2012). Photo courtesy of Stevenson, Cape Town/Johannesburg and Yancey Richardson, New York.

testimonies in full (notably, not spoken by the actual victims). Taken together, the multimedia, fragmented representations of violence captured the profound disorientation of experienced trauma. By displacing this experience onto so many tellers, Muholi suggested the pervasiveness of violence and its myriad echoes in black lesbian space, as well as how an atmosphere of diffuse homophobia made any centralized approach to its eradication near impossible.

In one small side room, Muholi recreated a township space of mourning, evoking the community ritual where the family of the dead would traditionally sit wrapped in blankets receiving guests throughout the day. A television sat in a central location, as it would have in the living room, playing footage of Noxolo Nogwaza's 2011 funeral on a loop, emphasizing the presence of many queer people supporting the family in their communities. By creating this "set," Muholi invited gallery audiences (primarily urban, often white) into the African ritual of mourning and evoked the real effects that these deaths have on families and communities in which they occur. By bringing the voices of Noxolo's family into the "home," Muholi placed black lesbians in a larger communal context, demonstrated the raw pain of familial loss (in the mother's looped wailing in the footage) and the rituals through which (even lesbian) dead were honored and remembered. In encountering this staged space in situ, white gallery visitors were called to account for their own body in relation to nearby locations where they rarely, if ever, visited. By reproducing the domestic "African" space in the gallery, Muholi drew upon histories of museum display, subtly implicating the audience's neocolonial gaze, as well as their desire to see the scene of the crime. *Mo(u)rning* posed an implicit provocation to its privileged audiences: why do you flock to see black experience when it is on display in a gallery, when so much of South Africa's continued inequalities are contingent on you *not* seeing the experiences of the majority?

In another room, the documentary *Difficult Love* was screened to introduce gallery viewers to Muholi's process and philosophy.[29] As viewers filed back out into the gallery, they were confronted by a small television screen broadcasting footage of two black women having sex. This depiction—once again only highlighting disjointed body parts to capture the intimacy of the act rather than identities of its participants—was by far the most explicit of Muholi's works on display. Where Xingwana had been horrified by the mere suggestion of same-sex intimacy, the video confronted the unsuspecting viewer with the sexual desire at the nexus of lesbian identity. Still photography may have allowed for a certain amount of critical distance between the viewer and implied sex act. In encountering the film, however, gallery visitors were forced to encounter, unfiltered and unprepared, their visceral responses to the action of two black women in the process of pleasuring each other: the emotions and desires evoked juxtaposed with the awareness that these bodies are vulnerable because of these enacted desires.

If the percepticide allowing sexual violence to pass unnoticed depends on the ability to see (and hear and speak) no evil, then Muholi's performative gallery exhibition engaged the senses one by one, simultaneously placing and displacing audiences in a variety of encounters with black lesbian South Africans. Having encountered the images, rhetoric, and testimony of black lesbians and narratives of Corrective Rape throughout the gallery, audiences finally confronted the politics of viewing itself: a small curtained-off area with a video projection of hundreds of eyes (presumably Muholi's collaborators) staring back at the viewer, occasionally blinking. This room, unlike the other side rooms, was completely silent, staging the encounter of the gaze. With the suggestive title *EyeMe*, this exchange of looking between the looker and the looked at might seem to provide the illusion of intimacy and connection between these women and their audiences. Yet the longer this spectator stared at these eyes, the more she was confronted with the realization that any sense of intimacy was, in fact, a projection of the viewer's own desires.

Mo(u)rning's staging of an extended performative encounter dramatized the process of looking that might go unmarked upon in an unmediated, superficial interaction between a Muholi photograph and an observer. In an early artist statement, Muholi expressed awareness of the vexed relationship between visibility and violation, writing of their process, "Many of [those photographed] had been violated; I did not want the camera to be a further violation."[30] Using the gallery space as their stage, Muholi facilitated an extended discomfiting encounter that avoided further violation of those photographed, by turning the gaze back onto the spectators' own perceptions of themselves and the distance between their lives and those of the black lesbians they had come to look at.

Mamela Nyamza: Choreographing Displacement and the Intimate Geographies of Violation

Mamela Nyamza's choreography inhabits the space between Western and African cultural forms, highlighting the ways they can be used by and against black female bodies. Her early dance pieces explored how costuming—particularly how certain clothes, whether ballet tutus or "traditional" African garb—dictated the sort of shapes the body could take and the work that it could do. Her art is frequently autobiographical: trained in ballet during apartheid at the Zama Dance School in the Cape Town township of Gugulethu, Nyamza received a one-year fellowship to the Alvin Ailey Conservatory in New York. This training, in which she was surrounded by other black dancers, helped her come to terms with her own body in relation to the dance forms that she had always seen as "white." She also discovered her attraction to women. Her mother's violent rape and murder, however, called her back to South Africa, where she reunited with a high school boyfriend, became pregnant, and married him.

As she tried to live up to the cultural expectations placed on a Xhosa mother and wife, Nyamza was haunted by her mother's death and felt increasingly detached from the role she was expected to play. Distanced from the work she wanted to complete and the life she wanted to live, Nyamza divorced her husband and committed to developing her choreographic repertoire away from the European and Afro-American traditions of her early training. She first received acclaim within South Africa for her dance piece *Hatch (2008)*. This piece—alongside its 2015 companion *Hatched*, which featured her son Mandla drawing in coloring books in the middle of the show—became her signature performance and first introduced the themes and tensions that would define her as a choreographer: the struggle to balance her identities as a lesbian, a Xhosa woman, a dancer, and a mother.

I Stand Corrected was not Nyamza's first piece to focus on sexual violence and the paradox of lesbian (in)visibility. Her 2009 work *Shift* explored the topic through the metaphor of sport: a trenchant commentary on how the sporting field can be a space of tentative acceptance for lesbian bodies, while also putting these bodies at risk in co-optation of what is seen as a masculine realm. She created the piece in part as a response to the death of Eudy Simelane, a player on the national women's soccer team Banyana Banyana who was stabbed to death in 2008. In *Shift*, Nyamza began her dance behind a scrim, with her sneaker-clad ankles the only part of her body visible to the audience. If her initial refusal to reveal herself to the audience frustrated their desires to see her perform, the dance, once the screen rose, shifted to the other extreme. Now in silver pumps, Nyamza encouraged the audience to pelt her with twenty-seven tennis balls, representing the number of times Simelane was stabbed. What the audience initially took as a playful invitation suddenly became sinister, as

Nyamza twisted in slow motion, as if under the weight of blows, curling into herself protectively.

This aggressive assault, the lesbian made visible through hyperviolence of participatory spectatorship, depended upon her initial invisibility as a lesbian. The resulting performance was, according to reviews, acutely unsettling. Performance critic Robyn Sassen commented that, even in Nyamza's "friendly" and "bold" enticement of the audience into what seemed to initially be a playful game, "there's an understated sense of danger in all of this and a child-like playfulness which sidestep definition, bringing complicity to the fray and a . . . sense of objectifying the body of the dancer." Indeed, Sassen found the final moments extremely unnerving because they did not deliver on the audience's expectations: "The work's final gesture leaves the audience feeling self-consciously awkward and unnecessary as the performer installs herself, in a foetal position behind the grouped crowd. You turn, you stare at her for a long time, waiting for her to do something, before you mutely shuffle off, maybe feeling cheated. Maybe pondering why you feel cheated."[31] By foiling her audience's desire for closure, the piece forced them to ponder the roots of their underlying expectation that the violated black lesbian body would somehow raise itself out of trauma to "do something" that would ease their own feelings of complicity. The black lesbian body, when visible, must always perform to its paying audiences.

I Stand Corrected, staged in both the United Kingdom and South Africa in 2012 and 2013, fulfilled this audience desire for a lesbian resurrection, but once again denied viewers the satisfaction of a single chronological narrative. Described rather glibly in promotional materials as an "eerie murder mystery where a queer wedding might have been," the story of *I Stand Corrected* is straightforward enough: alone at their Cape Town wedding, English-Nigerian Charlie (Adebayo) thinks she has been stood up by her female South African fiancée Zodwa (Nyamza). As her annoyance and embarrassment turn into anxiety and fear, scenes of Charlie's panicked attempts to get the police to take her partner's disappearance seriously are intercut with intimate moments from their relationship. Finally, it is revealed that Zodwa had been targeted for her sexuality and raped and murdered outside her township home the night before their wedding. The performance ends with Charlie speaking at the funeral and attempting to make sense of the loss.

As a piece of theater, *I Stand Corrected* avoided the tropes of linear storytelling that would have made it a didactic critique of homophobia. The different stylistic aspects each performer brought to the collaboration—Adebayo's training as an actor/playwright, Nyamza's experience as a choreographer—suggested the differences between the two characters' world viewpoints. Despite their attempts to unite (perhaps most explicitly in their wedding), these efforts were continuously foiled. Rather than staging this incommensurability as a failure of their relationship (as the archetypal "star-crossed lovers"), Nyamza and Adebayo suggested the factors that keep the lovers apart were far more structural.

From its beginning moments, the central violent act of *I Stand Corrected*—Zodwa's rape and murder—was both evoked and evaded, through the piece's sparse, symbolic objects and disjoined times and spaces. As the audience filed in, they received the play's program, doubling as wedding billet welcoming them to the marriage of Zodwa Ndlovu and Charlotte Browning. The stage was segmented, reflecting varying aspects of the symbolic regime of womanhood: a long white wedding dress hung upstage, seemingly suspended by several helium balloons. Downstage, two plastic garbage bags rested against a metallic trash can. The program's description of the play as a "supernatural love story" left audience members unprepared for Nyamza's intense, five-minute trash can dance described in this chapter's opening. The scene of violence was suggestive and disorienting, refusing to reveal either perpetrator or victim. The audience's experience of her trauma was similarly fragmented. Her performance was strangely silent, aside from the breath projected from within the metal container, echoing, and the staccato stamp of her feet.

Out of time and place, Nyamza's brutal duet with the trash can seemed to go on longer than it actually did. Other postapartheid theatricalizations of sexual violence have dwelt on the spectacle of the brutalized woman's body, every inch of the victim on display;[32] Nyamza's engulfed death dance became a reckoning of person and thing, Césaire's "thingification" that happens when a body is dehumanized.[33] Rather than turn Zodwa's rape and murder into a hypervisible, hyperreal spectacle—as Muholi did in photographic restaging of hate crimes—Nyamza withheld the literal enactment of the rape, accentuating its affects through her increasingly strenuous engagement with the trash can. Through her gasps, the tensing and untensing of her muscles, and the sweat pouring down her body, Nyamza's dance called the audience to make an empathetic leap for a body pushed to its extremes: to witness a violence that is not exposed, but experienced. At this point in the piece, Zodwa had yet to be introduced and no context had been given for the action. Yet Nyamza drew on the audience's familiarity with this body, or "the black lesbian body" in the process of being "Correctively Raped," and extended their moment of recognition (with its voyeuristic pleasures) into sympathetic pain.

The abruptness of this primary scene disrupted any pretense of a linear narrative suggested in the promised "murder mystery." Indeed, in the scene immediately following her "death," Nyamza emerged from the trash can, resurrected by the *kwaito* township beat. Nyamza's body—eyes empty, zombie-like—launched into the jerky jive steps of township movement and style, aesthetically placing her, while she remained temporally diffuse. This invisible death and sonic-induced resurrection suggested a narrative circularity and other similar events occurring outside the theater. Once resurrected, Nyamza repurposed the trash can as a toilet, as she sat, pants down, reading her horoscope and sounding out words like small child: "There's something delightfully feminine about Ms. Virgo, even when she's wearing tomboy clothes and having a bad hair day. . . . She just can't help being gorg-e-ous." This jarring juxtaposition sutured the ultimate violent act to other, smaller "corrections" made to the gender-nonconforming throughout their lives. Though the narrative properly commences with Charlie's entrance, the action of the play was ghosted by these two atemporal scenes.[34]

As Zodwa flips the pages of the magazine, Charlie finally enters the picture, crossing around her partner—still flipping pages on the toilet—and carrying a bouquet. For an extended moment the two exist in overlapping times and spaces, without connecting. Zodwa finally sinks into the trash can and out of sight as Charlie breaks the fourth wall, apologizing to the audience for her partner's lateness, cracking jokes about African time and finger food. The audience, having played an uncomfortable dual role as witness/voyeur to Zodwa's (symbolic) rape and bathroom time, is momentary placed, cast into the role of the friends and family of the brides and guests at the wedding. The moments of "wedding humor," settle the piece, at least momentarily, into a familiar genre. Yet the madcap wedding humor jars against the reality of Zodwa's situation, setting up the basic unequal dynamic between a mixed-race British cricket coach and her black South African partner. It is an imbalance that will, eventually, be revealed to have deadly consequences.

Throughout *I Stand Corrected*, Zodwa and Charlie inhabit different times and spaces, suggesting the divisions even among two superficially similar "queer black" women, as well as the uneven power dynamics between international couples and first-/third-world "queer" concerns.

Fig. 9. Charlie (Mojisola Adebayo) breaks the tension with a little wedding humor. Photo: Taryn Burger.

The piece's critique of the colonial histories of exploitation and prejudice is most explicit in Charlie's visit to the police to report Zodwa missing. At this point it is unclear whether Charlie is back at the wedding venue (or even who "we," the audience, are in this context). Adebayo delivers a monologue that begins as a scathing critique of southern African homophobia (with its selective versions of what is "natural"), before turning the rant inward to her own history, as the adopted "Coloured" daughter of white missionary parents who grew up in England always feeling different. Now, in the police office, baiting the African man with her anger, she has "never felt so white."[35]

Significantly, the vast majority of storytelling, at least in its traditional sense, falls on Adebayo's shoulders. It is Charlie who engages the audience during the "wedding that wasn't" that frames the moment of the play's "present"; who takes the lead on investigating her fiancée's disappearance; who translates their relationship to the audience through anecdotes. If Nyamza's Zodwa is the specter of sexual violence, shadowing the main narrative, then Adebayo's Charlie is the piece's medium, conjuring Zodwa across the time and distance for the audience. Charlie is by far the more richly drawn character, revealed to the audience through long, self-reflexive monologues, expressing feelings of ambiguity around her position as a British woman of color living in Africa.

Zodwa herself remains unknowable and opaque, speaking rarely. Indeed, her longest section of text comes late in the piece, where she disrupts Charlie's spoken narrative with another evocation of her rape and murder displaced onto a symbolic object. Zodwa stands on the trash can holding a wedding balloon, onto which she inscribes her attacker's face with a pen, as she describes his features: "Big eyes. A sharp mouth. A gold tooth in the middle." She speaks to him in both Xhosa and English, pointing out how any talk of tradition was perverted by the violence of the act, imploring him: "Is this what you wanted? Did you pay the bride price? Was I worth it?" Her final line turns the rhetoric of religion and judgment against her attacker: "What God has put together, no man can put asunder. You cannot divorce yourself from this. There will be consequences." The balloon pops and the scene ends. Though the scene is a powerful enactment of the confrontation that Zodwa did/could have had with her attacker, the symbolism of the balloon and the pen is far less clear than the earlier dance with the trash can. The words seem somewhat stilted, almost an imagined confrontation rather than an actual event. Is this Charlie's envisioned version of Zodwa's last moments? Once again, the out-of-time-

and-placeness of this scene renders Zodwa's experience of trauma opaque and unspecific.

That the performance did not seem particularly unbalanced is a testament to Nyamza's expressivity and her physical presence as a counterpoint to Charlie's monologues. While in part the obvious division of labor in a dance-theater collaboration, the displacement of narrative voice onto the British character and embodied trauma onto the South African replicated the problematic framing of Corrective Rape in transnational discourse: the black lesbian is silent/silenced and the (in this case, mixed-race) Western perspective is privileged. This disparity is further highlighted by the differentiated temporalities in which the characters live: if Charlie takes the audience with her in the present to discover the answer to the mystery of her disappearing fiancée, Zodwa exists in a temporality that is both past (flashbacks to the rape) and future (the audience knows that Charlie *will find* out the murder). Zodwa as an atemporal figure—a ghost, a memory—is in danger of replicating a romanticized timelessness with which Africa has been represented and exploited from the colonial era onward.

I would argue, however, that this staging draws attention to the subtle ways in which the stage is always overdetermined in the intimate geographies of colonialism; Charlie and Zodwa are kept apart because of the continuing legacies of apartheid and church-sponsored homophobia. *I Stand Corrected* was commissioned in 2012 by the British Counsel and had its longest run at London's Oval Playhouse, where it received rave reviews and six nominations for the Off West End Theatre Awards, including Best New Play. It also ran at Artscape Theatre in central Cape Town (where I observed the final dress rehearsal) and the township-based Soweto Theatre, where pay-what-you-can tickets were sold to those in the community. Its audiences were themselves geographically displaced; much like the characters and artists, the space of witnessing was crafted by varying points of identification and disidentification.

Part of the animating tension of the play comes from the staging that keeps the two in different temporalities, even as they share the same performing space. The audience straddles this dislocation uncomfortably, their knowledge of Zodwa's death and that the two will not be reunited overlaying their desire to see the union that cannot be. The moments when the tension is relieved—and the lovers are able to connect in a moment of temporal and spatial overlap and touch and really *see* each other—are structured to be some of the most emotionally powerful of the piece. The first instance comes in a flashback midway through the play, following

Charlie's visit to the police station, to the moment when Zodwa and Charlie met when Charlie coached Zodwa's cricket team. Zodwa teases her, playing a game of hide-and-go-seek, called *ndi-se ndi-se*: "Can I come? Not yet!" As they play, crawling on each other's bodies, this innocent game takes on sexual undertones and becomes increasingly erotic and urgent. Charlie supports Zodwa's legs over her shoulders and Zodwa drapes over her back, her head visible from between Charlie's legs. This moment of shared ecstasy and joy only makes the return to Charlie's reality more abrupt and painful.

The second instance the two share space-time occurs in the penultimate scene of the play. Charlie enters, dragging her suitcase, trailing deflated balloons behind. She has registered the loss, has given up hope. Zodwa mirrors her, unseen and spectral, unpacking the suitcase and taking out perfume, spraying it like breadcrumbs for Charlie to follow. In a dance that painfully mirrors the *ndi-se* hide-and-seek from earlier, Charlie catches the scent and follows it, searching for Zodwa. For a brief moment, they see each other and are in the same plane. Zodwa offers Charlie her hand and they laugh, relieved that they are together. Charlie pulls Zodwa into a kiss—one of the few times they touch each other—and they both embrace in the joy of the reunion. However, Zodwa slowly pulls away, unable to stay, but loathe to let go. It becomes clear that this moment of intimacy was never to be realized. This is the moment where the loss becomes real. As Charlie collapses to the ground sobbing, Zodwa unpacks the suitcase and lies lifelessly upon it.

The final scene mirrors the queer wedding-that-wasn't with the queer funeral that was. This, the third and final representation of the rape/murder, is narrated by Charlie to the audience. However, unlike the comic realism of the wedding scene, the funeral displaces the narration of the brutal details—the facts—onto both performers. Though Charlie begins telling the audience how it happened, it turns out to be a prerecorded voice-over. She stops speaking for a moment, as the details continue, before Nyamza (not Zodwa) takes over as Charlie-at-the-funeral, miming Adebayo's flat, emotionless voice-over. The recording continues, overlapping, as Charlie tries to make sense of the loss:

> CHARLIE: I remember there was a great storm that night. As if the heavens were raging. I imagine the winds sweeping through the bars of Robben Island prisons cells where, once, great black men in the fight for freedom dwelt . . .

Fig. 10. Zodwa (Nyamza) and Charlie (Adebayo) briefly connect across death. Photo: Taryn Burger.

CHARLIE VOICE-OVER: (mimed by Nyamza): *His hands around her throat . . . as she lay dying, he invaded her body and put out his cigarette on her clitoris.)*

CHARLIE: I couldn't sleep for fear and excitement. I wanted to jump to the taxi and go to her, because I know that heavy rain on corrugated iron is so loud and I was sure she wouldn't be able to sleep either. But we had agreed to spend the night before our wedding apart. As is the tradition.

CHARLIE VOICE-OVER: . . . *Set fire to her feet . . .*

CHARLIE: So I slept soundly under the white crisp sheets of my Sea Point hotel bed and covered my ears with a soft pillow. . . .

Why? Why are so many men in this country doing this? Something must have sparked that match, something much have fanned this flame, something must have started this fire. There must have been phosphorus. English-owned phosphorus.

This moment, the piece's most explicit account of sexual violation, further breaks down the lines between the world of the play and its varied audiences, as Nyamza (no longer Zodwa and not quite Charlie) takes over the telling of the assault to the funeral audience, and Adebayo (also not quite Charlie) breaks the fourth wall to pose some of the piece's most difficult questions directly to the audience. Outside of the framework of the narrative, momentarily, audiences—and particularly, British audiences—were asked to account for how they have benefited from colonialism and apartheid (as symbolized by Charlie's missionary adoptive parents' investment in phosphorus), as well as how they saw these crimes as separate from their own lives.

Despite this direct address/accusation, the play ends on a hopeful note. Charlie is left to eulogize Zodwa, whom she describes as being the home she hadn't known she had been seeking when she had come to South Africa. Drawing on the idea of ancestral wives—the often-forgotten tradition of African women taking an ancestor as a symbolic bride—Charlie claims Zodwa as her eternal partner, on a different, spiritual plane. Joined together, for a final time, the two lovers toss the bouquet into the audience, as the soundtrack blares the popular Zulu protest song (frequently employed by black South African lesbian activists): "Siyaya noba kubi." Even though it's bad, we still come.

This evocation of diasporic queer futurity linked to African queer pasts provides an alternate ending to a narrative whose roles seem at times to be overdetermined by History. *I Stand Corrected* unsettles these roles and narratives by existing in the in-between of space and time, of colony and colonizer, lover and beloved, life and death. Though the forward thrust of the action was contemporaneous to its performances, its parts moved back through time, the stories of its two main characters intertwining with the complex global legacies of colonialism and homophobia. Without reenacting the rape itself, the piece honored the lived experiences of those who have been victims of this sort of sexual violence. Like Muholi's stages of Mo(u)rning, the play emphasized the fragmentation of trauma, its shattering of time and place, and how violence can be simultaneously shocking and quotidian, both incomprehensible and inevitable.

Conclusion

Muholi's photography and Nyamza's choreography present the black lesbian in and between the context where she is most visible in the public sphere: the scene of her violation. Yet by staging the performative encounter between the viewer and the victim, these artists do more than just depict this violation; they actively turn the gaze of the viewer inward by engaging and evading the very tropes through which this body was constructed. Rather than directly depict the acts of sexual violence, their work continues to strategically engage the frameworks of representation itself, through a tactic I have called an *aesthetic of displacement*. In making visible the structures of seeing/avoiding that allow rape to be normalized, each artist addresses the violence experienced by many black South African lesbians in a way that avoids the material re-presentation of sexual trauma.

Despite their differing media and divergent careers, Muholi and Nyamza have collaborated on several occasions. Muholi took the production photographs when *I Stand Corrected* performed at the Soweto Theatre and promoted the show heavily on their website *Inkanyiso*. Perhaps more significantly, Muholi also provided an image for the play's poster art. The poster image, *Miss Lesbian I*, a Muholi self-portrait, is appropriately suggestive and evasive of the play's topic. In it, Muholi stands posed like a model, hands on hips, wearing a Wonder Woman leotard. A silver tiara sits in their hair. Muholi stares off to the side of the camera, eyes heavily made up in turquoise, expression inscrutable, standing in silver four-inch heels in the center of what seems to be a stage, the floor scuffed with paint. A white sash hangs across their chest, like a beauty queen's, hailing Muholi as *Black Lesbian*.

To an unsuspecting viewer encountering the poster, the image invites a number of provocations: is the Black Lesbian a superhero? A Barbie doll? An icon? Alongside the bold, red font advertising the play's title, the image becomes even more opaque. Who is the "I" center stage? Who is the unnamed "corrector?" What is broken in this relation? Who is the subject and who is the object? Who is looking? What is the relationship between the image of the Black Lesbian and the "correction" suggested by the performance title? The image's opacity begs the question: why choose to promote the production with this image and not an image of, say, Nyamza and Adebayo during their *ndi-se ndi-se* game, or of Nyamza in the midst of her trash can death dance?

Yet the poster reflects the overlapping, central preoccupations of each artist: the contradictory pressures of being a "representative lesbian," both invisible and hypervisible. When the viewer is able to see the "Black Lesbian" central to *I Stand Corrected* and Muholi's photography, it is only through the lens of her correction/violation. Zodwa, ostensibly the "I" in *I Stand Corrected,* is the antithesis of the high-femme Miss Lesbian or even the “delightfully feminine Ms. Virgo” mocked in the toilet scene. The contradiction immediately apparent between Muholi’s overproduced and hypervisible Miss Black Lesbian and Nyamza’s anonymous, dying lesbian-in-trash-can that opens the play suggests the overdetermined nature of any representations of black South African lesbians, particularly around discourses of violence and violation.

By focusing on the paradoxical interrelation of invisibility and hypervisibility crucial to the impossible action of Corrective Rape, both are able to craft work that, in the words of feminist cultural critic Pumla Gqola, writing about Muholi, is “less about making Black lesbians visible than it is about engaging with the regimes that have used these women’s hypervisibility as a way to violate them.”[36] Each artist uses refractive tactics that displace the viewer’s focus onto the limited scopic regimes that make black lesbians in(hyper)visible. By evoking the concept of *displacement*, I play on its many valances and connotations, particularly around the politics of witnessing in space. In psychoanalytic theory, displacement acts as a defense mechanism where the affects associated with a particular object deemed to be unacceptable are projected onto another object. By focusing not on the violated black lesbian body in its violation, but on its aftermath or symbolic objects—be it Muholi’s wall of testimony or Nyamza’s trash can—their audiences are able to see and experience violence differently.

If sexual violence is normalized and made invisible, its taboo nature also teases and incites the viewer to look. With South Africa’s history of public performances of bearing witness—perhaps most explicitly enacted in the hearings of the Truth and Reconciliation Commission—it might be argued that depictions of Corrective Rape come from a desire to acknowledge lesbian presence and “make visible” hidden pasts. Yet in focusing on the particular sexuality of the victims and defining the act from the perspective of the perpetrators, the phrase blurs the line between voyeur and witness and often sets up a false dichotomy between the rape of lesbians (as hate crimes) and everyday “normal rape.” The displaced aesthetic I argue that artists such as Muholi and Nyamza use to mitigate violence’s perverse draw also perpetually defers its enactment, making viewers uncomfortably aware of their own desire to see violence performed: left, in Sassen’s words, “pondering why you feel cheated.” In a Brechtian sense, the displacement of violence makes strange the drive to see violence enacted; by preventing its audiences from ever seeing the violence, it turns their gaze to their own (frustrated) desire to see, critically engaging their own complicity as (would-be) voyeurs of traumatic acts. Viewers made aware of their own optical desires—suspended uncomfortably between titillated voyeurism and compassionate witnessing—can never fully escape their implication (and inaction) in the act.

Finally, a displaced aesthetic is also innately a prismatic, postcolonial, and unsettled aesthetic connected to the subaltern, multiply situated body in transnational space. As discussed in the previous chapter, many black South African lesbians move between identities, translating these identities to their varied communities as feels necessary. By drawing attention to the displacement of black lesbian identity, these artists rehearse places where the motion of this translation is momentarily suspended and identity is allowed to be. This aesthetic also acknowledges the ways in which representations are never fully "placed," but are out of the control of those who create them.

Indeed, displacement also has its dangers. Muholi's images, particularly, circulate easily and—far from the specificity given the individual performances of self—tend to stand in for the unitary, violated, black lesbian that they are working against. Though circulation on the internet has won them acclaim as an artist and publicized the severity of sexual violence against South African lesbians, Muholi is never fully in control of how these images—so easily cut and pasted out of context—have been used. In response, Muholi has harnessed their popularity to set up a blog called *Inkanyiso*,[37] where individual black lesbian bloggers (authors, artists, and community activists) make daily posts, documenting their lives and the complexity of their experiences. The internet, in this context, also serves as a space of safety and collective knowledge production, where disembodiment and anonymity allow for paradoxical *em*placement in a variety of online communities. The prismatic, discursive space created by these online South African interpretive communities is the subject of this book's final chapter.

FOUR

When Jason Kissed Senzo

Prismatic Soap Opera Fandom on Gensblog

On September 1, 2009, over five million South Africans watched the South African Broadcasting Corporation's prime-time television show *Generations*, then the longest-running soap opera in South African history. The serialized soapie recounted the schemes, relationships, grudges, and aspirations of the members of two competing advertising conglomerates in Johannesburg. That evening, regular *Generations* viewers unknowingly tuned in to see something that had never been screened before on the soapie: two black men kissing. After circling each other for several weeks, Jason Malinga (Zolisa Xaluva) and Senzo Zondo (Thami Mngqolo) finally found themselves alone. Senzo had recently reunited with his father Sibusiso Dhlomo after a lifetime of estrangement. Jason had just returned from years spent working in New York to take up a position at Sibusiso's firm, but was being courted by the rival agency run by Sibusiso's sworn enemy, the devious Kenneth Mashaba. The two argued about business, drawing closer to each other. Finally, Jason reached out and grabbed Senzo by the neck, almost as if to throttle him . . . only to surprise him with a kiss. Senzo froze in shock, before reaching out and burying his hand in Jason's dreadlocks, pulling him closer.

In the two seconds between Jason's initiation of the kiss and the soaring synth of *Generations*' theme song heralding the blackout and the credits, something shifted in the South African cultural landscape. Radio talk shows—the soundtrack to the daily minibus taxi commutes of the majority of South Africans—were overwhelmed by viewers calling in, expressing disgust, shock, and excitement at the storyline. *Generations*, never one to shy away from controversial topics, had crossed a line, it was said. How could a man kiss another man? And more importantly, how would the proud, uber-masculine Sibusiso (also known as Ngamla, or "man with authority") react to finding out his son was *isistabane* (a gay man)? Already by far the most popular television show in the country, *Generations*' ratings shot up during this period. The Jason-Senzo storyline continued to build over the following months, culminating in Sibusiso's discovery of the two in bed together and attacking them in a rage with a sjambok whip.[1] With Jason in the hospital and Senzo repudiating his father, Ngamla spiraled out of control, turning to drink and alienating those around him. Forced to reckon with Senzo's sexuality, Sibusiso faced a choice: confront his own prejudices or risk losing his son.

Gay characters were not unheard of on South African television and, indeed, had been featured on other South African soap operas. Stone, the abused rent boy on *Rhythm City*, briefly had an affair with a "confused" friend Thula in 2008 before both returned to dating women. The regular character of genial and effeminate white man Paul on *Isidingo* had to deal with homophobia from his (mixed race) roommates when he came out. Why, then, did the Senzo-Jason storyline cause such popular outrage? Perhaps Stone and Paul were always coded as "Other," as embodying non-African forms of masculinity, damaged by trauma or already un-African (i.e.: white). Jason and Senzo were not marginalized, but successful black businessmen and competitive players in the Johannesburg media scene. They were not introduced for the purpose of making a one-note point about sexuality, but were each central to the soap's ever-shifting genealogies. Indeed, the discovery of Senzo's sexuality threatened the familial peace just as it had been restored at the heart of the show.

Generations was also different from other postapartheid soap operas. While the response to the gay characters on *Generations* created unprecedented dialogue around issues of black South African queerness in the public sphere, *Generations* had, from its premiere in January 1994 to its unexpected cancelation in August 2014, long reflected the lives and struggles of postapartheid South Africans. While the original iteration attempted to model the Rainbow Nation diversity of the multiracial, newly postapartheid South Africa, over its run *Generations* embraced an approach more akin to the affirmative action Black Economic Empowerment model: the majority of its nonblack, non-Nguni-speaking characters were gradually written off the show.[2] The denizens of *Generations*' Johannesburg at the debut of Jason and Senzo's storyline were almost entirely black, upper middle class or wealthy, and engaged in various forms of media and cultural production. Johannesburg, within the world of *Gen-*

erations, was portrayed as the ultimate cosmopolitan city, populated by coffee bars, parties, and relationship drama. Its viewers were by and large black, and lower to middle class. It was a space of fantasy, of aspiration, and—up until the kiss—of black heterosexual escapism. *Generations*' popularity over the first two decades of South Africa's democracy was in large part due to the long-term emotional investment of its viewers, an investment that encouraged them to "stick it out" through storylines that might otherwise morally offend or challenge them.

In 2008, around the time Senzo was first introduced as a promising young man with a mysterious past, a Johannesburg blogger named Thabo initiated *Generations*' first online fansite: www.gensblog.co.za. As Thabo daily posted his thoughts about the show, the blog began to grow exponentially, as *Generations*' viewers stumbled across the site in search of a space to engage with the storylines. Despite being an unofficial fansite with no direct link to the show, *Gensblog* quickly became a bustling hub of discussion and debate, clocking over one thousand comments daily by the time Jason and Senzo kissed. Its members almost all self-identified with the emergent black middle class: office workers, college students, or professionals, whose relationship to the soap opera tied into complex relationships with black (South) African modernities.

Where *Prismatic Performances* has thus far focused on the performing body as a prism into which audiences projected and reencountered their preconceived notions about South African identity, this chapter shifts focus to the often-elusive process of audience reception. In analyzing an audience's response to Jason and Senzo's storyline through its online traces over the course of several years, I track not only the content of the popular response, but its form and evolution over time. More broadly, I assess how the entanglement of new and old media has provided postapartheid audiences space for discussion and deliberation on the boundaries of "Africanness." Television has often been dismissed by theater scholars and practitioners as the proverbial "boob tube," critiqued as lacking the embodied frisson of live theater, its viewers seen as little more than passive consumers. Soap operas, due to their heightened register and association with female viewership, have perhaps more than any other televisual genre been dismissed as apolitical or even actively antithetical to critical spectatorial engagement.[3]

Gensblog, as a case study in prismatic and multiplatform audience engagement, works against these readings. I contend that both soap operas and their fan communities demonstrate the efficacy of active, performative spectatorship, where debate is energized (rather than deadened) by emotional investment. For regular viewers of the show—particularly those whose passion for the soapie prompted them to seek out online fandom—watching *Generations* became a dialogical process of identification and aspiration. Members of the self-appointed "Gensblog Family" projected their passion into the ether and saw themselves reflected anew through the comments of others. Through daily online interactions that, intentionally or not, emulated the heightened tone and structure of the serialized soap opera melodrama, participants both playacted idealized versions of themselves and shared the struggles of their physical, offline lives. Over the course of months and years the blog became a self-regulating space, created entirely for and by black South Africans, where (South) African unity was imagined and enacted across geography.

The virtual community was irreparably altered when Jason kissed Senzo. Members who had prided themselves on their civility and open-mindedness became polarized and lashed out at each other. Where once the potent combination of reality refracted through soap opera fantasy had dovetailed into a sustaining, supportive community, the kiss—and the introduction of homosexuality into the world of both the soapie and the board—had the effect of both revealing and disrupting established, unspoken norms. With emotions running high and real-world values and judgments suddenly brought to bear on what had seemed a harmonious online imagined community, *Generations*' gay storyline unveiled fractures and tensions within the urbane cosmopolitanism affected by the bloggers. Beyond providing an unusually extensive archive of a South African audience's reception of a particular soap opera storyline, *Gensblog* serves as a microcosm of how many black heterosexual South Africans reckon with and interpret a variety of narratives about gender, culture, and modern "Africanness."

Since emotional projection and passionate identification are central to both the soap opera genre and online fan communities, this chapter, more than any other in this book, enters into the nitty-gritty of its central prism metaphor to get at the triangulated relationship between audience, affect, and social change. I move beyond associative logics and surface qualities to probe its most basic functions and processes: What does a prism do? What circumstances shape particular optical outcomes? What factors change points of view? I approach my analysis of *Gensblog* and its reception of the "gay storyline" through the framework of three overlapping prismatic processes: reflection, refraction, and—drawing on recent feminist scholarship on difference—diffraction. While the metaphor is an inherently performative gesture on my part, it is particularly useful to unpack the complexity of a spectatorial experience, which rarely begins and ends with the act of witnessing. Indeed, for many Gensbloggers, the experience was extended across time and space: what was initially a pleasant distraction to fill life's pauses increasingly became entwined with the fabric of their lives and self-perceptions, influencing future actions.

Fandom—which might be defined as passionate, enhanced spectatorship—is located at a spatiotemporal triangulation: the physical (embodied viewing and blogging), the affective-aspirational (fantasizing alongside the soapie's glitzy melodrama), and the virtual (cocreated, immaterial, relational). Bound to neither one time nor one space, online fandom generates publics and attitude shifts that cannot always be traced offline. I am therefore not particularly interested in the content of the "gay storyline" itself, which in some ways is the quite traditional story of a prodigal son. Rather, I take the storyline as an example of what media scholar John Fiske has termed a media event: a public provocation that momentarily and spectacularly makes visible underlying cultural attitudes. Fiske likens culture to a river of discourses, where currents of meaning—particularly around race, gender, and sexuality—swirl into each other and "bubble up" at particular moments, allowing "invisible movements and workings [to] be theorized from the visible, because this inaccessible level typically carries the most significant connections between the points of visibility."[4] By virtue of its extensive virtual archive, *Gensblog* allows us to peek beneath the waves and coast upon its currents in a data set comprising 775 blog posts and 114,791 comments.

I approached *Gensblog* with the understanding that conducting an online ethnography of a fan community would require me to simultaneously serve as archivist/archeologist, ethnographer, and dramaturg.[5] As I entered the massive backlog of the *Gensblog* archive, I became drawn into a labyrinthine microdrama with an ever-expanding cast of characters, worthy of their own soap opera. Indeed, this chapter pays homage in form to the genre it chronicles. As any viewer of serialized television knows, the payoff is in the buildup; rather than jumping to the climactic kiss—the point of peak visibility—I begin my analysis by tracing the evolution of *Gensblog*, exploring its function as an African interpretive community and support system. I sketch out how the soap opera format, refracted through the blog, was able to open up previously unimagined forms of relationality and self-reflection. I argue that this delicate interplay between reflection (reality) and refraction (fantasy) was dependent on an unspoken set of conditions for communal inclusion: Africanness and heterosexuality. Once these assumptions were shattered through Jason and Senzo's kiss, the shards made visible the often-vexed attachments viewers had to previously stable concepts of "Africa," family, culture, and tradition. A close reading of an internet archive reveals not only the shockwaves caused by these "media events" but emphasizes the ways in which they are interpreted, internalized, and even changed through multifaceted spectatorial engagement.

Performing Virtual Spectatorship: Reflecting and Refracting an Afropolitan Family

When logging onto *Gensblog* (www.gensblog.co.za) in its 2009–2010 heyday, the viewer would have been confronted with a layout reflective of the urban, sophisticated aesthetic of Johannesburg's *Generations*: a sky-blue masthead, charcoal-colored text boxes on a slate-gray background, and blue, bolded teaser headlines over white text highlighting the most recent posts. Headshots of the cast rotated under these "teasers," familiar faces greeting the viewer. The men (Ajax! Sibusiso! Kenneth! Sam! Senzo! Khaphela!) all donned snazzy jackets, ties, or vests. The women (Karabo! Queen! Khetiwe! Dineo! Sharon!) all sported off-the-shoulder dresses, hair styled into soft, flowing curls, topped with hats or bows; their bare shoulders teased the viewer with ample skin, images cut off before the dress material began. In a neat moment of interactivity, the images either popped out or changed direction depending on the position of the viewer's cursor. As the viewer scrolled down, they were offered numerous options: they might read most recent posts, take the latest poll (for instance: "Who is more evil, Noluntu or Khetiwe?"), or visit the site's Facebook page. A box at the bottom of the screen registered the live traffic, pulling one out of any illusion of anonymity and situating them in a (literal) worldwide community of posters, lurkers, and fans (I was, for example, "A Visitor from Washington, DC, USA, 10 minutes ago").[6]

Unlike many television message boards—where users comment on the show and then leave—*Gensblog* operated more like a chat room, where people spoke to each other in real time. Indeed, by the time the Senzo-Jason storyline officially began—eighteen months after Thabo published his first post—the board had morphed into a multipurpose space. An individual blog post could receive upwards of seven hundred comments, often from fewer than ten regular commenters. From 8:00 a.m. to 4:30 p.m. Monday through Friday the bloggers, mostly bored office workers, would daily engage in debates, tease each other, and gossip. The "Comments" section spawned sprawling discussions on topics ranging from the soap opera itself to the actors' personal lives and, increasingly, the personal lives of those who "blogged" regularly.

The men and women who populated the board were all part of the distinctly postapartheid category of the black middle class. Almost all logged in from work and joked about using the company's time. While not necessarily representative of the average *Generations* viewer, this self-selected socioeconomic group in some ways reflected SABC 1's target audience, a segment of the population euphemistically referred to as the "Now Generation" in the broadcaster's advertising terminology. Judging from frequent mentions of cell phones, televisions, DVD players, and other household appliances, most members on *Gensblog* would likely be categorized as the most well-off segment of the desirable demographic.[7]

The internet urges its users to engage in "real time," to jot out quick responses, and to act on the immediacy of their emotions and first impressions. This "liveness" encourages a community of geotemporal simultaneity, of engagement and boredom, of repetition and revision, and play. Though sometimes considered ephemeral and placeless,[8] as communities of practice these virtual worlds encourage their users to inhabit multiple places simultaneously. Sidebars that track live-feed traffic, offsite links to other social media sites, and advertisements reminding the users of their bodily needs and desires compel users to recognize their presence as both grounded and virtual. Between 2008 and 2010, the period I chart, internet proliferation in South Africa increased threefold, spiking from around 8 percent of the population to over 24 percent.[9] By participating in the *Gensblog* community from its inception, these soap opera fans entered a largely uncharted territory, placing them among South Africa's technological vanguard. Unlike Facebook, another site popular with the bloggers, *Gensblog* did not require its members to share their offline identities, pictures, or any information other than a self-selected user name. The board encouraged its users to play with identity, in homage to the imaginary world of *Generations*. Their conversations struck a balance between play-acting and confessional, creating new, virtual relationships that coexisted with the situated geographies, languages, and rhythms of their offline lives.

These lives had been deeply disjointed and fragmented by postapartheid neoliberal economics. As previously noted, from its earliest years in power the ANC government had dismantled, privatized, and outsourced the very sources of income—such as a once-booming township textile industry—that had provided employment and self-sufficiency in black communities under apartheid.[10] The majority of the Gensbloggers reported migrating far from their home communities in order to gain entry to the emergent black professional class and to access the well-paying white-collar jobs in the urban metropoles. Many had previously only experienced city life through its televisual representations, in glitzy soapies or gritty crime dramas, and struggled to place themselves in radically unfamiliar environments. While employment at high-tech jobs in the central business districts of Johannesburg and Cape Town put them in proximity to a new socioeconomic status, many bloggers reported still renting rooms in peri-urban townships. Away from home and not yet "arrived" at definitive success, the bloggers spent much of their day commuting in packed minibus taxis, suspended between spaces, alone in a crowd.

In its first year, the blog became a haven for those who felt isolated and detached from community. One frequent participant, ChingChang, while expressing desire for grand soap opera romance, saw the blog as a social stopgap and balm to her isolation, commenting, "Blogging is what keeps me going without thinking of going home 2 b lonely."[11] With reality so dispiriting and precarious, the ritual of watching *Generations* had become for many an intensely meaningful act. Buoyed by the knowledge that people "back home" were likely doing the same thing, the nightly screening of the soap opera provided continuity between their current situation and previous, happier times, spaces, and selves. Carried to work the next day, their stored-up pleasures found an outlet and amplification through their conversations on the blog. In the physical space of their office, where they might be one of a few nonwhite people, they saw themselves, their languages, and passions reflected through the online platform. For some, even further afield, the blog was their only method of following the soap opera. Ntshantsha, a nanny in a country she referred to as "this frozen hell!" (Ireland), found the blog a cultural touchstone, a way of feeling seen and heard on the other side of the world: "You people i'm crying i just love you, especially when you say something in my language."[12] The compulsive relationship many users developed with the blog, checking in throughout the day and offering advice, was therefore only partially about the television show itself, which served as shorthand for a shared cultural vocabulary. The virtual spaces of both "soapie" and website became, in many ways, as "real" as—and perhaps in some cases, more than—the physical spaces where the Gensbloggers spent their lives.

The intensity and longevity of these attachments, where users drew daily emotional and creative sustenance in *Gensblog* over the course of several years, was likely in large part due to the fact that this "reality" was refracted through the hyper-emotional soap opera format that drew the bloggers together in the first place. Soap operas, as serialized melodramas, are structured to evoke powerful emotions from their audiences. Fan communities that cohere around affect-rich genres often have the effect of creating what Lauren Berlant terms "intimate publics": "porous, affective scene[s] of identification among strangers that promise a certain experience of belonging."[13] *Gensblog*, as a venue for conversation that joined both "real" and "virtual" worlds, became for its participants a dynamic and high-stakes intimate public.

The extended rollout of the storylines—where, as the saying goes, nothing ever happens—strongly appealed a group of regular viewers inclined toward self-dramatization with time on their hands. The conversation threads initially reflected the users' thoughts on the soap opera storylines, with occasional side commentary on the trials and triumphs of their daily lives. As the bloggers got to know each other better, however, the separation between soapie and self blurred, and their spectatorship became increasingly performative. Rather than merely reflecting their opinions on the storylines or reflecting on their daily lives, the bloggers joined the two to perform their lived experience as refracted *through* the lens of soapie-styled melodrama. The spectators, in essence, became the performance.

Prismatic language is particularly useful to understand the process of how a community of what I call performative spectators such as *Gensblog* came to function; indeed, Berlant draws on explicitly prismatic terms in her definition of an intimate public as both "a space of mediation in which the personal is refracted through the general" and "a place of recognition and reflection."[14] In the *Gensblog* community, these processes were not mutually exclusive. When its users directly commented on either the soap opera or events impacting their lives, the blog served what might be called a reflective function: a space where they received feedback on the information they projected onto the surface, without their perspectives or self-image being challenged in any substantive way. This function can be seen in the bloggers commiserating about the regular "load-shedding" blackouts that plagued South Africa in 2009, for instance, or when the message board became a support system when its members were distressed. They provided a positive feedback loop for ChingChang after she had gone on a disastrous second date that ended with her abandonment in downtown Johannesburg when she refused to sleep with her suitor. Similarly, regular commenter Dee asked and received advice when debating whether to date a coworker who had a history of dating women in her department. Even Tbos, who increasingly became the blog's resident agent provocateur, received sympathy when he expressed anguish that his wife was unwilling to forgive him after an affair. As a reflective space, the blog—much like a mirror's surface—served a relatively straightforward function.

Yet because of their passionate relationship to *Generations* and its heightened reality, the blog simultaneously served a more complex, refractive function, with users drawing on the dramatic repertoire of the soap opera to comment on and embellish their lives. The participants mimicked the heightened speech and narrative structure of their beloved soapie in never-ending relationship drama, excessive use of punctuation, and role-playing. The blog itself became a space outside of reality but not quite fantasy, akin to Michel Foucault's definition of a heterotopia. As a liminal "other" space, *Gensblog* provided a refractive mirror of the self that functioned through play and displacement: "It makes this place that I occupy at the moment when I look at myself in the glass at once absolutely real, connected with all the space that surrounds it, and absolutely unreal, since in order to be perceived it has to pass through this virtual point."[15] Much as the path and intensity of light is altered when refracted, passing from one medium to another, so did the bloggers' online interactions transform and intensify as they reenacted their daily lives and desires through the dual prisms of the internet and the soap opera. In transforming its users from passive audience to active performers, *Gensblog* was both reflective and refractive, simultaneously linked to and outside of other spaces. It was indeed "a space of illusion that exposes every real space, all the sites inside of which human life is partitioned . . . [even as it] create[s] a space that is other, another real space, as perfect, as meticulous, as well arranged as ours is messy, ill constructed, and jumbled."[16] The bloggers' interactions created a space that was radically other from their lives, through which they could engage the quotidian via the dramatic. Importantly, this particular heterotopia—beyond being perfect, meticulous, and well arranged—was a self-consciously cosmopolitan and explicitly African space.

Though unusual for a locally produced television show, the board hosted a large number of participants from elsewhere in Africa, due to *Generations*' availability via satellite in real time throughout the continent. This diversity created a platform for a shared pan-African identity that both celebrated and erased cultural difference. In creating an idealized Africa without the messiness of bodies or borders, the Gensbloggers increasingly referred to themselves and each other in familial terms. Several of the regular commenters logged in from outside of South Africa, blogging from Swaziland, Botswana, Zimbabwe, and Nigeria. Beyond demonstrating South African media's hegemony on the continent, the message board became a place where new definitions of Africanness could be tried out and exchanged. Zimbabwean poster Shawanda summarized the feelings of many when she exclaimed, "I am loving this blog more and more. There is such a diverse group of nationalities. I actually thought almost everyone on the blog is South African—now i am realising there is us Zimbos, Batswana, Nigerians. Ah- *Generations* is a true African Soap."[17] These pan-African solidarities continued to build an environment of cultural exchange, both surrounding the soap itself and within the board it inspired. Nigerian Olivia joked that watching *Generations* was like taking a correspondence course in Xhosa, and learned to say some rudimentary phrases, to the delight of the board.[18]

From early in its existence, the bloggers leaned on the metaphor of the virtual African family, with roots extending from South Africa through the continent and across the world. As members of the Gensblog Family, individual commenters were interpolated into a community that both drew on and extended beyond the television show they all loved. The archetype of the family looms large in soap opera melodrama. For all its interoffice intrigue, *Generations*, as its title suggests, was primarily focused on the dizzying family trees and relationship drama of the Mashabas, the Dhlomos, and their various illegitimate offspring. These storylines no doubt influenced the earliest emergence of the family metaphor, when the users initially joked that they were children to the proud papa Thabo. Yet the metaphor quickly took on a life of its own, becoming central to the board's self-image as an African space. Cemented through daily interactions and relationships, the familial metaphor crystalized the blog's existing social infrastructure into a formalized framework where spectators also became performers. As in real life, family became a double-edged sword, both giving the users a sense of mutual accountability and belonging and establishing and policing group norms. Though this kinship structure started off as a general metaphor (for example, an early user commented: "I really appreciate guys, each and everyone of us is getting this blog moving and i love it. We are family guys and this is a family discussion . . . keep up the good work"),[19] each family "member" was eventually given a specific role to play. When one of the most popular commenters, Dee ("Mama Dee") did not log onto the blog one day, Olivia (her "daughter" and a "twinny" to ChingChang) comforted those who were worried by assuring them that "she is working so hard to provide for the growing family since she is our mum,,,and i guess she is doing over-time today,,,,,,,hope she will be here soon,,,,,,,,,,lol."[20] By equating Dee's offline employment with her online role as mother to the Gensblog Family, Olivia both excused Dee's absence and affirmed her importance to their cohesion. Throughout her time on the board, Olivia was one of the users most invested in the family metaphor, frequently expressing joy at having found a community that allowed her to share her thoughts on *Generations* and other aspects of her life. At one point she enthused: "I am glad the family is growing uncontrollable, and ideas are flowing from cousin to sister..to aunt . . . to. . . . .brother etc. I really love airing my views and in turn getting other people's opinions on a certain subject."[21]

Which is not to say that Gensblog Family was a free-for-all. As the board gained an increasing number of regular commenters, hierarchies began to be upheld and maintained, often dependent on the perceived wit and knowledge of the commenter, as well as their level of commitment to the board. In her intensive study of the r.a.t.s. soap opera listserv, Nancy Baym noted the modes of discourse valued in the creation of what she terms a community of practice, through which "the social dimensions take over from the textual ones and an audience becomes a community."[22] As *Gensblog* members got to know and enjoy each other on a daily basis, they began to disclose information about their offline lives, including gender, location, jobs, and families. In some ways, these situations were similar to those explored on *Generations*—betrayal, intraoffice romance, infidelity—and definitely held a desirable appeal for those rushing to give advice. These confessions provided the bloggers the moral authority to weigh in and actively affect the course of these minidramas in a way that they could never do with any of the soap opera storylines. Yet beyond the thrill of private lives aired in a public forum, the board members' comments demonstrated a deepening connection between the members and the formation of the community as a safe, nonjudgmental social space.

Prior to the Jason-Senzo storyline, the ripples in the familial pond were relatively few. When conflict appeared, however, it notably emerged around questions of gender, morality, and the nature of African culture. When the board was in general agreement, this displeasure was primarily directed toward the characters and the show's producers, as was the case when Dineo—pregnant with the child of her husband's son—briefly considered getting an abortion. Other storylines, such as businessman Dumisane's decision to visit a *sangoma* (traditional healer) to rid him of bad luck in love and work, were more contentious. On this occasion the usually sanguine Tbos accused those who argued for African religions coexisting with Western ones of not being true Christians (provoking ChingChang's iconic response, riddled with characteristic punctuational extravagance: "so u saying we r disloyal 2 God Almighty & loyal 2 the Sangoma's Tbos??????").[23] This storyline brought up previously uncommented-upon contradictions about the role of representation, "tradition," and modernity in postapartheid South Africa, and demonstrated a variety of shifting cultural identifications and positions among those on the board. Tbos, for example, questioned the validity of African traditions, stating: "Tradition[!] where does tradition conme from ching ,,,who started tradition ??"[24] This comment was especially ironic coming from Tbos, who frequently expressed his approval for "traditional" behavior in women.

These debates—which in many ways foreshadowed the complex interplay of affiliations that would be revealed during the Jason-Senzo storyline—momentarily threatened to upend the rituals and norms that made *Gensblog* a safe, friendly space for its family members. In each case, however, the situation was quickly diffused, usually by Olivia, the self-appointed peacemaker of the group. Her typical response—as when tempers began to get heated in a discussion of poverty, related to a storyline about a homeless shelter—was to gently urge the members: "Let's leave this topic."[25] At another point, when fighting on the board had reached a peak, she weaponized familial shame to keep the bloggers in order: "Guys we are family. . . . .there is need to respect each other's comment regardless of how you feel about that. Cant you guys say something politely..oh no . . . guys you are letting me down."[26] Moments of disruption were thus quickly contained and dissent silenced. These small moments of tension, where outside prejudices and positions threatened the ways in which the posters perceived their multiple "selves," actually reinforced the norms structuring the blog.

Contrary to protestations that Senzo and Jason's kiss came out of nowhere, board members had been speculating about Senzo's sexuality for months, ever since his initial storyline establishing his paternity had wrapped up. Soap opera's serial structure dictates that when one storyline ends, another begins. Romance was the obvious next step for Senzo, who, being young, cute, and wronged, was almost universally popular with the board. That this storyline evolved over such a long period of time demonstrates the slow burn of soap opera and the painful pleasures of seriality. From his introduction, Senzo was a character shrouded in mystery without a clear origin and agenda. The viewers—especially those on the *Gensblog* board—were encouraged to participate in the "fact-finding mission" alongside the characters on screen, speculating on the "truth" and hypothesizing the twists and turns of the stories. Though the real-time nature of the soapie allowed for a sense of time as being coterminous with the watching viewers, they were also aware of the larger mechanisms through which the soap is produced, and familiar narrative patterns: an audience understands when the story being told is a romance and when it is not. During this period, Senzo's interactions with multiple available women did not follow the usual script. The bloggers created and debated possible counternarratives, each trying to fit him into a particular familiar storyline, such as the untried youth or the perfect, too-good-to-be-true romantic lead. Yet Senzo evaded these roles, and as it became increasingly clear that he was not interested in *any* of the women on the show, the gay hypothesis seemed increasingly likely.

With this realization—gradual but undeniable—came ambivalent pleasures: joy at having "decoded" the truth ahead of time, discomfort with what this truth would bring, and anticipation for the emotional fallout on the characters with whom the viewer had a long-standing relationship. If Senzo's interactions with women did not fit into the normative expectations of the romance storyline, his initial interactions with Jason definitely did. Their first meeting in a bar was suggestive and flirty, causing the bloggers to immediately—albeit begrudgingly—speculate on the possibility of the romance.

As much as they were office workers, students, mothers, and husbands—dealing with life's mundanity, paperwork, and reheated lunches—*Gensblog* and *Generations* gave its users permission instigate any number of microdramas, and build genuine relationships with people with whom they most likely would not have otherwise interacted. Yet even as it allowed for slippery identities, the interplay between reality and unreality—reflection and refraction—still held certain norms as sacrosanct, and desires unspeakable. The explosive reaction of the Gensblog Family to the gay storyline revealed that, on this issue, the fluid borders of Afropolitan tolerance remained rigid even in virtual and imagined spaces. While the family's spectatorial engagement with the soapie was both theatrical and performative—in the Butlerian sense, it created the community and its norms through sedimented discourse—the community remained basically reflective of the same gendered, heterosexual logics that governed larger society. When Jason kissed Senzo, this illusion of unity was shattered, and the fallout challenged and changed these guiding assumptions irrevocably.

The Kiss

If the spark of their flirty interactions discomfited the board, Jason and Senzo's actual kiss triggered a chain reaction of explosive vitriol, and marked a change from the board's expressed desire for tolerance and familial unity. In the days following the kiss, the majority of regular bloggers expressed their displeasure in no uncertain terms, blaming the storyline for changing their viewing experience of the show. Tbos, for one, felt that his own patriarchal role was being challenged and proclaimed, "I cant continue t watch men kissing it is sooo not on and I have to feel enbarassed in front of my wife and kids."[27] Despite having followed *Generations* for years, several bloggers expressed unadulterated hatred for the show and vowed to stop watching it if the storyline continued. When some bloggers tried to reason with those most loudly opposed, the naysayers refused to engage in debate. Thulie demurred, "unfotunately guyz i can pretend as if i like it . . . sorry. . . . sorry. . . . i rather stop watching gen."[28] BlackBeauty agreed: "i dnt thnk i wl b able 2 watch Gen if m gona c the gay couple,,,,,,."[29]

The flurry of comments from those first few days tended to express a shared, deeply held (though largely unarticulated previously) assumption that homosexuality had no place in African culture and went against both indigenous and Christian moralities. Thulie bluntly stated, "guyz to be honest gay thing is not for Africans,"[30] while Olivia asserted that "gays are not part of our African culture,,,,,its American."[31] Nosiphiwo B passionately appealed to any of the show's writers who might be lurking on the board to think of the impact the storyline would have on communities: "By adding gays and lesbians in my,our soap you are distroying the stats of soap, because Generations is a soap that is watched by families even in churches you will find leadership passing a positive comment about it. Guys we love the soap please do'nt kill our appeite on it by things that are not necessary."[32]

She followed up these remarks with increased urgency, revealing the close relationship between the communal religious practices, the quasi-religious practice of viewing of soap operas, the entwinement of each with national identity, and the necessity of enforcing normative gender roles and desires: "The whole South Africa will be lost! [. . .] i even get angry when the preacher does'nt stop and it's nearly 8hoo.We often lough when fathers are teasing thier daughters about Senzo promising the to get him for them, guys we were giving uSenzo the everything award please rewright Senzo's line please plase please we love him."[33] In telling phrasing ("my,our soap"), Nosiphiwo B claimed ownership of the soap both individually and for a larger collective "we," from which gays were explicitly excluded. As a wicked, imported other, homosexuality was aligned with the symbolic destruction of the church, the family, and "the whole South Africa." Her desperation to stop the storyline was specifically related to her and her community's feelings about Senzo ("we were giving [Senzo] the everything award"), and the love that they had previously held for his character as a positive example of black masculinity. Thus queered, the "family"—in its virtual, communal, and national sense—was thrown into peril.

Yet not all of the responses were negative. Among the overall tide of anger and outrage expressed on the board, several of the regular members showed tentative support, arguing that the soap opera was merely reflecting the reality on the ground. Dee, a longtime leading voice on the board, argued that "Mfundi [Vunda, *Generations*' executive producer] is not promoting anything he is just facing reality and a soapei is not only about promoting it is about educating."[34] Thando directly addressed Thulie's fears, arguing, "Thulie dear,i cant realy say its interestin 2c men kissin bt wen facing reality my darlin its happenin.Lets 4get abt interestin&focus on wats happenin on dis planet."[35]

Winston, a new voice on the blog, tried to contextualize viewer response in terms of larger structures of oppression, challenging what he saw as hypocritical policing of the boundaries of Africanness:

> I don't understand black people. *Uyazi* [you know], I really don't. For so many years, they fought against Apartheid, and opression, didn't understand how white people could hate them for being black. Something that they couldn't help. . . . Kanti, people mustn't come and say it's not part of the "African" culture. Whites, coloureds, blacks, gays, we are all african because we all live in Af-

rica. If you think it's not happening, it's happening out there. How about we try to start understanding, and stop hating. That's what this country needs.[36]

Winston's comments were meant to appeal to a geographical rather than cultural conception of Africanness as a tactical engagement of the board's previously espoused pan-Africanism. Tbos's response to Winston was deceptively simple, polite, and pointed: "Winston are you gay, my friend?"[37] This question, posed to almost everybody who did not condemn the storyline, served to intimidate and invalidate dissenting opinions. Thulie, piggybacking on Tbos's question, was more explicit in her shaming of Winston, overruling his appeal to shared Africanness by appealing to common Christian morality and drawing the line between family members and Others: "Morning Winston. no offense this gay thing its not even created by God . . . its demonic wheather u like it or not . . . and we cant stand it when mfundi is promoting demones. . . . nooooooooooooo Winston [. . .] are u also gay winston? that is not acceptable wheather u like it or not."[38] Dee, as the board's mama, increasingly became one of the few regulars with the authority to question the homophobia expressed by some family members. She urged, "Tbos stop it right there about questioning if winston is gay or not he is just telling the facts"[39] and "thulie stop it please we need to accept people for who they are and who they choose to becaome."[40]

As noted in relation to the Chosen FEW players, the concept of choice has played a large role in the construction of acceptable African modernities and can be used to both uphold and reject queer African identity. Where Dee saw gay people as exercising their right to express themselves ("who they choose to [become]"), Tbos saw same-sex object choice as going against the reproductive imperative that for him was central to African identity and continuity: "all these gays do have semen to produce kids mos,,I am not going to do it for them they must make babies for themselves and stop being cowards choice choice ,,what choise is this,,,, pls don't."[41] Members of the board, with their fixation on the new and the modern, expressed no sense of dissonance in picking and choosing which aspects of African modernities were desirable and which degenerate. Ironically, for a discussion taking place on an online forum, a number of posters were quick to comment on the corrupting forces of technology as partially to blame. Winnie faulted the accessibility of global mediascapes for changing mores: "The times has changed, our world has been exposed to this technology thing. we c what is happening in other areas of this earth so this generation is so fast."[42] Olivia, chatting from her job as an auditor in a shipping company in Nigeria, agreed, saying, "technology,,, its happening but its the fruits of the evil spirit."[43] Yet the following day, when Maqz berated the character of Dineo for being backward, Olivia was the first to agree: "dineo is not thinking like a modern lady,,,eish she only thinks stupid."[44]

In this destabilized atmosphere even "Mama Dee" was not immune to accusations of disloyalty, leading to the largest schism in *Gensblog*'s year-and-a-half existence. Both she and Tbos—as two of the board's most prolific posters—had recently been promoted to moderator status, in charge of writing the daily "recap" and "teaser" posts. Dee, who had become increasingly upset with the direction of the "kiss" conversation, posted an informative, motivational list entitled "What is a Gay or Lesbian (homosexual) Person or a Bisexual Person?"[45] This post served to redirect the anger from the soap opera and the storyline toward the perceived traitor in their midst. Dee's post provided them with an opportunity to air their views on homosexuality freely, to mock its rhetoric, and to circle the wagons by making explicit what was once implicit about the family.

Olivia asserted that "Gayness is a sickness indeed it is a confusion in the brain and it needs prayers coz there is no cure it is just like being mad."[46] Tbos, agreeing that "gays relationship are mostly about sex and nothing more,"[47] added that as a deacon in his church he has an obligation to "tell others to quit being GAY my friend ,,I mean do you know why this topic today and now at this point in time ,,that is because God is talking to you and me and all of us : so go and warn others the clock is ticking and I am not joking now."[48] Tbos's abrupt tonal shift from one of the board's most dramatic, provocative figures to his real-life role as a church deacon was just one of many examples of how quickly the playful performative norms of community folded when confronting deeply held personal and cultural beliefs. The abrupt emergence of psycho-socio-religious rhetoric in a space that previously had been one of fantasy and play brought the communal norms and rituals to a screeching halt. When someone tried to defuse the tension by teasing Olivia about her crush on (and imagined wedding to) Jason, for instance, she refused to engage in banter, demanding that the bloggers recognize the division between reality and fantasy: "the Jason thing was not real,,,,but [. . .] I am serious with what am saying today."[49]

The "gay storyline" seemed like none before it to have the power to disrupt the world-building on the board. By calling fellow Gensblog Family members to acknowledge reality outside of the heterotopic spaces of message board and soap opera—be it the lived reality of gay black South Africans or the moral reality of eternal damnation—Jason and Senzo's kiss stopped the playful, performative refection-refraction that had come to define *Gensblog* as a community. What had once prided itself on being a space of consensus and tolerance became increasingly riddled with discord and negative affect. Far from flowing "from cousin to sister..to aunt . . . to. . . . .brother," conversation following each episode seemed to further alienate the viewers from the world of the soapie, making role-play and escapist fantasy impossible. The kiss, and the strong emotions it evoked, lay bare the limitations and contradictions within the community that had once been smoothed over in the name of unity. Once the bloggers perceived the soapie's values as running counter to their own—even revealing the Gensblog Family members as potentially suspect—the once-seamless flow of reflected and refracted affect that had created and sustained the community became blocked, stemmed at the source. This disruption, occurring at the level of both optics and affect, opened to more existential questions leading to soul-searching and expressions of anguish. If Senzo—in so many ways the ideal African man—could also be a homosexual, then what other deeply held, foundational beliefs might suddenly be up for debate?

When Dee was confronted by the family turning in on itself, the aspects of her personality, including her open attitude toward sexuality, that had previously made her a hit on the board were suddenly called into question. Only the previous week, she had joked that she loved Sibusiso's wife Ntombi so much that "I want to try lesbian [. . .] I want to date Ntombi Khumalo [. . .] I want someone with big backseat like Ntombi."[50] In that context—of play, of trying on the fantasy—Dee's sexual openness was part of her persona, part of her joke. Then, Olivia delighted in Dee's subversive humor: "am still laughing,,,you guys are so naughty hey,,,Dee you wanna try lesbian."[51] At an earlier point, she had hinted that she was bisexual, but, tellingly, this reality had been ignored, enfolded into the family closet never to be mentioned again. Now Tbos rushed to label her as Other, announcing with faux solicitude: "Dee is just coming out of the closset guys and she is launching it on the blog,,I must say you've got style Dee."[52] Always insecure and jealous, ChingChang became incensed when Dee jokingly insinuated that ChingChang was dating Tbos. While this sort of microdrama was not unusual for Dee's trickster role on the board, in a context where even refractive play was suddenly suspect, ChingChang took offense and used Dee's waning popularity to stage a daylong "boycott" of the board with Maqz's and Olivia's support. Despite Tbos's attempts to moderate by calling a "family meeting," animosity between certain members overwhelmed the previous rituals of civility. Once the heterosexual heterotopia had been breached—and its unspoken assumptions revealed—all bets appeared to be off. Within two weeks of the kiss, the once-thriving family was in peril. As Thulie fretfully put it, "I think this blog is falling apart."[53]

The looming disintegration of the blog was a product of the spectators refusing to perform their expected roles, and more broadly, a result of a radical reconfiguration of spectatorial practices themselves. *Generations* had long been the televisual prism through which the majority of black South African viewers understood postapartheid success, to the extent that *Generations* producer Pulane Boesek confided to me: "People expect things of this show that they don't expect from [other local soap operas]. . . . It makes it hard to tell the good, relevant stories, while still being what they expect from a soap, while still giving them issues of national importance."[54] By shifting the national narrative of black success and belonging to include black gay men, *Generations* offered viewers an opportunity for a paradigm shift. Framed normatively within the romantic repertoire of the soap opera (star-crossed lovers, the grab-and-kiss), the particular, gendered configuration of kissing bodies brought the spectators up short by confronting them with queer desire as normal: *as African*.

When *Generations'* bodies and desires aligned with what the audience already perceived as natural, *Gensblog* joined reality and fantasy to become a space "as perfect, as meticulous, as well arranged as ours is messy, ill constructed, and jumbled."[55] When the bodies presented were at odds with norms, however, the reflection-refraction process of spectatorship that had sustained the board was effectively jumbled and blocked. Feminist scholars have turned to the process of diffraction—where light waves bend when encountering an obstacle—as a metaphor for such identificatory impasses. Where reflection and refraction are useful models to understand how intimate publics such as *Gensblog* found common ground and self-empowerment in and through fandom and fantasy, they are arguably insufficient frameworks to understand these communities in moments of crisis. Diffraction, as a metaphor, requires flexibility and change in the face of an obstacle—arguably, the same sort of patience and emotional investment required by soap opera fandom. The disjuncture between the audience's deeply held self-image and the storyline that asked them to accept a previously unacceptable identity ("the African homosexual") initially threw the community into disarray. Yet they did not, at least at that point, abandon the blog or the soap opera; and, as they continued to debate, bicker, and engage, things slowly began to shift.

If we look at *Gensblog*'s daily posts debating and reacting to the Jason-Senzo storyline as a diffractive processing of seemingly incompatible differences, we can see how these disruptive blockages—impasses—within these interactions over time changed the very ways people interacted. Rather than reproducing "'the same' displaced, as reflection and refraction do," Donna Haraway notes, "diffraction is a mapping of interference, not of replication, reflection, or reproduction. A diffraction pattern does not map where differences *appear*, but rather maps where the *effects* of difference appear" (emphasis mine).[56]

As an attempt to reflect reality on an outsized, melodramatic scale, *Generations* provided a landmark representation of LGBT identity in South African television, normalizing successful and well-adjusted black homosexuality (providing the *appearance* of difference). Yet *Gensblog* and its online archive give insight into an even rarer space: an extended record of participants' real-time reactions to the difference, the *effects* of which can be measured years after the fact. Its virtual traces document a moment of spectatorial confusion, of peak visibility, and of the collision of "(South) African" and "homosexual." These previously separate, and even oppositional, identities—marked with the implicit division of "us" and "them"—became blurred. They required a diffractive response: if the bloggers were unwilling to abandon the television show many had watched daily since childhood, they had to adapt their worldview to include successful, queer black African men.

While previous storylines had occasionally proved contentious, *Gensblog* had been able to incorporate or ignore them and remain essentially unchanged in its form and content—the storylines merely grazed and glanced off their communal identity. Only the shock of two black men kissing—bringing with it the (im)possibility of queer Africanness—was enough of an affective block to permanently alter the shape and function of the community. It is no wonder this impasse, a homosexual Senzo, initially seemed to some on the blog serious enough to portend national catastrophe. Yet the emotional engagements with the soap opera and the relationships built on the blog proved strong enough that, over time, the community shifted just enough for the family's desires and reflections to realign to make space for those previously invisible others (already always inside). Rather than consigning gay Africans to the invisibility that Trinh T. Minh-ha has called the "not-I's," a "shadow region, the space behind the mirror,"[57] the community, much like light reformulating around a blockage, created a space open to difference and change. In the weeks and months that followed, the *Gensblog* community allowed itself to bend and reshape into something new. Rather than rejecting the shadow or demonizing it as a negative other, a diffractive blockage incorporates the shadow as another part of the larger, unique pattern: shadow surrounded by light and then more shadow—different, yet part of a larger whole.

Mama Dee's refusal to back down from her initial support of the storyline, despite pressure from the family to prove her allegiance by denouncing gays, models one such diffractive performance. Her gesture served as a catalyst for others to enter the community. When pro-gay user Gee was being hazed by regulars on the board, Dee commented: "I am not scared of them we fight every day,"[58] a phrase intriguingly vague in its referents. Though the "them" was clearly the Gensblog Family, the "we" could have referred to either the family (with its tendency to infight) or have extended out to include Gee—and, by proxy, the larger "gay family"—having to "fight every day." When questioned about her sexual identity, a veiled threat in the context of the antigay sentiment on the board, Mama Dee took a clear stance: "I am everything."[59]

In a striking statement of omniscience, Dee refused the binary choice offered her: that one was either a demonic, selfish, foreign gay outsider or a moral, normal, African family member. Her refusal to play by the rules, supported by her history as the board's matriarch, complicated conservative notions of both African family and passive spectatorship. Her actions not only reflected and refracted but, in fact, reshaped the contours of what it meant to be African in that space.

The complete breakdown of the board's norms, coupled with Dee's authoritative insistence that family members should be allowed to be "both" and "everything," ushered in a second phase of the board's existence. In the weeks following The Kiss, for the first time, a number of gay posters flooded the message board. Answering the question "Are you gay?" with a definitive yes, they gave the bloggers' ignorant questions feedback from an unapologetically gay perspective. Zizi, for example, identified himself as someone who worked at the SABC in content development and answered user Thando's timid query on his sexuality by responding: "Now Thando dear, why would that offend me? there really is no need to tip toe around gay people. That is just a term to define someone of a different sexual preference, it's not derogatory."[60] In response to Tbos's warnings of the coming judgment, Zizi retorted, "Yes T Bos, that's if I believe in that sanctimonious babble, are you sure you going to heaven yourself? I know that God loves me no matter what these so-called 'christians' say, my struggles and successes bear testimony to that fact."[61] Duane commented on the presence of gays in their communities, saying, "Gay people do exist.i'm a rugby player myself and who would have thought that a rugby player can be gay?black *nogal* [moreover]!"[62] Duane and Zizi then began a side conversation on the merits of dating "straight men."

The "regulars" were initially taken aback by the influx of so many new posters, and seemed confused as how to address them. The following "side conversation" registered the queer, chaotic displacement of those used to adhering to the family's strict hierarchy and rituals. Much as the Jason and Senzo kiss made explicit the presence of queer desire in their favorite soapie, the regular commenters of *Gensblog* were suddenly forced to confront the literal gay presence in their midst.

MAZOW: Shooo the members r growing here,,,,,

THULIE: the family is increasing . . . . wow!

TBOS: But where does this family come from I think its a gay family here,,,

TSHILI: i was also confused 2day mazow,the family is growing big.

MAZOW: I agree with u TBos why now out of a suddern,,,,,,gay family,,,,

LINDI: family is growing problem is they don't introduce themselves so how can we welcome you guys sorry [. . .] Why are ppl commenting like this today there is no order here where madam Speaker sort this out please Dee am not used to this mess

KIKI: *Hayibo* [Wow] Duane a lot of gayz in the gen family I can't blive this.[63]

In an attempt to ignore the elephant in the (chat) room in the days immediately following the kiss and its explosive fallout, the board regulars decided that they would simply no longer discuss "this gay thing." Yet within a week, the slow burn of "Will they or won't they?" had the bloggers once again expressing interest in the storyline, despite their expressed distaste for it. Partially, this interest came from sympathy with Senzo's plight, as a potentially rejected lover and son (Thulie: "eish Senzo is real confuse. . . . I think he real love Jason" and ChingChang: "Eish i almost cried yesterday when Senzo was trying to explain to daddy eish poor guy").[64]

Jason's bisexuality, referred to colloquially as a "double adapter," provided a more recognizable, masculine pattern of same-sex desire. Indeed, as the storyline continued, the board increasingly took to feminizing Senzo, jokingly calling him "the princess" to fit the relationship into a familiar model. Even Maqz, one of the most adamantly antigay of the posters following the kiss, recognized Senzo as a potential heir to gripping family drama: "i think this senzo guy is going to have a complicated life in gens like karabo [the female lead]."[65] Later, she admitted rooting for him to find some self-acceptance, if for no reason than to move the story along: "Senzo should just accept who he is as he is getting in my nevs [nerves]."[66] Primarily, though, the anticipation inherent in the oft-repeated phrase "wait and see," especially in relation to Senzo's coming out to his uber-masculine father, propelled the continued interest of the Gensblog Family.

"We Were All Gay Today!"

Sibusiso's trajectory on the show over the course of the subsequent months was appropriately dramatic: after putting his son's partner in the hospital with a concussion led to soul-searching (and a brief bout of alcoholism), the manly *Ngamla* eventually accepted both men into his business and his family. This narrative—like many *Generations* storylines, an intensified version of reality—dramatized the immediate, visceral response of many of the viewers and, perhaps, subtly allowed them some distance from which to critique their initial reaction. Producer Boesak remarked that this was an intentional tactic, counting on the viewers' daily identification with the story and characters to move them to a more accepting place. She vocalized the viewers' thought process thus:

> "Ngamla hit his son, and I would have done the same thing, but shoo, look how far he's come, he's now accepted his son, isn't that wonderful?" Without knowing, they've gone through that whole journey with Ngamla. They were also mortified and disgusted and grossed out, and they would have fetched the sjambuck too. And when he came around, they came around with him. Amazingly enough.[67]

If the viewers eventually came around with Ngamla, it was through a prolonged parallel process of identification and the creation of new affective meaning. It might seem difficult to parse out the "deliberation"—that is, actual engagement and change—in the emotional outpour of anger and hate in *Gensblog*'s initial reaction to the storyline. And yet arguably this particular intimate public of performative spectators were primed to have an extended, evolving dialogue alongside the unfolding storyline of the "soapie." Indeed, they had been trained through years of viewership to respect narrative convention and to privilege "familial" bonds and love above all else. In a country deeply divided on issues of race, class, nationality, sexuality, and gender, few places exist where people can speak across these lines, without talking at cross-purposes. *Gensblog* provided an ideal blend of interpersonal intimacy and relative anonymity to have these difficult conversations, sharing the common ground of black African identity and aspirations for some version of the life reflected (and refracted) in the show they watched so compulsively: love, success, family. Though often painful, the dialogue opened on *Gensblog* mediated between the images reflected onscreen and the ways in which each commenter approached these issues in real life.[68]

Acceptance of the gay storyline (and African same-sex attraction) did not come quickly on *Gensblog* and, indeed, was part of a larger shift in the board's tone and membership. In the six months following the initial kiss, the blog underwent a number of changes, of which the storyline was but one motivator. Of those who threatened to abandon the show (and the blog), Olivia eventually stopped posting; BlackBeauty and Thulie continued. ChingChang moved to the Eastern Cape to return to school and did not have consistent internet access. Dee continued to post, but less frequently, as she was retrenched from her job (perhaps for her constant internet use?) and then became sick and had to work from home, where she had no computer. New bloggers joined the family. Meanwhile, Jason and Senzo's relationship unfolded slowly, often in the background to the heterosexual couples. The discussion about their relationship became increasingly about how their characters affected the plot, rather than a fixation on its homosexual nature.

However, it was Tbos—who remained the blog's most vocal champion and provocateur—whose beliefs underwent the most visible restructuring, in part due to several frank discussions that he had with Zizi. Zizi, the black gay man who worked at the SABC, returned to the board periodically, and his presence provided Tbos with an opportunity to pose questions that he otherwise would never have gotten answers to. Though these questions were often predictably graphic and focused on the scatological (e.g.: "isnt a gay relationship mainly about sex?" and "Another thing that I am interested in finding out is what do you feel in the ass I mean is it nice „or what?"),[69] they also gestured to a basic desire to understand what it meant for Zizi to be a black gay man and fellow human being. As Tbos haltingly explained, "you are a human being „gay or not but do you understand how weired this is,,, its just out of the ordinary."[70] When Zizi commented that he had decided to live his life as "a homosexual man, who doesn't understand why he is different, but has taken a conscious decision to embrace himself as also a human being who needs to love and be loved despite what mainstream society says,"[71] Tbos—who had previously stated that God had warned him to tell gays to "stop being gay" or else—encouraged Zizi to "keep coming to the blog hey „ppl can learn a lot through you."[72] As Zizi made his goodbyes that day, Tbos was practically effusive: "sorry zizi but you are the most inspiring gay person on the blogg we love you,,thats why when you come we feel the need to talk gay well even the heading says „*heita* [hey there!] to gays so we were all gay today,,,,,,,,with that its adios from moa [moi]!"[73]

The statement "we were all gay today" is striking on a number of levels. Tbos's farewell suggested a shared, cosmopolitan humanity: an empathetic leap to embrace a more inclusive vision of the self and the familial community on the board, whose playful, parodic mixture of French and Spanish further signaled worldly open-mindedness. Yet the phrase's acceptance was, importantly, time-bound; its future tolerance was in no way ensured. Indeed, where Senzo and Jason (and Zizi) created an acceptable model of visible black African homosexualities, it was a relatively nonthreatening and gender-normative version. Acceptance remained conditional. When Thulie asked if Zizi "walks with ur hands up, and do those funny talks,"[74] Tbos agreed that "yah thulie they exaggerate I think they are the ones that make ppl freak out about gays,,, they should keep it real like Senzo and Jason they look ok."[75] In order to have "good gays," there must be "bad gays," to blame and naturalize homophobia. Tbos's distaste for effeminate gays and the general "pass" given to Jason on the blog for being bisexual or "still a real man" demonstrated the limitations of acceptance.

Yet Tbos's defense of Jason and Senzo as "keeping it real," as well as his distancing himself from those who "freak out about gays," marked a change from his earlier visceral response and demonstrated a willingness to reposition himself as accepting and nonjudgmental. As he later counseled Zizi: "dont judge yourself its not your duty,,keep doing right and let God decide zizi."[76] A generous reading of this attitude, in which homosexuality could be viewed as authentic or "real" and equivalent to other types of differences, provided a diffractive escape or reconfiguring of the learned thought patterns that associated queerness as *particularly* untraditional and therefore un-African. As Tbos later mused, in a discussion on tradition and nature: "hey Dee „you and zizi were talking about Senzo and Jason,, and I was just thinking,,, neh,, some things are traditional some are natural,,,,, like circumsition „,it is traditional to have your *pipis* [penis] skin cut off but its not unnatural to leave the skin on."[77]

Tbos's occasional philosophizing didn't mean that board members were suddenly able to get past their hang-ups around homosexuality. Indeed, for every positive comment he made, Tbos would return with another comment that questioned the morality of homosexuality, or use casually homophobic words such as *stabane* and *moffie*. Eventually, Zizi stopped coming to the board, perhaps tiring of having to defend his sexual identity to people who never really seemed able to fully accept him. Yet Zizi's influence—and his comments from an African gay perspective—continued to be cited whenever gay issues were brought up.

Palm86, a twenty-four-year-old Xhosa man working in Cape Town, joined the blog around in the wake of Sibusiso's sjambok attack, and frequently made comments such as, "I am very homophobic, just like Dlomo!"[78] Upon hearing this, Tbos would call out to the board at large, wondering, "where is Zizi anyways he should come here and defend gay community . . . he does that so well that guy,,I miss him lots, but dont tell him."[79] When Palm86 later suggested violence toward gays, both Thulie and Tbos, earlier two of the most virulently antigay posters on the board, protested. Tbos viewed Palm86 as a cocky upstart and increasingly distanced himself from Palm86's homophobic taunts. Sensing Palm86's discomfort with homosexuality, Tbos took to flirting with Palm86 just to get a reaction out of him: "Palm I was persuing yuor pictures on FB and saw how good looking you were thats why I opted on being gay,, so what do you say? huh? huh. . . . huh?It will be our little secret."[80] Tbos's decision to position himself as a secret gay—however facetiously—demonstrated how normalized homosexuality had become over time, now incorporated into the repertoire of the family's identity play, making space for openly gay cousins and come-ons. Tbos's performative flirting converted Palm86's sexual anxiety into a laughing matter, rendering his homophobia ridiculous.

While Tbos and the others who regularly logged on to *Gensblog* may never identify as pro-gay, their experience with *Generations* and the blog provided a shift in perspective and dialogue, one that was far more nuanced than their initial shocked response to the kiss. Indeed, each subsequent kiss shared between Jason and Senzo (notably, there were not many), resulted in fewer and fewer outraged comments. Strikingly, the amount of emotional energy expended in initially repudiating the storyline seemed to only deepen many of the bloggers' passionate attachment to the show, the blog, and each other.

Virtual Archives, Invisible Repertoires

In a twist right out of a soapie, *Generations* was abruptly canceled in 2014, the result of an extended confrontation between defiant actors striking for higher wages and an intransigent, all-powerful executive producer. Facing a protracted contract negotiation with the main cast, Mfundi Vundla opted to cut his losses and shut down the production midseason. The following year Vundla's *Generations: The Legacy* premiered to fill its empty slot. Billed as the second coming of *Generations*, the show was, aside from two characters, entirely unrelated to the original. By all accounts, the show is nowhere as universally beloved as its predecessor.[81] How could it be? With its premiere preceding Nelson Mandela's inauguration by two months and its final episode airing nine months after his death, the original *Generations* carried with it a legacy of twenty years of postapartheid aspirations, interpreting the rise and fall of the rainbow dream for and alongside its many audiences. The rise and fall of *Generations* serves as good a bookend as any for South Africa's rainbow period.

Despite its absurd melodramatic twists and consumerist excesses, *Generations* remains a potent time capsule for the desires of a national intimate public longing to see black South Africans' success and their daily struggles of self-definition writ large. Cultural critic Danai Mapotsa sees the show as a window into the politics of democratic South Africa's first two decades: "*Generations* plays off the aspiration for [the ANC slogan] a better life for all, and . . . does not simply reflect broader social relations, but also offers powerful insights into the contradictions of contemporary South Africa."[82] The resistance encountered by Jason's and Senzo's inclusion in this narrative suggests that the televisual reflection—much like the everyday performances of the Chosen FEW discussed in chapter 2—remained subjunctive and, even as it offered a model of acceptance, largely aspirational. If, as Mapotsa argues, *Generations* offers insight into postapartheid contradictions, this insight is only compounded and given new dimension in the ways the storyline was taken up, refracted, accepted, rejected, and, in the case of *Gensblog*, diffracted—that is, fundamentally changed—by its audiences.

As the initial shock of seeing two men kissing on their soapie faded, members of the Gensblog Family, along with the majority of *Generations* viewers, stuck around to see what would happen next. Where queer black African identities had previously been consigned to the shadows and condemned from the pulpit, Jason and Senzo's relationship brought queer Africanness into the living rooms of millions of South Africans, inviting conversations in countless locations along the way. Though the initial impact of same-sex intimacy within *Generations* shook the viewing public to its core, the daily pleasure of watching and then discussing with friends and family (both on- and offline) made the affective bonds between the viewers and their soapie that much stronger. Without quite being aware of it, audiences had incorporated Jason and Senzo into their daily lives, and—through anticipatory narrative that teases catharsis and closure—started rooting for their reincorporation into the *Generations* family. For producer Boesak, this normalizing shift became most apparent when a law professor friend mentioned that she frequently used Jason and Senzo as a reference point for her students, so that "now, when they discuss [the legalization of gay marriage] they discuss the fact that *Generations* has made it acceptable in society. Even though the Case Law had been passed, what made it acceptable in society was that they saw it every night on *Generations*."[83]

For queer black South Africans, this increased societal acceptability forged by the show was profoundly meaningful. Even prior to the storyline, *Generations* had been for many queer viewers a disidentificatory pleasure, due to its superbly campy divas; longtime fan and avant-garde performance artist Athi-Patra Ruga, whose image graces this book's cover, counts leading lady Karabo as his first drag icon.[84] Yet in a dramaturgical context where villainous backstabbing and duplicity are par for the course, it was the normalcy of Jason and Senzo's relationship that made it so precious to those who rarely saw themselves as protagonists. At a group I facilitated at the LGBTQ archive Gay and Lesbian Memory in Action in 2011, for instance, a gay male college student from the University of Witwatersrand summed up the couple's appeal: "They have a home together, they live together, they get along with each other," he enthused. "They aren't cheating. Because being a gay person now and trying to navigate the relationship business, you know, it's treacherous, it's horrible. People cheat and lie to you. But with them, they're adults, they've reached the level that I hope to reach as well."[85] If *Generations*' original mandate was, in part, to show that black people could be successful, the Jason and Senzo storyline demonstrated that black men can be successful and love each other as well.

As an interpretive world parallel to the soap opera created through performative spectatorship, *Gensblog*'s long-term impact is less clear. Soap operas and websites, as spaces of performance, are ultimately always in motion. They exceed any attempts to document, summarize, or assign stable meaning. Where *Generations* went out with scandalous bang, *Gensblog* faded away with a whimper. Even as I conducted initial research for this chapter in 2012, the website had entered a period of decline, never quite recovering from *Generations*' monthlong preemption by the 2010 World Cup. When typing its URL into the address bar in October 2013 to check my citations for my doctoral thesis, I was confronted with a blank page: the website had been unceremoniously taken offline. Though a limited number of individual cached blog posts are still retrievable through archival sites such as the Wayback Machine (www.waybackmachine.org), the comments on the posts are no longer viewable. The traces have disappeared. In terms of their material existence—their accessibility—these conversations, processes of deliberation on which I have now spent so many years of my own life deliberating, may just as well have never happened at all.

Yet this disappearance echoes Peggy Phelan's definition of performance as a process that "honors the idea that a limited number of people in a specific time/space frame can have an experience of value which leaves no visible trace afterward."[86] *Gensblog*, as a time/space in which a small group of people shared an experience and created relationships that were profoundly important, is itself now a performance archived in these pages: a trace of a prismatic engagement of actors across the "time/space" of a real and imagined South Africa. *Gensblog*—initially a fragmented archive, now an invisible repertoire—provided its participants a space of reflection and imagination at a moment where people were struggling to shift alongside rather than abandon one of the cultural yardsticks against which they had long measured their identity.

Conclusion

On December 5, 2013, Nelson Mandela succumbed to a protracted illness at the age of ninety-five. Though he had not been actively involved in politics for over a decade, Mandela's death heralded a period of national mourning and introspection. For many it signaled the end of an era, the death of unified, if imperfectly enacted, sense of national possibility emerging from the aftermath of apartheid. For others, particularly the poor and unemployed, the rainbow shine had long since worn off. If Mandela's 1994 inauguration—marked by numerous multilingual and multicultural performances—had been an immaculately stage-managed introduction to the new Rainbow Nation, his 2013 state funeral threw this narrative's fragments and fractures into sharp and extremely public relief. Where the New South Africa had been inaugurated under blue skies and purple jacaranda trees outside Pretoria's Union Buildings, Mandela's memorial was held on a cold, rainy Tuesday at Soweto's FNB Stadium. While the organizers had no doubt chosen the location to show Mandela to be man of the people and to evoke the spirit of the antiapartheid struggle through the memorial's proximity to 1976 Soweto uprising, their choice unintentionally conjured a more recent and far more ambivalent narrative. The architecturally stunning calabash-shaped stadium had originally been designed for the 2010 World Cup Games at great public expense. Save for hosting the occasional club soccer match and serving as concert venue for touring international artists, the stadium has since stood largely empty. Dwarfing the surrounding modest township homes, it stands as a white elephant symbolizing the government's commitment to privatized spectacle over bettering the material conditions of its citizens.

The ceremony, viewed by millions across the globe, featured solemn tributes from luminaries such as Barack Obama and Ban-Ki Moon delivering well-scripted speeches about Mandela's dignity, compassion, and international legacy. Unlike his inauguration, however, where multiple political voices were folded into a unified state pageant, Mandela's memorial service was marked with numerous unruly, improvised performances that demonstrated to its audiences just how far the African National Congress had slipped in popular esteem. President Jacob Zuma's speech was frequently interrupted by large contingent from the far-left Economic Freedom Fighter Party. Their booes and chanted accusations that he had spent public funds on a mansion in his rural homestead of Nkandla foreshadowed the wave of popular anger that would result in his 2018 resignation. After the service ended, numerous deaf South Africans contacted the SABC to complain that the sign language interpreter, whose presence was required by the constitution's commitment to equal access, had been making meaningless gestures throughout the service. Mandela's own voice was largely eclipsed in international media coverage of the "fake interpreter" scandal, as commentators debated whether he was a con man or, as he claimed, in the middle of an unfortunately timed schizophrenic break. Twitter and Tumblr users, delighting in the absurdity, circulated GIFs and memes; each "Share" further divorced the ceremony in popular memory from its intended focus.

At each turn, the ANC government's attempts to invoke Mandela's rainbow repertoire—to capture the once-potent *Madiba magic*—seemed to reveal that South Africa was a nation disoriented and dislocated from its founding myths. Where Mandela's inauguration, in Loren Kruger's reading, performatively dramatized the act of union through an "amalgam of visual and aural diversity as well as the active responsiveness of participants,"[1] the audience-participants at Mandela's funeral were clearly no longer willing to play along and refused to be silently drafted into rehashed narratives of unity through diversity. To borrow from Ntozake Shange: after twenty years of postapartheid democracy, it seemed the rainbow was no longer enough. The question of what will fill this gap—postapartheid and post-Mandela—continues to be hotly debated, with no easy answer forthcoming.

Having long inhabited the contradictions of South Africa's multicultural democracy, the performances of its queer/LGBT citizens during its Rainbow era offer valuable insight into current existential crises and provide models for acting within and against dominant postapartheid narratives. The performances explored in this book have provided possible perspectives into how queerness might animate a socially fractured society and how audiences might adapt their particular affective attachments—

particularly to racialized concepts of Africanness—in relation to queer bodies in their midst. These performances occurred on different stages and scales and revealed the ways the norms governing these spaces could be challenged, disoriented, and reoriented through alternate ways of seeing, being, and feeling South African.

While *Prismatic Performances* employed its titular optical metaphor as a tool to think through discourses of identity and national belonging, the prismatic methods developed through these performances resist the discourses of "visibility" that often limit academic criticism and political activism. Even as they represented queer South African presence, the performers refused to present these identities as transparent or easily consumable. Zanele Muholi and Mamela Nyamza thus used the black lesbian's paradoxical relationship with visibility and violatability to draw attention to audiences' desire to see her victimhood performed. By avoiding a direct visual representation of rape, they gestured toward its experiential affects and the ways everyday violence both dehumanizes and objectifies. The members of the Chosen FEW, while harnessing the politicized rhetoric of queer visibility, did so through overperformed, citational embodiments (*swagga*) in order to shield those parts of themselves that felt the most vulnerable. The intimate relationships that developed between bloggers on *Gensblog* were able to flourish, in part, because the bodies of the participants were *in*visible to each other; the emergence of this disembodied space created a new form of performative spectatorship, where audience identities and receptivity to the gay storyline were created through daily interaction in virtual space.

The varying duration of each performance—be it an hour-long cabaret, the length of an exhibition, a few years of daily visits to a website, or the course of a lifetime—draws attention to both the spatial and temporal dimensions of the word "stage." Pieter-Dirk Uys and Steven Cohen used the immediate postapartheid moment to stage dramatically different versions of whiteness on a variety of stages; yet, as their performances were never accompanied by any meaningful economic transformation (and, unbeknownst to them, coincided with the early stages of South Africa's neoliberal policies), the alternative versions of white Africanness previewed were never to be fully realized. The first few decades of the postapartheid era could be said to follow a similar pattern: acts such as voting, once imbued with the possibility of enacting radical change and transformation, lost their meaning through repetition without any noticeable structural change. Indeed, the lesbian community members organizing the march against abuse by the Vosloorus police where I met Manika in 2010 were required to petition the very local police whose brutality they were protesting, in order to get their permit. By strategically allowing limited dissent and protest, the government bolstered its democratic narrative while avoiding any responsibility for systemic change.

None of the performances discussed in this book operated outside of the dominant frameworks of a profoundly racist, sexist, and homophobic society. Even where queerness has the potential to dislodge calcified narratives, it can just as easily be co-opted into those narratives. When space seems to be made for queer Africans, as it was on *Generations* and *Gensblog*, it still might be fleeting and perpetuate stereotypes that reiterate, rather than undo, trenchant gender norms. New images, such as Muholi's overwhelmingly butch *Faces and Phases* series, can, at times, create new limits for representation.

For all its disappointments, however, the fragmentation of the rainbow narrative has opened up possibilities for new solidarities and ways of being South African. I conclude by returning to this book's opening act, tracing the fallout from the One in Nine Campaign's die-in to see how a seemingly disorienting and disruptive act might have a number of creative, reorienting effects.

Though the One in Nine Campaign's interruption of the 2012 Joburg Pride march had no other stated goal than to draw attention to the "economic apartheid" of certain LGBT spaces in South Africa, the attention it drew and the affects it generated had an impact far beyond its goals. The entire corporate entity of Joburg Pride imploded within months, collapsing under the weight of bad publicity and infighting resulting from the fallout of the protest. Joburg Pride was effectively canceled. Blame was leveled at both the board and at the One in Nine protesters; subsequent meetings between various stakeholders to launch a new Pride organization were fraught with anger and accusations. In a move telling of the country's continued balkanization, *Joburg Pride* finally fractured into a number of *prides*, each with its own location and community-specific agenda. Having for many years already existed in parallel to the main pride celebration, locally organized township prides in Soweto and Ekhuruleni continued to pursue an agenda that addressed the needs of their communities. Another took place in Sandton, a suburb that is home to the Johannesburg Stock Exchange and the most dollar millionaires per capita on the entire African continent. Though "Sandton Pride," as it was dubbed in the media, took as its theme "Back to Our Roots," this explicit "rooting" of LGBT pride in the streets of white, neoliberal capital made clear that very little had changed in the previous year. Indeed, the move to Sandton resulted in the pride being further from the city center than ever before.

Yet in the face of this balkanization, a group of queer organizers and activists calling themselves People's Pride organized a march to take place in Hillbrow, the inner-city site of the original 1990 Johannesburg Pride March. These activists, many of them members of FEW and One in Nine, saw the destruction of LGBT pride as an opportunity to reenvision the relationship between queer South Africans and their communities and to connect queer struggles with those of other stigmatized communities. In 1990, as the ANC and National Party were on the cusp of negotiations that would officially end apartheid, Hillbrow had been a rare interracial urban neighborhood, known for its vibrant gay nightlife. Home to multiple bars and even a gay church,[2] it was one of the few "safe" spaces for queer South Africans to be publicly out. Following the transition to democracy, however, Johannesburg's inner city—once the center of apartheid's economic infrastructure—had seen huge population shifts, as its white inhabitants moved to the suburbs. Immigrants from the rest of the continent took advantage of the constitution's promise that South Africa "belongs to all who live in it" and migrated both legally and extralegally to the newly vacated high-rises of the inner city. Now the most densely populated mile in the southern hemisphere, Hillbrow has become a spatial boogeyman of the New South Africa, synonymous with crime and urban blight, a space seen as being "unsafe" for gays (and, indeed, for anyone who could afford to live elsewhere).

By returning to the site of the original 1990 parade, the organizers of People's Pride encouraged the marchers to performatively (re)imagine a future that would be a continuation of a larger struggle for a free and equal South Africa, built explicitly on feminist and antiracist politics. Hillbrow had undergone dramatic changes in the intervening twenty-three years, making clear that the battles for human dignity and recognition that had motivated the original protest were still being fought, albeit on a different ground. Their manifesto stated: "We call for a pride that is a microcosm of the society we wish to live in and not a mirror of the divided one that we currently live in. We wish Pride to be a space that all can access, where all can be free, and where every voice is important."[3]

On October 5, 2013, about five hundred people of all races and genders gathered at the Constitution Hill Complex, the "home" of the constitution, before marching into Hillbrow. As marchers made their way through the

Fig. 11. "Our Lady Justice": street theater at 2013 People's Pride, featuring performance artist Thokozani Ndaba (center). Photo by Gabriel Hoosain Khan, courtesy of Gay and Lesbian Memory in Action.

streets, dancing in outrageous drag, riding their bicycles under rainbow flags, and bringing out their best *swagga*, they did so under the watch of thousands of residents above. It was the largest audience that the parade had seen in years.

Despite the resulting collapse of the corporate entity that was Joburg Pride, One in Nine's performance at the 2012 pride was generative rather than destructive. It created space for an unusually public discussion on the nature of pride itself and how the struggle against homophobic oppression aligns or departs from the struggle against other systems of oppression. Through this realignment new lines and repertoires were created in old fractures. Where the "unity" narrative so important in both the earliest enactments of pride and earliest years of the democracy had become oppressive, 2013's multiple prides reflected the very real divisions that governed—and continue to govern—South African society. Yet, as

Fig. 12. Pride back in the city. People's Pride followed the path of the original 1991 march through Hillbrow as curious bystanders look on. Photo by Gabriel Hoosain Khan, courtesy of Gay and Lesbian Memory in Action.

the Johannesburg People's Pride's manifesto made clear, divisions did not have to serve as a mirror. Rather, they prismatically multiplied possibilities and crafted new alignments. Performance, beyond making visible the gaps between the ideal and the reality, played a crucial role in rehearsing new possibilities for action.

The People's Pride march involved a number of different types of performances. The parade began with a skit performed by activists from FEW, and was then led through the streets by a black "Lady Justice," her robe bloodied at its hem (see figure 11). She was escorted by several women (one of them Manika), wearing purple shirts proudly labeling them "Stabane" and "Feminist" and carrying papier-mâché ball and chains, labeled "Racism" and "Poverty." This street theater was backed by the soundtrack of the marchers' chants and repurposed protest songs; homemade signs fluttered in the spring breeze: "Queer Marches, Not Gay Parades!" "We Don't Need

Your Permission!" Volunteer parade marshals wore bright shirts in solid primary colors with the printed phrase "I March Because . . . ," suggesting that, like individual parts of the rainbow, the march was made up of many different individuals and stories. The People's Pride's manifesto, in reimagining what cartographies count as queer, interpolates many different types of bodies into its ranks: "queer and non-queer, workers and unemployed people, black and non-black, disabled and able-bodied activists, feminists, conscious and interested people," to recreate a sense of pride "where we can all be free and every voice is important."[4]

This endeavor might seem to be utopic, but it is a utopia firmly rooted in current realities. (And what is performance if not a space for imagining an elsewhere?). As I have argued throughout this book, it is the hints of the utopic, evoked through subjunctive performance, that make the everyday livable. The 2013 march and its subsequent yearly iterations were rooted in a shared queer South African experience, yet they contained equally important lines extending outward into a variety of communities. These events became occasions where joy and pain could coexist.

The ability for these actions to unite multiple, seemingly contradictory emotions and agendas was nowhere more apparent than the final two blocks of the 2013 march. The road alongside the Joburg Theatre leading back to Constitution Court was lined by black lesbians carrying "flags"—pieces of cardboard attached to sticks—bearing the names and sometimes images of those had been who had been murdered for their sexual orientation. As the marchers descended into the final stretch, they encountered signs asking for their silence as they walked through the "guard of honor." The solemnity, in contrast to the otherwise boisterous march, encouraged the marchers to contemplate those who were not able to be there and to remember their own losses.

By staging this last stretch of the march as a memorial, the organizers created a liminal space where the present was made thick with the ghosts of other marchers and past movements. Through this engagement with overlapping histories and current spatial realities, the marchers were able to reorient the horizon of possibility for South African queer identities and rescript the vocabularies of struggle to more inclusive enactments. No longer held hostage to an attractive, if vacuous rainbow metaphor, this queer politic may yet forge new configurations of South African identity.

Notes

Introduction

1. From Section 9 of the constitution: "The state may not unfairly discriminate directly or indirectly against anyone on one or more grounds, including race, gender, sex, pregnancy, marital status, ethnic or social origin, colour, sexual orientation, age, disability, religion, conscience, belief, culture, language and birth." Constitution of the Republic of South Africa, 1996.

2. Simon Nkoli, "Opening Address at the 1990 Johannesburg Pride March," in *Pride: Protest and Celebration*, ed. Shaun de Waal and Anthony Manion (Johannesburg: Fanele, 2006), 37.

As becomes apparent even in this brief quotation, the terminology used to describe nonheterosexual South Africans is central to the construction of both citizenship and racial and ethnic belonging. Scholarship often risks erasing culturally specific identities, such as the Afrikaans *moffie* referenced by Nkoli, by uncritically replacing them with terms that make them intelligible to Western audiences (such as my imperfect replacement, "queer"). The question of language is central to this project and is one to which I will return throughout the chapters that follow.

3. "Theme 2012," *Joburg Pride*, accessed October 25, 2013, http://joburgpride.org/sample-page/theme-2012

4. Townships, the peri-urban communities outside of major South African cities, are a remnant of apartheid's spatial segregation policies. Historically home to a black labor force working (but banned from living) in cities, these communities remain home to over one-third of the country's population. While individual townships contain a vibrant spectrum of economic and cultural diversity, they—alongside "informal settlements"—often house the country's most economically marginalized; they are perceived, particularly by those who don't live there, as spaces of poverty, crime, and blight. The white marcher's derogatory use of the term *lokshin* holds a dual injury, referencing the township's apartheid history as "native locations" as well as mocking the pronunciation/translation of the word by black South Africans.

5. Nyx McClain, "The Digital as Enabler: A Case Study of the Joburg 2012 Pride Clash," *Feminist Africa* 18 (2013): 26–42.

6. "Homonationalism" and "pinkwashing," concepts initially theorized by Jasbir Puar and Sarah Schulman respectively, describe the relationship of complicity between

LGBT-identified people and the state. See Jasbir Puar, *Terrorist Assemblages: Homonationalism in Queer Times* (Durham, NC: Duke University Press, 2007); and Sarah Schulman, *Israel/Palestine and the Queer International* (Durham, NC: Duke University Press, 2012).

7. Gqola comments that rainbowism requires its adherents to ignore "the common knowledge that gold is dug up (mainly) by black male mine workers from the belly of the earth who remain poor because they have no power within capitalism to own the product of their labor, or indeed, even their labor itself. There is no mention of their labor when we mythologize about the pot of gold at the end of the rainbow." Pumla Gqola, "Defining People: Analysing Power, Language and Representation in Metaphors of the New South Africa," *Transformation* 47 (2001): 100.

8. Brenna Munro, *South Africa and the Dream of Love to Come: Queer Sexuality and the Struggle for Freedom* (Minneapolis: University of Minnesota Press, 2012), xxiv.

9. Munro, *South Africa*, 173.

10. Andrew Kohut, *The Global Divide on Homosexuality: Greater Acceptance in More Secular and Affluent Countries* (Washington, DC: Pew Research Center, 2013).

11. Thabo Mbeki's evocation of South Africa as ground zero for a continent-wide renaissance very much continued and expanded Mandela's rainbow narrative. Mbeki also used the phrase to advocate for neoliberal economic policies adopted during his presidency.

12. World Bank, "Gini Estimate: South Africa," https://data.worldbank.org/indicator/SI.POV.GINI?locations=Z

13. Emma Seery and Ana Caistor Arendar, *Even It Up: Time to End Extreme Inequality* (New York: Oxfam International, 2014), 11.

14. Recent scholarship by Pumla Gqola and Melanie Judge provides a comprehensive and nuanced overview on the factors contributing to the high rates of sexual violence. I address the particular narrative of so-called Corrective Rape at length in chapter 3. See Gqola, *Rape: A South African Nightmare* (Cape Town: Jacana, 2016) and Judge, *Blackwashing Homophobia: Violence and the Politics of Gender, Sexuality, and Race* (London: Routledge, 2017).

15. For in-depth analysis of early postapartheid nation-building performances, see Loren Kruger's discussion of the Mandela inauguration's theatrical nationhood in *The Drama of South Africa* (New York: Routledge, 1999), Catherine Cole's *Performing South Africa's Truth Commission: Stages of Transition* (Bloomington: Indiana University Press, 2010), and Yvette Hutchison's *South African Performance and the Archives of Memory* (Oxford: Oxford University Press, 2013).

16. The rainbow first emerged as a reoccurring motif in Archbishop Desmond Tutu's sermons during the volatile five-year period immediately preceding the country's transition to democracy (1989–1994), where he referenced South Africa's population as a "Rainbow People of God." During this time, as newly released Nelson Mandela and his former captors hammered out the details and compromises that would define the postapartheid era, fifteen thousand South Africans died engaged in bloody internecine skirmishes between the primarily Zulu Inkatha Freedom Party and the mostly Xhosa African National Congress. Tutu, ever the peacemaker at home and abroad, offered the rainbow as a quasi-biblical alternative to the racial and ethnic brinkmanship then hold-

ing the country hostage. The 1990–1994 interregnum, Tutu's sermons suggest, was not South Africa's end but rather its version of the biblical flood: full of loss and requiring faith, but, weathered together, the promise for a fresh start. Where the rainbow proved God's covenant with Noah, Tutu's metaphor suggested that South Africa's multicultural people were God's promise for the future and that their actions that would ensure the possibility of a lasting peace. Mandela echoed this narrative in his inaugural address, using his platform to convert the rainbow people into citizens of a new Rainbow Nation: "Out of the experience of an extraordinary human disaster that lasted too long . . . we enter into a covenant . . . a rainbow nation at peace with itself and the world." See Mandela, "Nelson Mandela at His Inauguration as President of South Africa," http://www.mandela.gov.za/mandela_speeches/1994/940510_inauguration.htm

17. For instance, possession of images of Mandela was a punishable crime. The writings of activist Steve Biko—leader of the 1970s Black Consciousness Movement, assassinated in police detention—were similarly embargoed. While the apartheid state was often paranoid, it fully understood the power of the image: in Biko's case, the "proof" of his 1979 murder only emerged when pictures of his tortured body were snuck out of the country by journalists and published in newspapers worldwide.

18. Marcia Blumberg and Dennis Walder, introduction to *South African Theatre and/as Intervention* (Amsterdam: Rodopi, 1999), 6.

19. The *toyi-toyi*—part jog, part war dance—emerged as an intimidation tactic during the 1980s state of emergency. It continues to be a staple of South Africa's protest repertoire.

20. David Graver, *Drama for a New South Africa: Seven Plays* (Bloomington: Indiana University Press, 1999), 2.

21. One reviewer, covering Mbongeni Ngema's *Asinamali* in 1986 for the *Chicago Tribune* described the piece as a "ritual of rage and purification. . . . This is not a reasoned answer to social wrongs. It is a distinctive assault on the denial of their humanity and it erupts in overpowering waves of emotions." Regarding black struggle theater favorably in comparison to Athol Fugard's drama, the critic notes, "For all their passion, Fugard's painstakingly crafted works seem genteel" compared to "the chaos of black South Africa's existence . . . miraculously mirror[ed]" in the performance. While this review captures the affective power of *Asinamali*'s physical theater and pared-down storytelling, it also reproduces discourses of black African authenticity, where performers draw on emotionality and ritual rather than reason and craft. In this critic's estimation, the English-Afrikaans Fugard, South Africa's most famous playwright, dramatizes and interprets; struggle theater, like *Asinamali*, can only mirror. Richard Christianson, "Asinamali: A South African Ritual of Rage," *Chicago Tribune*, May 6, 1986, http://articles.chicagotribune.com/1986-05-06/news/8602010826_1_south-africa-apartheid-system-asinamali

22. Despite Barack Obama's hagiographic eulogy at his memorial service (which drew parallels to Mahatma Gandhi, Abraham Lincoln, and Martin Luther King), Mandela was, by his own account, no saint. His support of armed struggle and of Palestinian independence were strategically played down during his presidency, in favor of a grandfatherly public persona and a legacy of reconciliation. His worldwide goodwill tour following his release from prison was, in part, a tactic to regain international trust and investment in the New South Africa. Importantly, while criticism of neoliberal eco-

nomic policies has largely fallen on Thabo Mbeki, they were initiated under Mandela. Despite (or perhaps because of) Mandela's absence from public life in his final years, his image remains one of South Africa's biggest exports.

23. I refer here only to those who ascended to the presidency through national general elections, thus excluding Kgalema Motlanthe (internally appointed to the presidency by parliament to bridge the eight months between Mbeki's 2008 resignation and Zuma's 2009 election).

24. Gibson Cima, "Postconflict Nostalgia: Postapartheid South African Theatre, 1990–2010," PhD diss., University of Washington (2012).

25. For more about the role community-based theater played in countering the HIV/AIDS epidemic in Africa, see *Acting on HIV: Using Drama to Create Possibilities for Change*, ed. Dennis Francis (Rotterdam: Sense Publishers, 2012) and Ola Johansson, *Community Theatre and AIDS* (London: Routledge, 2011), writing in Tanzania.

26. Ismail Mohomed, director of country's National Arts Festival from 2008 to 2016, contends that, at a time when Andrew Lloyd Webber musicals were some of the top imports, most practitioners shied away from controversial material: "The majority of South African playwrights . . . tinkered away on their keyboards churning out quick-fixed romanticised plots about racial reconciliation or badly hatched plays about Hiv and Aids [*sic*]. The latter could solicit easy and unfocused funding." See "Ismail Mohomed Reflects on the Last 20 Years of South African Theatre," *Theatre Times*, May 8, 2014, http://www.thetheatretimes.com/ismail-mahomed/

27. While the internet had been available to the public since 1992, it was only due to the advances and proliferation of mobile technology during this time period that it became widely accessible: in 2008, only 8.4 percent of the population accessed the internet on a regular basis; by 2013, this figure had quintupled to 46.5 percent. World Bank, "Internet Users," http://data.worldbank.org/indicator/IT.NET.USER.P2?locations=ZA

28. Staff Writer, "Cape Town in the Pink over Gay Tourism," *Cape Times*, February 22, 2012, http://www.iol.co.za/capetimes/cape-town-in-the-pink-over-gay-tourism-numbers-1239878

29. Alok Vaid-Menon, "Rainbows Are Just Refracted White Light: Settler Homonationalism in Neo-apartheid South Africa," master's thesis, Stanford University (2012).

30. See, for instance, Stephen O. Murray and Will Roscoe, *Boy-Wives and Female Husbands: Studies of African Homosexualities* (New York: Palgrave, 1998); and Ruth Morgan and Saskia Wieringa, *Tommy Boys, Lesbian Men, and Ancestral Wives: Female Same-Sex Practices in Africa* (Johannesburg: Jacana Media, 2005).

31. See Marc Epprecht, *Hungochani: The History of a Dissident Sexuality in Southern Africa* (Montreal: McGill-Queens University Press, 2004); and Neville Hoad, *African Intimacies: Race, Homosexuality, and Globalization* (Minneapolis: University of Minnesota Press, 2007). Both authors also intriguingly read their subjects across multiple countries, denaturalizing the geopolitical boundaries established by the 1884 Berlin Conference.

32. See T. J. Tallie, *Queering Colonial Natal: Indigeneity and the Violence of Belonging in Southern Africa* (Minneapolis: University of Minnesota Press, 2019).

33. South Africa remains vastly overrepresented among these ethnographies, likely a result of its legal protection of sexual minorities.

34. See Graeme Reid, *How to Be a Real Gay: Gay Identities in Small-Town South Af-*

rica (Scottsville: UKZN Press, 2013); and Bryce Lease, "Dragging Rights, Queering Publics: Realness, Self-Fashioning and the Miss Gay Western Cape Pageant," *Safundi* 18, no. 2 (2017): 131–146.

35. See Andrew Tucker, *Queer Visibilities: Space, Identity, and Interaction in Cape Town* (Oxford: Wiley Blackwell, 2009); Zethu Matebeni, "Exploring Black Lesbian Sexualities and Identities in Johannesburg," PhD diss., University of the Witwatersrand (2011); Amanda Lock Swarr, *Sex in Transition: Remaking Gender and Race in South Africa* (Albany: SUNY Press, 2012); and Xavier Livermon, "Queer(y)ing Freedom: Black Queer Visibilities in Postapartheid South Africa," *GLQ* 18, nos. 2–3 (2012): 297–323.

36. See Graeme Reid, *Above the Skyline: Reverend Tsietsi Thandekiso and the Founding of an African Gay Church* (Johannesburg: UNISA Press, 2010); Melissa Hackman: *Desire Work: Ex-Gay and Pentecostal Masculinities in South Africa* (Durham, NC: Duke University Press, 2018); and Casey Golomski, "Queering Myth in a Southern African Gay and Lesbian Pentecostal Church," *Transforming Anthropology* 28 (2020)

37. See Cheryl Stobie, *Somewhere over the Double Rainbow: Representations of Bisexuality in Post-apartheid Novels* (Scottsville: UKZN Press, 2009); and Munro, *South Africa*.

38. See, for instance, Ifi Amadumbe, *Male Wives and Female Husbands: Gender and Sex in an African Society* (London: Zed Press, 1987); Oyèrónkẹ́ Oyěwùmí, *The Invention of Women: Making an African Sense of Western Gender Discourse* (Minneapolis: University of Minnesota Press, 1997); Signe Arnfred, ed., *Re-thinking Sexualities in Africa* (Uppsala: Nordiska Afrikainstitutet, 2004).

39. I situate the discipline's public "coming out" to 2016, when Ashley Currier and Thérèse Migraine-George coauthored three articles on the topic in leading queer and women's studies journals. See "Queer Studies / African Studies: An (Im)possible Transaction?," *GLQ* 22, no. 2 (2016): 281–305; "'Lesbian'/Female Same-Sex Sexualities in Africa," *Journal of Lesbian Studies* 21, no. 2 (2016): 133–150; and "Queering Queer African Archives: Methods and Movements," *WSQ: Women's Studies Quarterly* 44, nos. 3–4 (2016): 190–207.

40. Marc Epprecht, *Heterosexual Africa? The History of an Idea from the Age of Exploration to the Age of AIDS* (Athens: Ohio University Press, 2008), 16.

41. Keguro Macharia, "Africa : Queer : Anthropology," *New Inquiry*, July 28, 2018, https://thenewinquiry.com/blog/africa-queer-anthropology/

42. Sylvia Tamale, "Researching and Theorizing Sexualities in Africa," in *African Sexualities: A Reader*, ed. Sylvia Tamale (Cape Town: Pambazuka Press, 2011), 28. Tamale locates Michel Foucault's work on power relations, Judith Butler's theory of performativity, and Gayle Rubin's conception of sexual hierarchy as being particularly relevant to the study of African sexualities.

43. Ibid., 29. The *Reader* also, notably, includes poetry and fiction alongside more traditionally academic work, challenging the hierarchies within the "academic anthology" as well as adding space for creative engagement and dialogue among the texts.

44. Stella Nyanzi, "Queering Queer Africa," in *Reclaiming Afrikan: Queer Perspectives on Sexual and Gender Identities*, ed. Zethu Matebeni (Athlone: Modjaji Books, 2014), 63.

45. Dwight Conquergood, "Performance Studies: Interventions and Radical Research," *TDR* 46, no. 2 (2002): 145.

46. Megan Lewis's *Performing Whitely in the Post-colony: Afrikaners in South African*

Theatrical and Public Life (Iowa City: University of Iowa Press, 2016), it should be noted, does important work unpacking racialized gender expectations in Afrikaans cultural production (including discussion of Pieter-Dirk Uys's drag performance); queerness, however, is not its central analytic.

47. Joseph Massad, "Reorienting Desire: The Gay International in the Arab World," *Public Culture* 14, no. 2 (2002): 361–385.

48. Zethu Matebeni and Jabu Pereira, "Preface," in Matebeni, *Reclaiming Afrikan*, 7.

Chapter 1

1. Pieter-Dirk Uys, *Between the Devil and the Deep: A Memoir of Acting and Reacting* (Cape Town: Zebra, 2005), 159.

2. In his autobiography, Uys recounts Mandela's political savvy in reaching audiences he might not reach through a different medium: "I want to be on Evita's show because I have important things to say. And no one watches the news" (ibid.).

3. Mandela, "Nelson Mandela at His Inauguration."

4. Pieter-Dirk Uys, *Elections and Erections: A Memoir of Fear and Fun* (Cape Town: Zebra, 2002), 70.

5. Gembok horns hold a particularly gendered and ethnic resonance for white South African masculinity, as Megan Lewis's explores in her work of Afrikaans performance artist Peter Van Heerden. See Lewis's *Performing Whitely* for a comprehensive overview of the dramaturgy of Afrikaans masculinities.

6. Marjorie Garber, *Vested Interests: Cross-Dressing and Cultural Anxiety* (New York: Routledge, 1997).

7. Laurence Senelick, *The Changing Room: Sex, Drag, and Theatre* (New York: Routledge, 2000), 7.

8. Also deeply important: the social location of the performer. While Garber's and Senelick's arguments are relevant to the social function of drag in the context about which I write here, it is imperative not to romanticize gender subversion and "drag" or to overtheorize embodiments in contexts where gender nonconformity comes with life-or-death stakes. While this book does not largely focus on trans/nonbinary identities (in part because such identities were only beginning to be recognized in South Africa during this period), I address the performative stakes of everyday gender nonconformity more fully in the next chapter.

9. José Muñoz, *Disidentifications: Queers of Color and the Performance of Politics* (Minneapolis: University of Minnesota Press, 1999).

10. See, for instance, Eric Lott, *Love & Theft: Blackface Minstrelsy and the American Working Class* (Oxford: Oxford University Press, 1993); and Alfred J. Lopez, ed., *Postcolonial Whiteness: A Critical Reader on Race and Empire* (Albany: SUNY Press, 2012).

11. Megan Lewis has compellingly argued that performances of South African whiteness—particularly the gendered Afrikaans *trekboer* iconography that undergirded apartheid—has always contained the seeds of its undoing: "a site of potential transgres-

sions, unspoken crossings, and external threats . . . [whiteness] is more porous and more tenuous than it is monolithic. See Lewis, *Performing Whitely*, 28.

12. A note on method: writing about performances from the recent past presents a challenge to the researcher. Though I have witnessed multiple live performances by Uys (as himself, Evita, and her chanteuse sister Bambi) and Cohen's 2012 piece *The Cradle of Human Kind*, my archive comprises autobiographical writings, interviews (both my own and others'), and performance footage. Where it is difficult to capture or quantify audience response for a performance, particularly the sort of community interventions about which I write, my analysis draws on accounts from the performers' autobiographical writings, interviews, performance reviews, and video footage.

13. Bantustans were small, self-governing "countries" parceled out by the apartheid government amounting to 13 percent of South Africa's least-farmable land. From 1951 to 1989, over 55 percent of South African blacks were relocated from urban centers to these rural outposts.

14. *Minister of Home Affairs v. Fourie*, Case CCT 60/04 (2005). Notably, Sachs was also responsible for presiding over the formation of the interim constitution's Equality Clause. In its inclusion of sexual orientation as a protected category, the new constitution (and the legislation it spawned) validated the experiences and identities of lesbians, gays, and bisexuals as necessary in constituting a new body politic.

15. Pieter-Dirk Uys, *A Part Hate, a Part Love: The Legend of Evita Bezuidenhout* (Johannesburg: Radix, 1990), 514.

16. Melissa Steyn, *Whiteness Just Isn't What It Used to Be: White Identity in a Changing South Africa* (Albany: SUNY Press, 2001).

17. Ibid., 20.

18. Richard Dyer, *White: Essays on Race and Culture* (New York: Taylor and Francis, 1997), 2.

19. Njabulo Ndebele, "Iph'indlela? Finding Our Way into the Future," in *Fine Lines from the Box: Further Thoughts about Our Country* (Houghton: Umuzi, 2007), 137.

20. *Ubuntu*, often simplistically translated as "shared humanity," is in fact shorthand for the longer Zulu saying, *umuntu ngumuntu ngabantu*: a person is a person through other people. This saying is conceptually prismatic (reflecting the self through the refraction of the other) and linguistically performative: in his analysis of the phrase, Mark Sanders has noted that each part of the phrase only exists in relation to the others. Mark Sanders, *Ambiguities of Witnessing: Law and Literature in the Time of a Truth Commission* (Palo Alto, CA: Stanford University Press, 2007), 26–28.

21. Pieter-Dirk Uys, *The Great Comedy Trek*, VHS (Johannesburg: Nu Metro Home Entertainment, 2007).

22. Katrin Seig, *Ethnic Drag: Performing Race, Nation, and Sexuality in West Germany* (Ann Arbor: University of Michigan Press, 2002), 2.

23. *Indaba* is an *Nguni* (Zulu and Xhosa) word with a number of meanings and cultural resonances. While the most direct translation is "news," it can also mean a meeting of a chief or leader with his or her people. Evita's election *indaba* retains the word's localized political element, while reframing it as a democratic process: a people's *indaba*.

In 2009, Uys would use a similar strategy when he announced that Evita would run for president, as representative of Evita's People's Party.

24. Uys, *Elections and Erections*, 86.

25. Pieter-Dirk Uys, interview with the author, Darling, South Africa, August 3, 2008.

26. J. Bishop, "The Man behind the Woman," in *Conversations* (Sloane Park: Premier, 1991), 198.

27. Uys, *Part Hate*, 35.

28. Uys, interview.

29. Literally, "farm girl" (Afrikaans).

30. Uys's and Cohen's identities as Jews raised within the context of white minority rule deserve closer attention. Throughout its history, white South Africa enthusiastically accepted its Jews and granted them full privileges of whiteness. Jews took an ambivalent role in the drama of race and national identity. Legally enfranchised, they were often vulnerable to anti-Semitism (particularly after the Holocaust) and had an ambivalent investment in the state. Some became leading activists in the antiapartheid movement; others continued to identify with the ideology of white supremacy. See Milton Shain and Richard Mendelsohn, *The Jews in South Africa: An Illustrated History* (Johannesburg: Jonathan Ball Publishing, 2009).

31. Morwenna Bosch, "Limping into the African Renaissance: The Abject Art of Steven Cohen," *South African Theatre Journal* 19 (2005): 121.

32. My reference to Camp's bracketing effect draws on Susan Sontag's contention that "camp sees everything in quotation marks. It's not a lamp, but a 'lamp'; not a woman, but a 'woman.' To perceive Camp in objects and persons is to understand Being-as-Playing-a-Role. It is the farthest extension, in sensibility, of the metaphor of life as theater." See Susan Sontag, "Notes on Camp," in *Camp: Queer Aesthetics and the Performing Subject—a Reader*, edited by Fabio Cleto (Ann Arbor: University of Michigan Press, 1999), 69.

33. The "explicitness" of the body is central to the mission of performance art, a medium that emerged out of the 1960s American avant-garde movement that found expressions in South Africa postapartheid (with Cohen being one of the first and most famous practitioners). Performance theorist Rebecca Schneider has commented that the body in performance art becomes a space for staging—making explicit—its construction, arguing that, as "a mass of orifices and appendages, details and tactile surfaces the explicit body in representation is foremost a site of social markings, physical parts and gestural signatures of gender, race, class, and sexuality, all of which bear ghosts of historical meaning, marking and delineating social hierarchies of privilege and disprivilege." If identities are supposedly read on the skin, Schneider—in reference, particularly, to feminist artists—notes that these performances enact a symbolic flaying, a "peeling at signification." See Rebecca Schneider, *The Explicit Body in Performance* (New York: Routledge, 1997), 2.

34. Uys, *Elections and Erections*, 20.

35. Sigmund Freud, "Mourning and Melancholia," in *The Standard Edition of the Complete Psychological Works of Sigmund Freud*, trans. James Strachey (London: Hogarth Press, 1955), 250. Following the death of his longtime partner and collaborator Elu, Cohen would go on to literalize this cannibalistic urge to merge oneself with a lost

Other: in each performance of *Put Your Heart under Your Feet . . . and Walk* (2017–2018) Cohen ritually consumed a spoonful of Elu's ashes as audiences looked on. Yet what Freud would deem pathological Cohen transformed into a deeply personal ceremony of shared presence and pain. For further accounts of this performance, see Catherine Cole, "Johannesburg Dance Umbrella: Thirty Years On (Review)," *Theatre Journal* 70, no. 4 (2018): 539–542; and Robyn Sassen, "For the Love of Elu: Steven Cohen's Gentle Endocannibalism," *Performance Research* 23 (2018): 83–87.

36. See Robyn Sassen, "Steven Cohen / Princess Menorah: Coming Out Jewish in South African Art," master's thesis, University of the Witwatersrand (2005); and Meyer Taub, "The Practical Etymology of Seeing Oneself While Listening to Others," *South African Theatre Journal* 24, no. 1 (2011): 156–175.

37. See Liza Christofides, "Embodying Prejudice: Abjection in the Performance Art of Steven Cohen," master's thesis, University of Witwatersrand (2003); Liese van der Watt, "Imagining Alternative White Masculinities: Steven Cohen's Living Art," in *Under Construction: "Race" and Identity in South Africa Today*, ed. Natasha Distiller (London: Heinemann, 2004); Bosch, "Limping into the African Renaissance."

38. The "Red Ants" are privatized security workers, given their nickname from their distinctive red coveralls and tendency to swarm squatter camps en masse, evict their inhabitants, and raze the informal settlements to the ground. The Red Ants have come to symbolize for many the post-1994 government's failed promise of delivering housing to all, in favor of protecting private property for a few.

39. Steven Cohen, "The Chandelier Project: Creating amidst Destruction," http://vweb.isisp.net/~elu@artslink.co.za/stevencohen/chandelier.htm

40. A three-part handshake that consists of clasped palms, sliding forward so that thumbs interlink loosely, before returning to clasped palms.

41. Cohen, "The Chandelier Project."

42. Ibid.

43. This is not to say that white interests were less served by the new regime. A 2014 study by Oxfam found that the two wealthiest South Africans (both white men) have as much money as the 26.5 million of the country's (mostly black) poor. See Seery and Arendar, *Even It Up*.

44. See, for instance, Alice Nevin, "Instant Mutuality: The Development of Maboneng in Inner-City Johannesburg," *Anthropology Southern Africa* 37, nos. 3–4 (2014): 187–201.

45. Nikki Moore, "An Old Act in a New Age of Satire," *Cue Online*, http://cue.ru.ac.za/2015/07/an-old-act-in-a-new-age-of-satire/

46. *The Cradle of Human Kind* was made in collaboration with Nomsa Dhlamini, the nonagenarian domestic servant who raised him and who spends much of the production naked alongside Cohen as an evocation of Original Woman. Controversy erupted when audience members accused Cohen of exploiting Dhlamini, comparing the display of her body to that of Saartjie Baartman's. For my critique of this piece, see April Sizemore-Barber, "South Africa's National Arts Festival (review)," *Theatre Journal* 65, no. 2 (2013): 261–264.

47. Kymberley Feltham, "Spotlight South Africa: Chandelier," *My Entertainment World*, http://www.myentertainmentworld.ca/2015/05/spotlight-south-africa-chandelier/

48. The SA Human Rights Commission has reported a surge in racist violence and rhetoric in the past five years, particularly among the "Born Frees," those too young to remember apartheid. See "SAHRC: Spike in Racism-Related Incidents in SA," *News24*, http://www.news24.com/SouthAfrica/News/SAHRC-probed-over-500-racism-cases-20140731

49. "Athi-Patra Ruga: Design Is the Discipline to Art," YouTube video, wmv, 5:38, posted by Design Indaba on May 9, 2014, https://www.youtube.com/watch?v=taNVPk8_Cso

50. Ibid.

51. Andrew Brown notes that Ruga's performances reveal the ways white LGBT South Africans have benefited from black activism without engaging their own privilege and racism: "It is no coincidence that the person processing around like a banner for the Rainbow Nation is a white character built upon, but at the same time obfuscating, the labor of a black queer man." Andrew Brown, "Performing Blackness in the 'Rainbow Nation': Athi-Patra Ruga's *The Future White Women of Azania*," *Women and Performance* 27, no. 1 (2017): 76.

Chapter 2

1. Manika, interview with the author, April 14, 2011, Vosloorus, Gauteng, South Africa.

2. Nira Yuval-Davies, *Gender and Nation* (London: Sage, 1997); and Anne McClintock, *Imperial Leather* (New York: Routledge, 1995).

3. This term intentionally plays on one of the underpinning concepts of Western dramatic realism, Constantin Stanislavski's so-called "Magic if." Here a performer can create the emotional life of the character through a creative and empathetic engagement with the given circumstances of the situation: "*If* acts as a lever to lift us out of the world of actuality into the realm of the imagination" (*An Actor Prepares*, trans. Elizabeth Reynolds Hapgood [New York: Routledge, 1989], 46). I argue that by living as if, black lesbians are able to think outside of their lived reality into an imagined space where their constitutional rights are enacted.

4. The presentation of the self in the everyday is not random, but often a series of mediated performances calculated to give off a certain effect of authenticity. Erving Goffman's notion of everyday "impression management" in terms of "frontstage/backstage" is especially apt in regards to members of the Chosen FEW, who were under numerous forms of surveillance in their communities at that time. They were required to perform "lesbian," "black," "soccer player," "South African," "Zulu/Xhosa/Ndebele/etc.," among any number of more personal, relational roles (daughter, neighbor, etc.). The public character of their self-presentation rendered all of their everyday performances in CAPS, cited in quotation marks as both individual and representative: THE Black-Lesbian-from-the-Township (Who-Plays-Soccer). See Erving Goffman, *The Presentation of Self in Everyday Life* (New York: Anchor, 1959).

5. Ann Pellegrini, "Religion, Secularism, and a Democratic Politics of 'As If,'" Social Research 76, no. 4 (2009): 1349.

6. J. Halberstam, *In a Queer Time and Place: Transgender Bodies, Subcultural Lives* (New York: NYU Press, 2005).

7. See, for example, Lee Edelman, *No Future: Queer Theory and the Death Drive* (Durham, NC: Duke University Press, 2004); José Esteban Muñoz, *Cruising Utopia* (New York: NYU Press, 2009); Catherine Bond-Stockton, *The Queer Child: or Growing Sideways in 20th Century America* (Durham, NC: Duke University Press, 2009); Elizabeth Freeman, *Time Binds: Queer Temporalities, Queer Histories* (Durham, NC: Duke University Press, 2010).

8. See Puar, *Terrorist Assemblages*.

9. Muñoz, *Cruising Utopia*, 1.

10. Tavia Nyong'o, *Afro-Fabulations: The Queer Drama of Black Life* (New York: NYU Press, 2019), 25.

11. See Dwight Conquergood, "Rethinking Ethnography," *Communication Monographs* 59 (1991): 179–194; D. Soyini Madison, *Critical Ethnography: Method, Ethics, and Performance* (Thousand Oaks, CA: Sage, 2011); and Marlon Bailey, *Butch Queens up in Pumps* (Ann Arbor: University of Michigan Press, 2013).

12. Edelman, *No Future*, 30.

13. Jafari Allen, "Black/Queer Rhizomatics: Train Up a Child in the Way Ze Should Grow . . . ," in *No Tea No Shade: New Writings in Black Queer Studies*, ed. E. Patrick Johnson (Durham, NC: Duke University Press, 2016), 30.

14. Mlondolozi Zondi, "Black Performance Theory (Review)," *Text and Performance Quarterly* 37, nos. 3–4 (2017): 278–281.

15. Manika, interview. The Chosen FEW present a challenge to the researcher in terms of pseudonyms. From one perspective, they are public figures and have been given extensive coverage in the international media, who use their full names (see *The Guardian*, *New York Times*, etc.). Their images and names are easily accessible to those with internet access. However, as out lesbians in communities where this is highly stigmatized identity, they fall under the category of vulnerable populations. Yet they are experts in self-promotion and often refer to themselves, proudly, as local celebrities. Moreover, as visible out lesbians, their decision to reveal their names and faces to me (and others) is an explicitly political one. In order to respond to the tensions of the quasi-public nature of their identities—as well as gesture to the importance of naming and being named—I have decided to refer to the team members by their nicknames, given to them from a variety of sources and often more important to their senses of self than their given names. By doing this, I hope to preserve the privacy of the individuals while still respecting their personalities, experiences, and embodiments.

16. Chosen FEW members often use the phrase "lesbian woman" as opposed to simply "lesbian" when speaking about their political stances. I found this interesting and somewhat redundant, until I met with Phindi Malaza, the programs coordinator at FEW, whose constant use of the phrase as a noun describing same-sex-attracted women (with "lesbian" being more often an adjective) and their engagements with their communities made it clear to me that this is a political point, a way of emphasizing that lesbians *are* women and are connected to the larger struggles for women's equality. This affiliation allows lesbian issues to be taken up by the women's movement, as well as strategically positions FEW as a partner for civil society organizations focused on gender issues.

17. Manika's destabilization of "everyday" township norms echoes Halberstam's contention that female masculinity denaturalizes "heroic," normative masculinities and critiques the ideologies that support them, as well as Marjorie Garber's work on the cross-dresser as the catalyst for a larger societal "category crisis." I would argue that the visibility of gays and lesbians within black South African communities has become a flashpoint for larger discussions about the meaning of blackness, and becomes shorthand for larger discussions on the role of (racial, ethnic, national) difference in postapartheid society. See J. Halberstam, *Female Masculinity* (Durham, NC: Duke University Press, 1998) and Garber, *Vested Interests.*

18. Zulu slang: My homie, my friend.

19. Manika, interview.

20. Ibid.

21. Zulu: *nika*—to give.

22. Beyond both of its local and transnational meanings, "this Manika name" had deeper, culture-specific resonances. In many parts of South Africa, the process of naming has a number of important cultural meanings, often linked to oral performance and praise poetry (*izibongo* or *lithoko*). Though most famously crafted for great chiefs—such as Shaka or Moshoeshoe—many clan names within South Africa's main ethnic/tribal groupings have long histories of *izibongo* attached to them, linking modern identity with a larger tribal cosmology of chiefs and warriors. This tradition is not merely sentiment. During apartheid—when black identities were reduced to *dompas* (passbook), a Christianized name, and a number—naming became a tactical necessity for locating the self in a larger context than the present. The importance of naming is reflected in a number of ways: some children are given the name of a deceased relative; others' names have direct correlation to the circumstances of their birth or to a personal characteristic (for example, a popular Zulu girls name, Thandeka directly translates to "the one who is loved").

It is important to note that "nigga," the racial epithet that has often been reclaimed in African American hip-hop cultures, does not have the same affective punch in South African youth cultures as it does in America. Indeed, the equivalent Afrikaans word, *kaffir* ("The 'K' word") has yet to be reappropriated in any large degree by those it denigrates.

23. Victor Turner, *The Ritual Process* (New York: Aldine de Gruyter, 1969). Notably, Turner's widely cited theory of *communitas*, a central tenet in the performance studies canon, has its origins in his Namibian fieldwork. Yet both the southern African connection and the theoretical labor of Turner's Ndembu interlocutors are frequently obscured or erased attempts to streamline the field's formation, going unmentioned in the field's most frequently taught textbook, *Performance Studies: An Introduction*, ed. Richard Schechner and Sara Brady (New York: Routledge, 2017). I reengage *communitas* here, privileging the black South African lesbian perspective, as a pointed effort to resituate and recenter this geographical erasure.

24. For an in-depth reading of the cultural politics of the *isistabane* label, see Swarr, *Sex in Transition.*

25. K. K., interview with author, November 27, 2010, in Soweto, Gauteng, South Africa.

26. Sarah Nuttall, in her analysis of postapartheid youth-oriented magazines and

shopping malls, has noted that the generation of postapartheid black youth—despite being overwhelmingly poor—has crafted a new, individualized identity through a process of "cultural accessorization." Sarah Nuttall, "Stylizing the Self: The Y Generation in Rosebank, Johannesburg," *Public Culture* 16, no. 3 (2004): 439.

27. Khambi, interview with the author, January 12, 2011, Katlehong, Gauteng, South Africa.

28. Ibid.

29. Ashley Currier, *Out in Africa: LGBT Organizing in Namibia and South Africa* (Minneapolis: University of Minnesota Press, 2012). Currier draws on extensive ethnographic research with four organizations, including Forum for Empowerment of Women, to theorize the strategic and fluid mobilization of visibility within African LGBT movements.

30. Khambi, interview, January 12, 2011.

31. J. L. Austin, *How to Do Things with Words* (Cambridge: Harvard University Press, 1962).

32. Inderpal Grewal, *Transnational America: Feminisms, Diaspora, Neoliberalisms* (Durham, NC: Duke University Press, 2005).

33. Epprecht, *Heterosexual Africa?*

34. Manika, interview.

35. K. K., interview.

36. See Lila Abu-Lughod, "The Romance of Resistance: Tracing Transformation of Power through Bedouin Women," *American Ethnologist* 17, no. 1 (1990): 41–55; and Saba Mahmood, *The Politics of Piety: The Islamic Revival and the Feminist Subject* (Princeton, NJ: Princeton University Press, 2004).

37. I borrow these terms from social psychology, especially the work of E. Tory Higgins, "Self-Discrepancy: A Theory Relating Self and Affect," *Psychological Review* 94, no. 3 (1987): 319–340.

38. K. K., interview.

39. Patrick Barth, "In South Africa, the Chosen Few," *New York Times* video, July 8, 2010, http://www.nytimes.com/video/sports/soccer/1247468408867/the-chosen-few.html

40. Thully, interview with the author, January 10, 2011, Johannesburg, Gauteng, South Africa.

41. Ibid.

42. Ibid.

43. Skaaps, interview with author, April 21, 2011, Johannesburg, Gauteng, South Africa.

44. Religion was an ambivalent topic for all of the women I interviewed. All were raised in practicing Christian households, and most had struggled with relatives using religion as justification for (at least initially) rejecting them. The majority of interviewees listed religion alongside traditional culture as largest source of homophobia in their lives. Yet church frequently factored into their narratives as spaces of conditional acceptance and communal support. Thully was the most actively engaged in organized religion (wearing skirts on Sundays, in spite of her generally butch attire). All, however, expressed some belief in a higher power, often preferring to craft meaningful personal

relationships with a Christian God outside of an institution that they viewed as virulently homophobic. Some of their personal beliefs also combined Christianity with indigenous spiritual traditions, as is common practice throughout South Africa.

45. Linguistically, *ikultcha* falls under the category of Class Four Zulu prefixes: words that have been adapted (or Zulu-ized) from English or Afrikaans. By adding the prefix "i" to a word where the Zulu word is either nonexistent or inadequate (for example, i-cellphone) language is manipulated to provide a broader, more fluid range of meanings.

46. Note: not Thully, the Chosen FEW player of the similar name.

47. Manika, interview.

48. Sotho: dew, the totem for the Bafokeng "clan name" (*diboko*); Manika's family totem.

49. Ibid.

50. Here, I draw on Harold Scheub's analysis in, *The Tongue Is Fire: South African Storytellers and Apartheid* (Madison: University of Wisconsin Press, 1996), xxi.

51. Manika, interview.

52. Elizabeth Gunner, *Musho! Zulu Popular Praises* (East Lansing: Michigan State University Press, 1991), 19–20.

53. Notably, in her account of her youth, *Zami: A New Spelling of My Name* (New York: Random House, 1982), Lorde undergoes a process of self-definition, traced by the "new spellings" of her name.

54. Heather Russell, *Legba's Crossing: Narratology in the African Atlantic* (Athens: University of Georgia Press, 2009), 60.

55. Atlantic Philanthropies, a US-based grant agency had invested in LGBTQ non-profits. Without outside funding, many LGBT organizations struggled to remain solvent; some, such as Behind the Mask (an LGBT media NGO) and the Out in Africa Film Festival, shuttered. Though the Forum for Empowerment of Women weathered this change, it was no longer able to fund the Chosen FEW.

56. The only player I was unable to reach was Thully. Her former teammates reported that no one had seen her for quite some time.

57. Jill Dolan, *Utopia in Performance: Finding Hope at the Theatre* (Durham, NC: Duke University Press, 2005).

58. Khambi, interview, January 12, 2011.

Chapter 3

1. Keguro Macharia, "Archive and Method in Queer African Studies," *Agenda* 22, no. 1 (2015): 145.

2. April Sizemore-Barber, "Archival Movements: South Africa's Gay and Lesbian Memory in Action," *Safundi* 18, no. 2 (2017): 117–130.

3. Prior to global attention turning to South Africa during the May 2010 competition, Corrective Rape had received scant mention in news media, primarily in local South African news sources (mentioned in 10 articles in 2008; 28 in 2009). Coverage increased exponentially in 2010 and reached its Zenith in 2011 (the term appearing in 81 and 208 articles, respectively). Aside from a spike in renewed interest in 2013

(145 mentions), the global focus has lessened as the Western eye turned elsewhere (43 mentions in 2017) (Lexus Nexus). The popularity of the term among online users can likewise be traced via Google Trends, where it peaked in January 2011 (coinciding with international interest in the Change.org petition).

4. Tavia Nyong'o, "Queer Africa and the Fantasy of Virtual Participation," *WSQ: Women's Studies Quarterly* 40 (2012): 49.

5. Ibid., 50.

6. Achille Mbembe, *On the Postcolony* (Berkeley: University of California Press, 2001), 2.

7. "South Africa: Take Action to Stop Corrective Rape," Change.org.

8. Gayatri Chakravorty Spivak, "Can the Subaltern Speak?," in *Can the Subaltern Speak? Reflections on the History of an Idea*, ed. Rosalind Morris (New York: Columbia University Press, 1988).

9. While reliable statistics are hampered by barriers to reporting, a 2009 study by the Medical Research Council reported nearly one in four South African men admitted to having had nonconsensual sex with a woman. See Rachel Jewkes et al., "Understanding Men's Health and Use of Violence: Interface between Rape and HIV in South Africa," on *Women's Net*, http://www.womensnet.org.za/sites/www.womensnet.org.za/files/resources/men_exec_smry.pdf

10. Deborah Posel, "The Scandal of Manhood: 'Baby Rape' and the Politicization of Sexual Violence in Post-apartheid South Africa," *Culture, Health and Sexuality* 7, no. 3 (2005): 239–252.

11. Ibid.

12. One particularly vivid, performative example emerged in then-deputy president Jacob Zuma's 2006 trial for the rape of his friend's daughter, in part through his defense team's argument that she had "asked for it" by sleeping in a *kanga*, a traditional, sarong-like garment. "Khwezi," as his accuser was known, was publicly excoriated for her HIV positive status, which marked her as a loose woman, and for daring to accuse her elder, the extremely popular Zuma. Outside the courthouse, effigies of Khwezi were burned to chants of "Kill the bitch" and "Zuma, rape me!" from his supporters. Following the trial, Khwezi fled the country and Zuma was elected South African president in 2009 on a platform that emphasized his Zulu masculinity, virility, and a return to "traditional African values." Significantly, Khwezi's bisexuality was little remarked upon, by either the media or in public discourse during the trial. When it was brought up in court, it was used—alongside her HIV status and previous rapes—to prove her an unreliable witness. Her sexuality was made simultaneously both invisible (i.e., not discussed) and hypervisible as part of what made her allegedly "deserving" of rape. Zuma's very public acquittal and subsequent ascent to the presidency seemed to many to further entrench the gap between a constitution that protected bodily dignity of its citizens and an "African" culture that policed its legitimacy on and through gendered—and, particularly, black—bodies. Khwezi eventually returned to South Africa, where she died at the age of forty-one in 2016. The following year, a posthumous biography publicly revealed her identity for the first time as Fezekile Ntsukela Kuzwayo. See Redi Thlabi, *Khwezi: The Remarkable Story of Fezekile Ntsukela Kuzwayo* (Johannesburg: Jonathan Ball Press, 2017).

13. See, for instance, Mary Hames, "Violence against Black Lesbians: Minding Our

Language," *Agenda* 25, no. 4 (2011): 87–91; Henriette Gunkel, "Some Reflections on Postcolonial Homophobia, Local Interventions, and LGBTI Solidarity Online: The Politics of Global Petitions," *African Studies Review* 52, no. 2 (2013); and Zethu Matebeni, "Deconstructing Violence towards Black Lesbians in South Africa," in *Queer African Reader*, ed. Hakima Abbas and Sokari Ekine (Dakar: Pambazuka, 2013).

14. Nicole R. Fleetwood, *Troubling Vision: Performance, Visuality, and Blackness* (Chicago: University of Chicago Press, 2011), 6.

15. Judge, *Blackwashing Homophobia*, 77.

16. Diana Taylor, *Disappearing Acts: Spectacles of Gender and Nationalism in Argentina's "Dirty War"* (Durham, NC: Duke University Press, 1997), 123–124.

17. While they continue to produce prolifically, for the purpose of this book's periodization, this chapter primarily focuses on Muholi's work prior to what might be seen as their emergence into the global arts scene: a six-month solo exhibition at the Brooklyn Museum's Elizabeth Sackler Center for Feminist Art in 2015.

18. Staff Reporter, "Lulu Xingwana Describes Lesbian Photos as Immoral," *Mail and Guardian Online*, March 3, 2010, http://mg.co.za/article/2010-03-03-lulu-xingwana-describes-lesbian-photos-as-immoral

19. Lulu Xingwana, "Statement by Minister of Arts and Culture, Ms. Lulu Xingwana on Media Reports around the Innovative Art Exhibition," Media Release, Department of Arts and Culture, March 4, 2010, http://www.dac.gov.za/media_releases/2010/04-03-10.html

20. Zanele Muholi, "Faces and Phases Artist Statement," in *Faces and Phases* (Munich: Prestel, 2010).

21. While Muholi's coming out as nonbinary in 2018 no doubt fruitfully complicates any future interpretation of their work, the contours and impact of this identity are outside the time period covered in this study (1994–2013), when they publicly—and very politically—identified as a lesbian woman.

22. In Henriette Gunkel, "Through the Postcolonial Eyes: Images of Gender and Female Sexuality in Contemporary South Africa," *Journal of Lesbian Studies* 13, no. 1 (2009): 80.

23. Muholi, attentive to the dangers of the object/subject dichotomy, asks that those writing about their work refer to those photographed as "participants" rather than "subjects" (a condition of gaining permission to use their images). I have respected their wishes throughout this chapter.

24.Bim Adewunmi, "Zanele Muholi: 'I Cannot Give Up Myself and My Soul Simply Because I Need Some Exposure,'" *New Statesman*, March 30, 2013, http://www.newstatesman.com/bim-adewunmi/2013/03/zanele-muholi-i-cannot-give-myself-and-my-soul-simply-because-i-need-some-expos. Sarah (or Saartjie) Baartman, the so-called Venus Hottentot, was widely displayed in medical and public exhibitions throughout Europe in the early nineteenth century. Known for her "large buttocks," her body was dissected following her death in 1815 and was returned to a state burial in South Africa in 2002. She remains an important cultural touchstone for many South African and diasporic artists.

25. Andrew van der Vlies, "Queer Knowledge and the Politics of the Gaze in Contemporary South African Photography: Zanele Muholi and Others," *Journal of African Cultural Studies* 24, no. 2 (2012): 141.

26. Kylie Thomas, "Zanele Muholi's Intimate Archive: Photography and Post-apartheid Lesbian Lives," *Safundi* 11, no. 4 (2010): 434.

27. For indeed, she is not. Fish, who passed away from illness, is one of several women whom Muholi mentions in the introduction to the book version of *Faces and Phases* as having died prior to its publication.

28. See, for instance, Rachel Lewis, "Queering Vulnerability: Visualizing Black Lesbian Desire in Post-apartheid South Africa," *Feminist Formations* 28, no. 1 (2016): 205–232; Z'étoile Imma, "(Re)visualizing Black Lesbian Lives, (Trans) Masculinity, and Township Space in the Documentary Work of Zanele Muholi," *Journal of Lesbian Studies* 21, no. 2 (2017): 219–241; Stephanie Selvick, "Positive Bleeding: Violence and Desire in Works by Mlu Zondi, Zanele Muholi, and Makhosazana Xaba," *Safundi* 16, no. 4 (2015): 443–465.

29. Zanele Muholi and Peter Golsmid, *A Difficult Love,* video, 48:00, http://www.imdb.com/video/wab/vi3128728089/

30. Muholi, "Faces and Phases Artist Statement."

31. Robyn Sassen, "Dance Umbrella: Shift," *Arts Link*, March 6, 2011, http://www.artlink.co.za/news_article.htm?contentID=26629http://www.artlink.co.za/news_article.htm?contentID=26629

32. This spectacularization of sexual assault is perhaps exemplified in the mimed rape that begins Mpumelelo Paul Grootboom's *Relativity: Township Stories*. Grootboom's focus on violence and sexuality has earned him the title "the Tarantino of the townships" and made him something of an enfant terrible of postapartheid theater. His work has been critiqued for glorifying violence, particularly violence against women. The opening to *Relativity*—the rape of a woman perceived to be promiscuous—is an extremely graphic depiction of sexual violence (with a conveniently absent perpetrator); the victim eventually asphyxiates, strangled on her own thong. Nyamza's trash can dance, rather than revealing her body, obscures the act of violence. The audience members are disoriented and, rather than looking away in horror, crane their necks to see more.

33. Aimé Césaire, *Discourse on Colonialism*, trans. Joan Pinkham (New York: Monthly Review Press, 1972).

34. Writing about the play and its performances can be similarly temporally disorienting. For stylistic purposes, in order to capture the immediacy of the story as experienced by its audiences, I recount the text and performance of *I Stand Corrected* in the present tense. When referring to its performance history and reception, I revert to the past.

35. Adebayo reflects at length on the piece in an essay in *Queer Dramaturgies* (2016), commenting that her collaboration with Nyamza played a key role in articulating the black, queer, Afro-diasporic performance aesthetic she terms *Afri-Quia*. See Mojisola Adebayo, "Everything You Know about Queerness, You Learned from Blackness: The Afri-Quia Theatre of Black Dykes, Crips and Kids," in *Queer Dramaturgies: International Perspectives on Where Performance Leads Queer*, ed. Alyson Campbell and Stephen Farrier (London: Routledge, 2016).

36. Pumla Dineo Gqola, "In Zanele Muholi's Eyes: Re/imagining Ways of Seeing Black Lesbians," in Tamale, *African Sexualities*, 623.

37. Inkanyiso.org

Chapter 4

1. The sjambok (a rubber whip, usually between three and five feet long) would have carried a number of connotations for *Generations* viewers. Originally used to herd cattle in the rural areas and then adopted by the apartheid police to beat protestors into submission, it is a weapon that carries the heft of tradition and violent discipline.

2. Nguni languages are a subset of the sub-Saharan Bantu language family, and are also found in Zimbabwe and Botswana. Zulu, Xhosa, and Sotho are the primary Nguni languages spoken in South Africa (and on *Generations*).

3. South African theater scholar Loren Kruger has notably bucked this trend, arguing persuasively for television's central role in shaping postapartheid publics. Indeed, her articulation of the central paradox of the SABC as a privatized public broadcaster has shaped my understanding of the relationship between producer and consumer of postapartheid television. Yet even in an essay that acknowledges the pedagogical potential of soap opera, such as soap-inflected SABC edutainment series *Soul City* and *The Lab*, Kruger differentiates between regular nightly "soapies" and the soap operas that she perceives as operating via a Brechtian "critique by stealth." Where she does briefly reference *Generations*, it is only as a straw man counterpoint to the other, more critical shows she discusses. While I would in no way argue that *Generations* operates through Brechtian alienation, to reject its critical potential *tout court* is to underestimate the dialogical possibilities of affective investment, and dismiss the many varied, complex ways viewers take up the soap opera genre. See Loren Kruger, "Theatre for Development and TV Nation: Notes on an Educational Soap Opera in South Africa," *Research in African Literatures* 30, no. 4 (1999): 106–126 and "Critique by Stealth: Aspiration, Consumption and Class and Post Apartheid Television Drama," *Critical Arts* 24, no. 1 (2010): 75–98.

4. John Fiske, *Media Matters: Everyday Culture and Political Change* (Minneapolis: University of Minnesota Press, 1996), 7.

5. I analyzed blog entries and comments posted from the blog's March 4, 2008 debut to June 9, 2010. By selecting these dates, I chart the evolution of the community from its inception (2008) through the introduction of the gay storyline (2009) and its denouement (2010). While the blog would not slide fully into inactivity until 2013, the monthlong disruption of *Generations*' nightly broadcasts by the 2010 World Cup led to a noticeable decline in the blog's daily activity and a sharp falloff of regular participants. This time-bound analysis allows me a longitudinal observation a particular group of fans' reactions to the storyline in real time; importantly, it allows me to trace how their interactions with each other and the soap opera shaped their perceptions of the storyline and queer Africanness more generally.

6. As I conducted primary research in January–April 2012, I wrote down the locations listed on the scrolling Live Traffic Feed. Though this is by no means a thorough account and was collected randomly (i.e., just when I happened to log on), it provides a useful cross-section of those who sought out the website, whether actively posting or, like myself, silently "lurking." Tellingly, only about half of those who visited the blog were from South Africa. International visitors hailed from locations as diverse as Auckland, New Zealand; Brookline, Massachusetts (USA), Gaborone, Botswana; Halifax, Canada; Harare, Zimbabwe; Jacksonville, Florida (USA); Kingston, Jamaica; Lagos, Nigeria;

London, UK; Maseru, Lesotho; Miami, Florida (USA); Oakland, California (USA); Ontario, Canada; Orapa, Botswana; Oslo, Norway; Reykjavik, Iceland; Richmond, Virginia (USA); and Warsaw, Poland.

7. In our 2011 interview Pulane Boesek, then one of *Generations*' producers, defined this audience as rating 1–8 on the network's LSM (Living Standard Measure) scale. In a sardonic aside, Boesek represented SABC 1's viewership to me as being "your young, your hip. Very much into celebrity, very shallow. Basically sixteen to twenty-four. Very ambitious, but basically more materialistic ambition than anything else" (personal interview). According to South African Advertising Research Foundation, LSM is determined by twenty-nine variables, ranging from running water to number of radios and televisions, owning a PC, and hiring a domestic worker, among others ("Living Standards Measure," http://www.saarf.co.za/LSM/lsms.asp). While this system of classification was meant to categorize viewers outside of the apartheid-era racial categories, it ironically shows the impossibility of separating race and class in postapartheid society: as of 2005, almost two-thirds of adult South Africans were classified LSM 1–5. LSM 9–10 were primarily white (74%) and LSM 1–5 were almost entirely black (95%) (South African Television Authority, "What's Your LSM?," *TVSA*, http://www.tvsa.co.za/default.asp?blogname=news&articleID=4931).

8. The democratic potential of "cyberspace" has been famously, and perhaps overly enthusiastically, espoused—and subsequently critiqued—by many. For representative examples of both sides of this debate, see Howard Reingold's in *Virtual Communities: Homesteading on the Electronic Frontier* (Cambridge: MIT Press, 1993); and Douglass E. Cowan, "Online U-topia: Cyberspace and the Mythology of Placelessness," *Journal for the Scientific Study of Religion* 44, no. 3 (2005): 257–263. The recent proliferation of social media and smartphones productively complicates these earlier analyses, in ways that are only now beginning to be theorized. See, for instance: #identity: Hashtagging Race, Gender, Sexuality, and Nation, ed. Abigail de Kosnik and Keith Feldman (Ann Arbor: University of Michigan Press, 2019).

9. See World Bank, "Internet Users," http://data.worldbank.org/indicator/IT.NET.USER.P2?locations=ZA

10. Gillian Hart provides an in-depth case study of this displacement in her excellent analysis of globalization's impact on the local garment industry in KwaZulu Natal, *Disabling Globalization* (Berkeley: University of California Press, 2002).

11. ChingChang, "What Happened to Them?????????," *Gensblog* (blog), September 8, 2009, http://www.gensblog.co.za/2009/09/08/what-happened-to-them

12. Ntshantsha, "Dineo Can't Take It Anymore," *Gensblog*, June 29, 2009, www.gensblog.co.za/2009/06/24/dineo-cant-take-it-anymore

13. Lauren Berlant, *The Female Complaint* (Durham, NC: Duke University Press, 2008), viii.

14. Ibid.

15. Michel Foucault, "Of Other Spaces: Heterotopias," trans. Jay Miskowiec, *Diacritics* 16, no. 1 (1967): 8.

16. Ibid.

17. Shawanda, "Senzo and Sharon," *Gensblog*, May 25, 2009, www.gensblog.co.za/2009/05/25/senzo-and-sharon

18. Language and its uses became especially important as signifying belonging to the

board. Most members made a concerted effort to keep the board in English, presumed to be understood by all speakers of South Africa's eleven official languages as well as those logging in from other countries abroad. This occasionally led to skirmishes about who got to determine the languages spoken, with accusations of self-loathing bandied about. Generally, the board comments were in English, with a smattering of words from South Africa's other official languages (especially Tswana, Zulu, Xhosa, and—to a lesser degree—Afrikaans) as well as slang (*Tsotsitaal*). The blogger's use of "text-speak," abbreviations, and ellipses created a snappy, slangy rhetorical style, mimicking the tone of *Generations*' code-switching "vernac" dialogue.

19. Olivia, "Congratulations to Olivia!," *Gensblog*, May 31, 2009, http://www.gensblog.co.za/2009/05/31/congratulations-to-olivia

20. Olivia, "Tuesday 14 July 2009," *Gensblog*, July 14, 2009, http://www.gensblog.co.za/2009/07/14/tuesday-14-july-2009

21. Olivia, "What Does Sibusiso Not Want Dolly's Sister to Tell Senzo?," *Gensblog*, June 2, 2009, http://www.gensblog.co.za/2009/06/02/what-does-sibusiso-not-want-dollys-sister-to-tell-senzo. Gaining access to the familial space of *Gensblog* did not come easily, however. There were certain codes of conduct to be followed, ways of gaining cultural capital to truly earn membership in the family. At a minimum, those who wanted to be family members had to consistently participate in the daily life of the blog, commenting on either the narratives of the soap or the (often unrelated) discussions and banter between the members. As the blog moved away from its initial designation as a discussion board for the soap opera, so did the patience of the members wane for those who de-lurked only to never return.

22. See Nancy Baym, *Tune In, Log On: Soaps, Fandom, and Online Community* (Thousand Oaks, CA: Sage, 2005), 19. Baym isolates a variety of genres of online soap opera "talk" as facilitating community, including sharing knowledge on a soap opera's pasts; humor, especially that which demonstrates awareness of the soap opera's own failings; and criticism that allows for creative engagement and rescripting of the perceived weaknesses. These discourses, mixed in with the daily gripes and the rituals of greeting and leave-taking, allowed for the development of individual performed identities of the participants, of interpersonal relationships, and, perhaps most importantly, of a sense of play.

23. ChingChang, "Thursday 6 August 2009," *Gensblog*, August 6, 2009, http://www.gensblog.co.za/2009/08/06/thursday-6-august-2009

24. Tbos, ibid.

25. Olivia, "Dineo Did Not Have the Abortion," *Gensblog*, August 13, 2009, http://www.gensblog.co.za/2009/08/13/dineo-did-not-have-the-abortion

26. Olivia, "Why Does Abi Not Want to Go Back to Nigeria?," *Gensblog*, June 10, 2009, http://www.gensblog.co.za/2009/06/10/why-does-abi-not-want-to-go-back-to-nigeria

27. Tbos, "Tuesday 1 September 2009," *Gensblog*, September 1, 2009, www.gensblog.co.za/2009/09/01/tuesday-1-september-2009

28. Thulie, ibid.

29. Black Beauty, ibid.

30. Thulie, ibid.

31. Olivia, ibid.

32. Nosiphiwo B, "Thursday 3 September 2009," *Gensblog*, September 3, 2009, http://www.gensblog.co.za/2009/09/03/thursday-3-september-2009

33. Ibid.

34. Dee, "What Is a Gay or Lesbian (Homosexual) or Bi-sexual Person?," *Gensblog*, September 2, 2009, http://www.gensblog.co.za/2009/09/02/what-is-a-gay-or-lesbian-homosexual-person-or-a-bi-sexual-person

35. Thando, "Oh My G . . . ," *Gensblog*, September 2, 2009, http://www.gensblog.co.za/2009/09/02/oh-my-g

36. Winston, "Senzo, Senzo, Senzo!," *Gensblog*, September 1, 2009, www.gensblog.co.za/2009/09/11/senzo-senzo-senzo

37. Tbos, ibid.

38. Thulie, "Tuesday 1 September 2009."

39. Dee, ibid.

40. Dee, "What Is a Gay or Lesbian."

41. Tbos, "Jason and Linda—Where Does Senzo Fit In?," *Gensblog*, September 10, 2009, http://www.gensblog.co.za/2009/09/10/jason-and-linda-where-does-senzo-fit-in. Senzo and Jason's storyline coincided with another popular discussion in South African media around runner Caster Semenya's controversial (alleged) intersex identity. Dee, especially, had been enraged by the racist global coverage of Semenya's win. Tellingly, at the same time that they were condemning Jason and Senzo's relationship, members of the board were very sympathetic to Semenya's plight: for ChingChang, "what i like in her is she is proud of who she is & she is not ashamed of the way God created her" ("Little Dini's Luxury Life Is No More," *Gensblog*, September 8, 2009, www.gensblog.co.za/2009/09/08/little-dini's-luxury-life-is-no-more).

42. Winnie, "What Is a Gay or Lesbian."

43. Olivia, "Tuesday 1 September 2009."

44. Maqz, "Kenneth Is Still in Love," *Gensblog*, September 3, 2009, www.gensblog.co.za/2009/09/03/kenneth-is-still-in-love

45. Dee, "What Is a Gay or Lesbian."

46. Olivia, ibid.

47. Tbos, ibid.

48. Ibid.

49. Olivia, ibid.

50. Dee, "Thursday 20 August 2009," *Gensblog*, August 20, 2009, www.gensblog.co.za/2009/08/20/thursday-20-august-2009

51. Ibid.

52. Tbos, ibid.

53. Thulie, "Monday 14 September 2009," *Gensblog*, September 15, 2009, www.gensblog.co.za/2009/09/14/monday-14-september-2009

54. Boesek, interview.

55. Foucault, "Of Other Spaces," 8.

56. In Karen Barad, "Diffracting diffraction: Cutting together-apart." *Parallax* 20.3 (2014): 168–187.

57. Ibid., 170.

58. Dee, "Thursday 20 August 2009,".

59. Ibid.

60. Zizi, "Oh My G . . . ."
61. Ibid.
62. Duane, ibid.
63. Mazow, Thuli, Tshili, Lindi, and Kiki, "Oh my G . . . ."
64. Thulie, "Jason and Linda"; ChingChang, ibid.
65. Maqz, ibid.
66. Maqz, "You Can Run but You Can't Hide," *Gensblog*, September 29, 2009, www.gensblog.co.za/2009/09/29/you-can-run-but-you-cant-hide/
67. Boesak, interview.
68. This was not only the case with the Jason-Senzo storyline, but also of a concurrent storyline where young professional Khetiwe is repeatedly abused by her boyfriend Dumisane. This plot brought out painful, personal stories from both abused and abusers on the board (and caused several members to briefly leave *Gensblog*). It also laid the ground for a passionate and unusually frank debate about gender roles, the definition of abuse—how emotional and physical abuse differed—and what was necessary to make modern marriages work. The high emotional stakes—intensified by the identification with the characters on the soapie—upped the incentive to find a workable solution. Because of board members' support and the dialogue that resulted from watching the Dumisane/Khetiwe storyline, Stacy—a Zimbabwean poster in an abusive marriage—decided to leave her husband.
69. Tbos, "Heita Gays!," *Gensblog*, December 11, 2009, www.gensblog.co.za/2009/12/11/heita-gays
70. Ibid.
71. Zizi, ibid.
72. Tbos, ibid.
73. Ibid.
74. Thulie, ibid.
75. Tbos, ibid.
76. Tbos, "Ajax Is Also Gay?," *Gensblog*, January 5, 2010, www.gensblog.co.za/2010/01/05/ajax-is-also-gay
77. Tbos, "Tradition Sucks!," *Gensblog*, January 7, 2010, www.gensblog.co.za/2010/01/07/tradition-sucks. It is common for Xhosa South African men to go through a process of initiation in "bush schools" when they reach puberty, where they are then circumcised by an elder. Circumcision is closely linked with manhood in these contexts.
78. Palm86, "Rethabile Retaliates!," *Gensblog*, April 4, 2010, www.gensblog.co.za/2010/04/29/rethabile-retaliates
79. Tbos, ibid.
80. Tbos, "Heartbreak Hotel," *Gensblog*, June 3, 2010, www.gensblog.co.za/2010/06/03/heart-break-hotel
81. Though, as Twitter user @Mr_Skota pointed out, quality is relative: "The old generations . . . wasn't better. Its just that people were more used to that trash. New trash shock today. So chill."
82. Danai Mupotsa, "Sophie's Special Secret: Public Feeling, Consumption, and Celebrity Activism in Post-apartheid South Africa," in *Celebrity Humanitarianism and North-South Relations: Politics, Place and Power*, ed. Lisa Ann Richey (London: Routledge, 2016).

83. Boesak, interview.

84. Athi Patra-Ruga, interview with author, Cape Town, South Africa, July 2016.

85. Focus Group on LGBT Media, Gay and Lesbian Memory in Action, Johannesburg, South Africa, April 5, 2011.

86. Peggy Phelan, *Unmarked: The Politics of Performance* (New York: Routledge, 2004), 149.

Conclusion

1. Kruger, *Drama of South Africa*, 17.

2. Graeme Reid has written a compelling ethnography of Hope and Unity Metropolitan Community Church, a vibrant gay church in the 1990s, located in Hillbrow above a popular gay bar. See Reid, *Above the Skyline*.

3. "Our Manifesto," *JHB People's Pride*, June 10, 2013, http://peoplespride.blogspot.com/p/pride-movement-of-protest-celebration.html

4. Ibid.

Bibliography

Abu-Lughod, Lila. "The Romance of Resistance: Tracing Transformation of Power through Bedouin Women." *American Ethnologist* 17, no. 1 (1990): 41–55.

Adebayo, Mojisola. "Everything You Know about Queerness, You Learned from Blackness: The Afri-Quia Theatre of Black Dykes, Crips and Kids." In *Queer Dramaturgies: International Perspectives on Where Performance Leads Queer*, ed. Alyson Campbell and Stephen Farrier. London: Routledge, 2016.

Allen, Jafari. "Black/Queer Rhizomatics: Train Up a Child in the Way Ze Should Grow . . . ." In *No Tea No Shade: New Writings in Black Queer Studies*, ed. E. Patrick Johnson. Durham, NC: Duke University Press, 2016.

Amadumbe, Ifi. *Male Wives and Female Husbands: Gender and Sex in an African Society*. London: Zed Press, 1987.

Arnfred, Signe, ed. *Re-thinking Sexualities in Africa*. Uppsala: Nordiska Afrikainstitutet, 2004.

Austin, J. L. *How to Do Things with Words*. Cambridge: Harvard University Press, 1962.

Bailey, Marlon. *Butch Queens up in Pumps*. Ann Arbor: University of Michigan Press, 2013.

Barad, Karen. "Diffracting Diffraction: Cutting Together-Apart." *Parallax* 20, no. 3 (2014): 168–187.

Baym, Nancy. *Tune In, Log On: Soaps, Fandom, and Online Community*. Thousand Oaks, CA: Sage, 2005.

Berlant, Lauren. *The Female Complaint: The Unfinished Business of Sentimentality in American Culture*. Durham, NC: Duke University Press, 2008.

Bishop, J. "The Man behind the Woman." In *Conversations*. Sloane Park: Premier, 1991.

Blumberg, Marcia, and Dennis Walder. "Introduction." In *South African Theatre and/as Intervention*. Amsterdam: Rodopi, 1999.

Bond-Stockton, Catherine. *The Queer Child: or, Growing Sideways in 20th-Century America*. Durham, NC: Duke University Press, 2009.

Bosch, Morwenna. "Limping into the African Renaissance: The Abject Art of Steven Cohen." *South African Theatre Journal* 19 (2005): 116–129.

Brown, Andrew. "Performing Blackness in the 'Rainbow Nation': Athi-Patra Ruga's *The Future White Women of Azania*." *Women and Performance* 27, no. 1 (2017): 67–80.

Christofides, Liza. "Embodying Prejudice: Abjection in the Performance Art of Steven Cohen." MA thesis, University of Witwatersrand, 2003.

Cima, Gibson. "Postconflict Nostalgia: Postapartheid South African Theatre, 1990–2010." PhD diss., University of Washington, 2012.

Cole, Catherine. "Johannesburg Dance Umbrella: Thirty Years On (Review)." *Theatre Journal* 70, no. 4 (2018): 539–542.

Cole, Catherine. *Performing South Africa's Truth Commission: Stages of Transition*. Bloomington: Indiana University Press, 2010.

Conquergood, Dwight. "Performance Studies: Interventions and Radical Research." *TDR* 46, no. 2 (2002): 142–156.

Conquergood, Dwight. "Rethinking Ethnography: Towards a Critical Cultural Politics." *Communication Monographs* 59 (1991): 179–194.

Cowan, Douglass E. "Online U-topia: Cyberspace and the Mythology of Placelessness." *Journal for the Scientific Study of Religion* 44, no. 3 (2005): 257–263.

Currier, Ashley. *Out in Africa: LGBT Organizing in Namibia and South Africa*. Minneapolis: University of Minnesota Press, 2012.

Currier, Ashley, and Thérèse Migraine-George. "'Lesbian'/Female Same-Sex Sexualities in Africa." *Journal of Lesbian Studies* 21, no. 2 (2016): 133–150.

Currier, Ashley, and Thérèse Migraine-George. "Queer Studies / African Studies: An (Im)possible Transaction?" *GLQ* 22, no. 2 (2016): 281–305.

Currier, Ashley, and Thérèse Migraine-George. "Queering Queer African Archives: Methods and Movements." *WSQ: Women's Studies Quarterly* 44, nos. 3–4 (2016): 190–207.

Dolan, Jill. *Utopia in Performance: Finding Hope at the Theatre*. Durham, NC: Duke University Press, 2005.

Dyer, Richard. *White: Essays on Race and Culture*. New York: Taylor and Francis, 1997.

Edelman, Lee. *No Future: Queer Theory and the Death Drive*. Durham, NC: Duke University Press, 2004.

Epprecht, Marc. *Heterosexual Africa? The History of an Idea from the Age of Exploration to the Age of AIDS*. Athens: Ohio University Press, 2008.

Epprecht, Marc. *Hungochani: The History of a Dissident Sexuality in Southern Africa*. Montreal: McGill-Queens University Press, 2004.

Fiske, John. *Media Matters: Everyday Culture and Political Change*. Minneapolis: University of Minnesota Press, 1996.

Fleetwood, Nicole R. *Troubling Vision: Performance, Visuality, and Blackness*. Chicago: University of Chicago Press, 2011.

Foucault, Michel. "Of Other Spaces: Heterotopias." Trans. Jay Miskowiec. *Diacritics* 16, no. 1 (1967): 22–27.

Francis, Dennis, ed. *Acting on HIV: Using Drama to Create Possibilities for Change*. Rotterdam: Sense Publishers, 2012.

Freeman, Elizabeth. *Time Binds: Queer Temporalities, Queer Histories*. Durham, NC: Duke University Press, 2010.

Freud, Sigmund. "Mourning and Melancholia." In *The Standard Edition of the Complete Psychological Works of Sigmund Freud*, trans. James Strachey. London: Hogarth Press, 1955.

Garber, Marjorie. *Vested Interests: Cross-Dressing and Cultural Anxiety*. New York: Routledge, 1997.

Goffman, Erving. *The Presentation of Self in Everyday Life*. New York: Anchor, 1959.

Golomski, Casey. "Queering Myth in a Southern African Gay and Lesbian Pentecostal Church." *Transforming Anthropology* (forthcoming).

Gqola, Pumla Dineo. "Defining People: Analysing Power, Language and Representation in Metaphors of the New South Africa." *Transformation* 47 (2001): 94–106.

Gqola, Pumla Dineo. "In Zanele Muholi's eyes: Re/imagining Ways of Seeing Black Lesbians." In *African Sexualities: A Reader*, ed. Sylvia Tamale. Dakar: Pambazuka Press, 2011.

Gqola, Pumla Dineo. *Rape: A South African Nightmare*. Cape Town: Jacana, 2016.

Grewal, Inderpal. *Transnational America: Feminisms, Diaspora, Neoliberalisms*. Durham, NC: Duke University Press, 2005.

Gunkel, Henriette. *The Cultural Politics of Female Sexuality in South Africa*. London: Routledge, 2010.

Gunkel, Henriette. "Through the Postcolonial Eyes: Images of Gender and Female Sexuality in Contemporary South Africa." *Journal of Lesbian Studies* 13, no. 1 (2009): 77–87.

Gunkel, Henriette. "Some Reflections on Postcolonial Homophobia, Local Interventions, and LGBTI Solidarity Online: The Politics of Global Petitions." *African Studies Review* 52, no. 2 (2013): 67–81.

Gunner, Elizabeth. *Musho! Zulu Popular Praises*. East Lansing: Michigan State University Press, 1991.

Halberstam, J. *Female Masculinity*. Durham, NC: Duke University Press, 1998.

Halberstam, J. *In a Queer Time and Place: Transgender Bodies, Subcultural Lives*. New York: NYU Press, 2005.

Hames, Mary. "Violence against Black Lesbians: Minding Our Language." *Agenda* 25, no. 4 (2011): 87–91.

Hart, Gillian. *Disabling Globalization: Places of Power in Post-apartheid South Africa* Berkeley: University of California Press, 2002.

Higgins, E. Tory. "Self-Discrepancy: A Theory Relating Self and Affect." *Psychological Review* 94, no. 3 (1987): 319–340.

Hoad, Neville. *African Intimacies: Race, Homosexuality, and Globalization*. Minneapolis: University of Minnesota Press, 2007.

Hutchison, Yvette. *South African Performance and the Archives of Memory*. Oxford: Oxford University Press, 2013.

Imma, Z'étoile. "(Re)visualizing Black Lesbian Lives, (Trans) Masculinity, and Township Space in the Documentary Work of Zanele Muholi." *Journal of Lesbian Studies* 21, no. 2 (2017): 219–241.

Johansson, Ola. *Community Theatre and AIDS*. London: Routledge, 2011.

Johnson, E. Patrick. *Appropriating Blackness: Performance and the Politics of Authenticity*. Durham, NC: Duke University Press, 2003.

Judge, Melanie. *Blackwashing Homophobia: Violence and the Politics of Gender, Sexuality, and Race*. London: Routledge, 2017.

Kruger, Loren. "Critique by Stealth: Aspiration, Consumption and Class and Post-apartheid Television Drama." *Critical Arts* 24, no. 1 (2010): 75–98.

Kruger, Loren. *The Drama of South Africa: Plays, Pageants, and Publics since 1910*. New York: Routledge, 1999.

Kruger, Loren. "Theatre for Development and TV Nation: Notes on an Educational Soap Opera in South Africa." *Research in African Literatures* 30, no. 4 (1999): 106–126.

Lease, Bryce. "Dragging Rights, Queering Publics: Realness, Self-Fashioning and the Miss Gay Western Cape Pageant." *Safundi* 18, no. 2 (2017): 131–146.

Lewis, Megan. *Performing Whitely in the Postcolony: Afrikaners in South African Theatrical and Public Life*. Iowa City: University of Iowa Press, 2016.

Lewis, Rachel. "Queering Vulnerability: Visualizing Black Lesbian Desire in Post-apartheid South Africa." *Feminist Formations* 28, no. 1 (2016): 205–232.

Lieberfeld, Daniel. "Crossing Apartheid's Lines: An Interview." *TDR* 41, no. 1 (1997): 61–71.

Livermon, Xavier. "Queer(y)ing Freedom: Black Queer Visibilities in Postapartheid South Africa." *GLQ* 18, nos. 2–3 (2012): 297–323.

Lopez, Alfred, ed. *Postcolonial Whiteness: A Critical Reader on Race and Empire*. Albany: SUNY Press, 2012.

Lorde, Audre. *Zami: A New Spelling of My Name*. New York: Random House, 1982.

Lott, Eric. *Love & Theft: Blackface Minstrelsy and the American Working Class*. Oxford: Oxford University Press, 1993.

Macharia, Keguro. "Archive and Method in Queer African Studies." *Agenda* 22, no. 1 (2015): 140–146.

Macharia, Keguro. "Africa : Queer : Anthropology." *New Inquiry*, July 28, 2018. https://thenewinquiry.com/blog/africa-queer-anthropology/

Madison, D. Soyini. *Critical Ethnography: Method, Ethics, and Performance*. Thousand Oaks, CA: Sage, 2011.

Mahmood, Saba. *The Politics of Piety: The Islamic Revival and the Feminist Subject*. Princeton, NJ: Princeton University Press, 2004.

Massad, Joseph. "Reorienting Desire: The Gay International in the Arab World." *Public Culture* 14, no. 2 (2002): 361–386.

Matebeni, Zethu. "Deconstructing Violence towards Black Lesbians in South Africa." In *Queer African Reader*, ed. Hakima Abbas and Sokari Ekine. Dakar: Pambazuka, 2013.

Matebeni, Zethu. "Exploring Black Lesbian Sexualities and Identities in Johannesburg." PhD diss., University of the Witwatersrand, 2011.

Matebeni, Zethu, and Jabu Pereira. "Preface." In *Reclaiming Afrikan: Queer Perspectives on Sexual and Gender Identities*, ed. Zethu Matebeni. Athlone: Modjaji Press, 2014.

Mbembe, Achille. *On the Postcolony*. Berkeley: University of California Press, 2001.

McClain, Nyx. "The Digital as Enabler: A Case Study of the Joburg 2012 Pride Clash." *Feminist Africa 18* (2013): 26–42.

McClintock, Anne. *Imperial Leather: Race, Gender, and Sexuality in the Imperial Conquest*. New York: Routledge, 1995.

Moffett, Helen. "'These Women, They Force Us to Rape Them': Rape as Narrative of Social Control in Post-apartheid South Africa." *Journal of Southern African Studies* 32, no. 1 (2006): 129–144.

Morgan, Ruth, and Saskia Wieringa. *Tommy Boys, Lesbian Men, and Ancestral Wives: Female Same-Sex Practices in Africa*. Johannesburg: Jacana Media, 2005.

Muholi, Zanele. *Faces and Phases*. Munich: Prestel. 2010.

Muñoz, José. *Cruising Utopia: The Then and Now of Queer Futurities*. New York: NYU Press, 2009.

Muñoz, José. *Disidentifications: Queers of Color and the Performance of Politics*. Minneapolis: University of Minnesota Press, 1999.

Munro, Brenna. *South Africa and the Dream of Love Yet to Come: Queer Sexuality and the Struggle for Freedom*. Minneapolis: University of Minnesota Press, 2012.

Mupotsa, Danai. "Sophie's Special Secret: Public Feeling, Consumption, and Celebrity Activism in Post-Apartheid South Africa." In *Celebrity Humanitarianism and North-South Relations: Politics, Place and Power*, ed. Lisa Ann Richey. London: Routledge, 2016.

Murray, Stephen O., and Will Roscoe. *Boy-Wives and Female Husbands: Studies of African Homosexualities*. New York: Palgrave, 1998.

Ndebele, Njabulo. "Iph'indlela? Finding Our Way into the Future." *Social Dynamics* 26, no. 1 (2000): 43–55.

Nevin, Alice. "Instant Mutuality: The Development of Maboneng in Inner-City Johannesburg." *Anthropology Southern Africa* 37, nos. 3–4 (2014): 187–201.

Nkoli, Simon Tseko. "Opening Address at the 1990 Johannesburg Pride March." In *Pride: Protest and Celebration*, ed. Shaun de Waal and Anthony Manion. Johannesburg: Fanele, 2006.

Nuttall, Sarah. "Stylizing the Self: The Y Generation in Rosebank, Johannesburg." *Public Culture* 16, no. 3 (2004): 430–452.

Nyanzi, Stella. "Queering Queer Africa." In *Reclaiming Afrikan: Queer Perspectives on Sexual and Gender Identities*, ed. Zethu Matebeni. Athlone: Modjaji Books, 2014.

Nyong'o, Tavia. "Queer Africa and the Fantasy of Virtual Participation." *WSQ: Women's Studies Quarterly* 40, nos. 1–2 (2012): 40–63.

Nyong'o, Tavia. *Afro-Fabulations: The Queer Drama of Black Life*. New York: NYU Press, 2019.

Oyěwùmí, Oyèrónkẹ́. *The Invention of Women: Making an African Sense of Western Gender Discourse*. Minneapolis: University of Minnesota Press, 1997.

Pellegrini, Ann. "Religion, Secularism, and a Democratic Politics of 'As If.'" *Social Research* 76, no. 4 (2009): 1345–1350.

Phelan, Peggy. *Unmarked: The Politics of Performance*. New York: Routledge, 2004.

Posel, Deborah. "The Scandal of Manhood: 'Baby Rape' and the Politicization of Sexual Violence in Post-apartheid South Africa." *Culture, Health and Sexuality* 7, no. 3 (2005): 239–252.

Puar, Jasbir. *Terrorist Assemblages: Homonationalism in Queer Times*. Durham, NC: Duke University Press, 2009.

Reid, Graeme. *Above the Skyline: Reverend Tsietsi Thandekiso and the Founding of an African Gay Church*. Johannesburg: UNISA Press, 2010.

Reid, Graeme. *How to Be a Real Gay: Gay Identities in Small-Town South Africa*. Scottsville: UKZN Press, 2013.

Reingold, Howard. *Virtual Communities: Homesteading on the Electronic Frontier*. Cambridge: MIT Press, 1993.

Russell, Heather. *Legba's Crossing: Narratology in the African Atlantic*. Athens: University of Georgia Press, 2009.

Sassen, Robyn. "For the Love of Elu: Steven Cohen's Gentle Endocannibalism." *Performance Research* 23 (2018): 83–87.

Sassen, Robyn. "Steven Cohen / Princess Menorah: Coming Out Jewish in South African Art." MA thesis, University of the Witwatersrand, 2005.

Schechner, Richard, and Sara Brady, eds. *Performance Studies: An Introduction*. 3rd ed. New York: Routledge, 2017.

Scheub, Harold. *The Tongue Is Fire: South African Storytellers and Apartheid*. Madison: University of Wisconsin Press, 1996.

Schneider, Rebecca. *The Explicit Body in Performance*. New York: Routledge, 1997.

Schulman, Sarah. *Israel/Palestine and the Queer International*. Durham, NC: Duke University Press, 2012.

Seig, Katrin. *Ethnic Drag: Performing Race, Nation, and Sexuality in West Germany*. Ann Arbor: University of Michigan Press, 2002.

Selvick, Stephanie. "Positive Bleeding: Violence and Desire in Works by Mlu Zondi, Zanele Muholi, and Makhosazana Xaba." *Safundi* 16, no. 4 (2016): 443–465.

Senelick, Laurence. *The Changing Room: Sex, Drag, and Theatre*. New York: Routledge, 2000.

Shain, Milton, and Richard Mendelsohn. *The Jews in South Africa: An Illustrated History* Johannesburg: Jonathan Ball Publishing, 2009.

Sizemore-Barber, April. "Archival Movements: South Africa's Gay and Lesbian Memory in Action." *Safundi* 18, no. 2 (2017): 117–130.

Sizemore-Barber, April. "Queer Transition: Whiteness in the Prismatic, Post-apartheid Drag Performances of Pieter-Dirk Uys and Steven Cohen." *Theatre Journal* 68, no. 2 (2016): 191–211.

Sizemore-Barber, April. "South Africa's National Arts Festival (Review)." *Theatre Journal* 65, no. 2 (2013): 261–264.

Sontag, Susan. "Notes on Camp." In *Against Interpretation and Other Essays*. New York: Picador, 2001.

Spivak, Gayatri Chakravorty. "Can the Subaltern Speak?" In *Can the Subaltern Speak? Reflections on the History of an Idea*, ed. Rosalind Morris. New York: Columbia University Press, 1988.

Stanislavski, Constantin. *An Actor Prepares*. Trans. Elizabeth Reynolds Hapgood. New York: Routledge, 1989.

Steyn, Melissa. *Whiteness Just Isn't What It Used to Be: White Identity in a Changing South Africa*. Albany: SUNY Press, 2001.

Stobie, Cheryl. *Somewhere over the Double Rainbow: Representations of Bisexuality in Post-apartheid Novels*. Scottsville: UKZN Press, 2009.

Swarr, Amanda Lock. *Sex in Transition: Remaking Gender and Race in South Africa*. Albany: SUNY Press, 2012.

Tallie, T. J. *Queering Colonial Natal: Indigeneity and the Violence of Belonging in Southern Africa*. Minneapolis: University of Minnesota Press, 2019.

Tamale, Sylvia. "Researching and Theorizing Sexualities in Africa." In *African Sexualities: A Reader*, ed. Sylvia Tamale. Dakar: Pambazuka Press, 2011.

Taub, Meyer. "The Practical Etymology of Seeing Oneself While Listening to Others." *South African Theatre Journal* 24, no. 1 (2011): 156–175.

Taylor, Diana. *Disappearing Acts: Spectacles of Gender and Nationalism in Argentina's "Dirty War"*. Durham, NC: Duke University Press, 1997.

Thlabi, Redi. *Khwezi: The Remarkable Story of Fezekile Ntsukela Kuzwayo*. Johannesburg: Jonathan Ball Press, 2017.

Thomas, Kylie. "Zanele Muholi's Intimate Archive: Photography and Post-apartheid Lesbian Lives." *Safundi* 11, no. 4 (2010): 421–436.

Tucker, Andrew. *Queer Visibilities: Space, Identity, and Interaction in Cape Town.* Oxford: Wiley Blackwell, 2009.

Turner, Victor. *The Ritual Process: Structure and Anti-structure.* New York: Aldine de Gruyter, 1969.

Uys, Pieter-Dirk. *A Part Hate, a Part Love.* Johannesburg: Radix, 1990.

Uys, Pieter-Dirk. *Between the Devil and the Deep: A Memoir of Acting and Reacting.* Cape Town: Zebra, 2005.

Uys, Pieter-Dirk. *Elections and Erections: A Memoir of Fear and Fun.* Cape Town: Zebra, 2003.

Vaid-Menon, Alok. "Rainbows Are Just Refracted White Light: Settler Homonationalism in Neo-apartheid South Africa." Master's thesis, Stanford University, 2012.

Van der Vlies, Andrew. "Queer Knowledge and the Politics of the Gaze in Contemporary South African Photography: Zanele Muholi and Others." *Journal of African Cultural Studies* 24, no. 2 (2012): 140–156.

Van der Watt, Liese. "Imagining Alternative White Masculinities: Steven Cohen's Living Art." In *Under Construction: "Race" and Identity in South Africa Today*, ed. Natasha Distiller and Melissa Steyn. London: Heinemann, 2004.

Yuval-Davies, Nira. *Gender and Nation.* London: Sage, 1997.

Zondi, Mlondolozi. "Black Performance Theory (Review)." *Text and Performance Quarterly* 37, nos. 3–4 (2017): 278–281.

Index

Abu-Lughod, Lila, 63
Adebayo, Mojisola, 75, 94–95, 97–98, 101–103, 161
African National Congress, 6, 10, 22, 31, 43, 82, 113, 133, 137, 140, 146
Afrikaans, 18, 22, 31–32, 150
Afrikaner, 9, 22, 26, 28, 32
"after nines," 49
antiapartheid, 1, 3, 8, 46, 65, 72, 136
antigay
  feelings, 6, 127, 129, 132
  leaders, 49
apartheid
  antigay law, 1
  censorship under, 9, 35
  and citizenship, 8, 24
  cross-racial intimacy during, 29
  economic, 5–6, 43, 113, 139
  end of, 6, 28–29, 57, 136, 140
  gender and racial difference under, 24–25, 29
  government, 9, 29–31
  in history, 7, 81
  legacies of, 4, 13, 22, 42, 66, 99, 102
  mixed race under, 29
  and sexual puritanism, 12
  struggle against, 1, 8–9, 121
  visual and performance cultures under, 9, 11, 33, 93
  whiteness under, 26–27, 29, 42
art
  dance, 75, 79, 83, 93–95, 98–100, 103
  performance, 13, 19, 24, 36, 44, 134, 141
  photography, 6, 14, 20, 78–79, 82–84, 86–89, 91–92, 95, 102–103
  visual, 84
Artscape Theatre, 99
"as-if," 47, 50, 52–53, 74, 154
audience
  complicity, 6, 79, 91–92, 95–96, 102, 104
  creation of, 11, 21, 39, 115, 117, 138
  engagement with, 24–25, 32, 34, 37, 49, 59, 92–93, 95, 98, 108, 114
  exchange with, 5, 8, 25, 43, 88, 92–94, 99–100, 102, 117, 134, 137–138
  expectations, 33, 35, 59, 79, 94–96, 98, 125, 138
  intended, 11, 30, 112
  international, 10, 59
  reception, 7–8, 15, 31–33, 37, 108–109, 137
  understanding, 7, 21, 26, 30–32, 42, 75, 79, 81, 87, 93–94, 98–99, 104, 108–109, 119
  varied, 16, 25, 32, 59, 133
  Western, 10, 76, 78, 102
  white, 11, 22, 25, 29–31, 42, 91
Austin, J.L., 61

Baartman, Sarah, 86, 153, 160
Bahati, David, 49
Bailey, Marlon, 51
Ban Ki-Moon, 136
Baxter Theatre, 11, 31
Berlant, Lauren, 114

Biko, Stephen, 147
bisexual, 63–64, 123–124, 129, 131, 159
Black Economic Empowerment, 42, 107
blood
  menstrual, 84
  stains, 84
  used in performance, 36–37, 46, 84, 142
Blumberg, Marcia, 9
bodies
  absent, 89
  African, 86
  and belonging, 14
  Black, 4, 7, 9, 30, 79, 82–83, 85–86, 88, 93–94, 96, 104, 143
  dead, 76
  dignity of, 30
  gendered, 78, 125, 143
  invisible, 138
  Jewish, 35
  lesbian, 70, 78–82, 84–85, 88–89, 93–94, 96, 104
  limitations of, 24, 35
  live, 17, 76
  messiness, 116
  mixed-race, 29
  naked (stripped), 30
  national, 46, 86
  non-conforming, 96, 160
  in performance, 9, 16, 20, 25, 70, 86, 93–96, 100, 108, 125, 152
  politic, 18, 78, 86
  in protest, 3–4, 17
  postapartheid, 24
  queer, 4–6, 12, 16, 18, 35–36, 39, 41, 46, 53, 77–78, 138, 143
  raced, 20
  sexed, 54
  violated, 20, 30, 75, 79, 89, 95, 101
  vulnerability of, 30, 70, 92
  white, 26, 30, 35–37, 41
  women's, 54, 78, 83, 86, 93
Born Free Generation, 11, 57, 154
boundaries/borders, 5, 19–20, 35, 37, 42, 49, 70, 74, 77, 83–84, 87, 108, 116, 119, 121
Braamfontein, 13, 42, 59
Brown, Andrew, 154
Butler, Judith, 120, 149

camp, 13, 26, 36, 46
cannibalism, 37, 152
Cape Town, 11, 31, 38, 79, 85, 87–88, 90, 93–94, 99, 113, 132
capital
  capitalism, 18, 37, 53
  global, 12
Césaire, Aimé, 95
choice
  and coming out, 49, 61, 64, 122, 127
  and democracy, 58
  and LGBT identity, 61, 64, 122, 127
  limitations of, 60–61, 107, 127
  and modernity, 107
  rhetoric, 60–61
Chosen FEW, 13–14, 18–19, 47–53, 55–59, 61–68, 70, 72–75, 86–87, 122, 133, 138, 154–155, 158
Christianity, 49, 118, 120, 122, 128, 157–158
cisgender, 18
citizenship
  Black, 9, 74
  cosmopolitan, 18
  cultural, 30, 51, 72, 74
  democratic, 51
  full, 2, 8, 49
  LGBT, 1, 5, 18, 51, 77, 137, 145
  multiracial, 8
  performative, 52
  postapartheid, 6, 39
  white, 42, 81
class
  elite, 42
  middle class, 20, 35, 107–108, 112
  poor, 4, 12, 17, 42, 76, 118, 128, 136, 142
  upper class, 16, 18, 42
closet (as metaphor), 57–58, 62, 70, 124
clothing, 33–34, 54, 57–58, 93, 96
Cohen, Steven
  Chandelier, 13, 38–42, 44, 153
  Cock/Coq, 44
  The Cradle of Human Kind, 44, 153

Dog (persona), 35
Faggot (persona), 35–36
Jew (persona), 35–36
Put Your Heart under Your Feet . . . and Walk, 44, 153
Taste, 36
Ugly Girl (persona), 35–37
Virgin Penetrated, 37
Cole, Catherine, 156, 163
Cole, Teju, 77
colonialism, 7–8, 10, 15, 17, 19, 22, 27, 30, 42, 62, 76, 78–79, 86, 98–99, 102
Coloured, 9, 29, 98, 121
Constitution (1996), 1–2, 12, 19–20, 24, 49, 51–52, 60–61, 80, 137, 145, 151
Conquergood, Dwight, 17, 51
contradiction, 5, 10, 19, 21, 25, 34, 41–42, 52–53, 63–64, 70, 103–104, 118, 124, 133–134, 137
cultural accessorization, 57
Currier, Ashley, 59

death
from HIV/AIDS, 10
murder, 7, 68, 70, 85, 87, 89, 93–96, 98–100, 143
LGBT, 7, 52, 68, 78, 91, 93, 102, 143
performed, 75, 95–96, 99, 101–103
suicide, 35, 65
deKlerk, F.W., 23
Deleuze, Gilles, 74
diamonds, 27, 42
diversity
as cosmopolitanism, 1, 32, 52, 112
cultural, 52, 112
of LGBT identity, 64, 70, 82–83
narrative of, 4, 11–12, 25, 57, 107, 137
nation, 4, 8, 11, 25, 107
as unifying, 4, 8, 25, 137
of whiteness, 31, 36
Dolan, Jill, 74
drag
cross-dressing, 25
ethnic, 31
performance, 6, 19, 22–26, 31, 33, 35–36, 41–42, 46, 134, 141, 150
queen, 2, 22, 26, 36
and race, 25, 27, 44
as subversion, 42
transvestite, 25
dramaturgy, 10, 72, 110, 134
Dyer, Richard, 30

Edelman, Lee, 51
Ekhureleni Muncipality, 47
English, 8–9, 67, 94, 98, 101
Epprecht, Marc, 16, 62, 148

Facebook, 88, 111–112
family
and heterosexuality, 66
and identity, 58, 66, 116–119, 122–130, 132, 134, 164
and nation, 121
and performance, 27, 29, 116
queer, 6, 50, 53, 67, 121
and tradition, 66, 68–69, 111, 127
and white supremacy, 9
fandom, 6, 20, 106, 109–110, 125, 127, 164
femininity
feminine, 45, 54, 64, 66, 96, 104
femme, 54–55, 60, 88, 109
ladyhood, 54
feminism, 48, 53, 69
FIFA World Cup, 6, 19, 48, 65, 72, 77, 135–136, 162
Fleetwood, Nicole, 81
fluidity
of borders, 119
cultural, 53, 67
gender, 54
queer, 59
racial, 54
temporal, 4, 18
Forum for the Empowerment of Women (FEW), 13–14, 18–19, 47–53, 55–59, 61–68, 70, 72–75, 82, 86–87, 122, 130, 138, 140, 142
Foucault, Michel, 115, 149
fracture, 7, 18–19, 21, 27, 31, 36, 42, 46, 109, 136–137, 139, 141

freedom/liberation, 1, 11, 37, 56–57, 61, 65, 70, 72, 100, 123, 140, 143
Freud, Sigmund, 37, 153
Fugard Theatre, 11

Garber, Marjorie, 25, 150, 156
gay, 1–2, 5–7, 11–15, 18, 20, 25, 34, 48–50, 53–55, 57–58, 69, 72–73, 76–77, 107, 109–110, 119–125, 127–132, 134–135, 138, 140, 142
Gay and Lesbian Memory in Action, 141–142
gender
  ambiguity, 26, 36
  and citizenship, 6, 52
  diversity, 1, 117, 130, 140
  fluidity, 46
  nonconformity, 18, 58, 62, 64, 66, 77, 84, 86, 96
  normativity, 7, 37, 48, 63, 80, 121, 131, 139
  performance, 15, 25, 31, 33, 36, 46, 54, 64, 79, 88
  subversion, 19, 24, 27, 42
  and whiteness, 42
genitalia
  breasts/nipples, 62, 84
  penis, 34, 36, 44, 132
  vagina/vulva, 84
Generations, 14, 20, 106–109, 111–113, 115–117, 119–121, 125–126, 129, 132–135, 139, 162
Generations: The Legacy, 133
Gensblog, 6, 11, 20, 106, 108–119, 123–130, 132, 134–135, 138–139, 162, 164
Goffman, Erving, 154
gold, 27, 39, 42, 98
gospel, 14
Gqola, Pumla, 5, 104, 146
grandmother (*gogo*), 33, 40
Graver, David, 10
Grewal, Inderpal, 61
Grootboom, Mpumelelo Paul, 161
Gunner, Elizabeth, 70–71

Halberstam, J. 156
Haraway, Donna, 126
heterosexuality, 6, 16, 18, 20, 34–35, 48–49, 54, 56, 62, 64–66, 78, 80, 86, 108–109, 111, 120, 125, 130
Hillbrow, 140
hip-hop, 71
HIV/AIDS
  and Black South Africans, 66
  denialism, 33
  education, 43
  struggle against, 11
Homeland (Bantustan), 9, 28, 46, 151
homonationalism, 4, 12, 145
homophobia, 15, 19, 21, 47–48, 50, 54, 60, 73, 83–84, 87, 89, 91, 95, 98–99, 102, 107, 122, 131–132, 139, 141
homosexuality, 6, 9, 15, 17, 36, 49, 56, 62, 67, 109, 120–121, 123–124, 126, 130–132
humanity, 9–10, 29–31, 34, 36, 41, 51, 76, 81, 131
Hutchison, Yvette, 156

Ikultcha (culture), 47–48, 50, 53, 67, 70, 72, 74
imagination
  community, 32, 70, 109
  as decolonial, 19
  freedom, 11
  future, 8, 46, 50, 123, 140
  geographies/cartographies, 21, 58, 109, 143
  identities, 14, 17, 39, 84
  imagining otherwise, 51
  national, 14, 24, 46, 49, 109, 135
  (neo)colonial, 78
  precolonial past, 66
  popular, 82
  queer, 12, 51
  Western, 77–78
Immorality Act, 24
Indian, 9, 29
inequality, 7, 13
intimacy, 13, 15, 29, 64, 91–92, 94, 99–100, 114, 125, 130, 133–134, 138

Jews
  under Apartheid, 35, 152

immigrants to South Africa, 27
Jewishness, 37, 44
Star of David, 36
and whiteness, 27, 35
Johannesburg, 1, 6, 13–14, 18, 39, 42–44, 47–48, 68, 79, 84, 106–108, 113, 115, 139–140, 142
Johannesburg People's Pride, 142
Joint Working Group, 12
Judge, Melanie, 81, 146

Khoisan (Khoi/San), 8, 26
Krueger, Anton, 12
Kruger, Loren, 132, 146, 167
Kwaito, 14, 96
labor, 9, 27, 46, 58, 66, 99
lesbian
Black, 3, 6–7, 15, 18–20, 47–52, 57, 59, 63, 67, 72, 74–75, 77–80, 82–88, 91–92, 94, 96, 99, 102–105, 138, 143
butch (amabutchie), 54–55, 60, 63–66, 87–88, 139
characters, 11
churches, 15
dyke, 54–55, 57, 60
femme (amafemme), 54–55, 60, 88, 103, 113
identity, 1, 12–13, 19, 46–50, 53–70, 72–73, 75, 77–89, 91, 93–94, 102, 105, 120, 123–124, 134, 138, 155
mothers, 64–66, 93
and rape, 20, 65, 68, 76, 78, 83, 86, 89, 104–105
and the state, 5, 47
Lewis, Megan, 150, 151
LGBT, 1–5, 7, 12, 51, 59, 61–62, 68, 72–73, 76–77, 80–81, 89, 126, 134, 137, 139–140
Lorde, Audre, 71, 158

Maboneng Precinct, 43
Macharia, Keguro, 16, 76
Madison, D. Soyini, 51
Mahmood, Saba, 63
Malinga, Jason (character), 106–109, 111, 117–120, 123–124, 126, 128–135
Mamelodi Township, 32
Mandela, Nelson, 1, 5–6, 8, 10, 13, 19, 21–23, 26–27, 39, 42, 44, 57, 77, 133, 136–137, 146–147, 150
Mandela, Winnie, 31
Market Theatre, 9, 43, 65
masculinity, 7, 25–26, 54, 80, 84, 93, 107, 121, 129
Massad, Joseph, 18
Matebeni, Zethu, 18
Mbeki, Thabo, 10, 43
Mbembe, Achille, 78
McClain, Nyx, 4
McClintock, Anne, 49
MNet, 22
Mngqolo, Thami, 106
Moffett, Helen, 80
monstrosity, 13, 24, 26, 34–36, 41
mourning, 31, 37, 86, 89, 91, 136
Muholi, Zanele
Bra, 84–85
EyeMe, 92
Faces and Phases, 83, 86–90, 139, 161
Hate Crime Survivor, 84
ID Crisis, 84
Isilumo Siyaluma (Period Pains), 84
Miss Lesbian I, 103, 109
Mo(u)rning, 88, 90–92, 102
Murder, 84
Only Half the Picture, 83–86
Rape, 84
Status Unknown, 84
multiculturalism, 5, 7, 12, 18, 37, 42, 46, 77, 136–137
Muñoz, José, 26, 51, 67, 74
Munro, Brenna, 5–6
Mupotsa, Danai, 133

naming, 56, 57, 61, 66, 70–71, 155–156
National Arts Festival, 43, 45
National Coalition for Gay and Lesbian Equality, 12
nation-state, 5, 18
natural/unnatural, 33, 60–61, 98, 125, 131–132
Ndebele, 59
Ndebele, Njabulo, 30
neoliberalism, 7, 10–11, 18, 61, 113, 138, 140

Newtown, 13, 39, 42, 44
NGO, 2, 47–48, 72–73, 76, 158
Nguni, 30, 70, 89, 107
Nkoli, Simon, 1, 145
nonbinary, 79, 82, 86
Nuttall, Sarah, 67, 166–167
Nyamza, Mamela
  Hatch, 93
  Hatched, 93
  I Stand Corrected, 75–76, 93–96, 99, 102–103, 161
  Shift, 93
Nyanzi, Stella, 17
Nyong'o, Tavia, 51, 77–78

Obama, Barack, 136, 147
obscenity, 36
One in Nine Campaign, 2–4, 7, 14, 17–18, 21, 47, 73, 139–141

Pan-African, 49, 116, 122
Pellegrini, Ann, 50, 74
Pereira, Jabu, 17
performativity, 2, 6–8, 20, 27, 42–43, 50, 52, 59, 61–62, 67, 72, 74, 80, 88, 92, 102, 110, 114, 120, 123–124, 130, 132, 135, 137–138, 140
Phelan, Peggy, 135
piercings, 47, 57
Pink Rand, 2, 4
Pinkwashing, 4, 145
play, 20, 26, 32–33, 35–36, 41, 46, 57, 71, 87, 93–94, 112, 115, 123–124, 131
pleasure
  ambivalent, 119
  audience, 10, 16, 78, 96, 113, 134
  dis-, 117, 120
  painful, 119
  pluralism, 5, 50
  seeking, 36
  taking, 60, 70
pornography, 40, 82
postapartheid, 1, 4–7, 10–13, 15, 17–19, 21–25, 29–30, 32–33, 35–37, 42, 46, 57, 61–62, 77, 80, 82, 88, 95, 107–108, 112, 118, 125, 133–134, 137–138
postcolonial, 5–7, 48, 62, 86, 105
Pretoria, 27, 79, 136
Pride, 1–4, 7, 12, 14, 18, 21, 35, 47, 52, 57, 73, 139
prism, 1–2, 6, 10, 31, 43, 77
propaganda, 9
protest, 2–4, 7, 11, 14, 17, 21, 47–48, 52–53, 65, 102, 118, 132, 139–140, 142

queer
  activism, 4, 21, 61, 140, 142–143
  and Africanness, 5–6, 13–20, 25, 42, 48, 50, 71, 76–79, 82, 107, 122, 126, 132, 134, 138–139, 149
  and Blackness, 4, 52, 96, 126, 134
  bodies, 4–5, 12–13, 16–18, 27, 35–37, 41, 52, 77, 138, 143
  citizenship, 24, 77, 137
  desire, 125, 128
  family, 6, 91, 121, 128
  gaze, 56, 134
  identities, 1, 12, 52, 55, 57–58, 61, 63, 65, 71, 134, 138, 143
  and Judaism, 27, 35, 37
  men, 126
  nationalism, 6, 24, 46
  performance, 5, 7, 14, 18, 21, 34, 36, 42, 46, 53, 70–71, 78–79, 138
  theory, 14–19, 51–52, 62, 67, 76, 81–82, 139
  visibility, 35, 59, 80–82, 138
  and whiteness, 6, 26–27, 32, 35, 37, 41–42
  women, 2, 66–67, 70–71, 96
Queer African Studies (field), 14–15, 149
queer temporality
  queer futurity, 51, 86, 102
  queer pasts, 15, 51, 102
  queer utopia, 18, 51, 74

rainbow
  as national signifier, 5–8, 11–13, 18–19, 21, 25, 39, 41–42, 44, 46, 133, 136–137, 139, 143
  and Pride/gay symbol, 1–3, 7, 25, 57, 141, 143

Rainbow Nation, 4–5, 8, 10, 19, 21, 24–25, 30, 42, 46, 77, 107, 136, 146, 154
Ramaphosa, Cyril, 10
rape (*see* sexual violence)
Red Ants (security and demolition company), 39–40, 42, 153
representation, 5–6, 8, 11, 15, 20, 22, 49, 60, 62, 64, 71, 75, 78, 81, 83, 86, 88–89, 91, 100, 103–105, 113, 118, 126, 138–139
reproduction
  adoption, 2, 65, 98, 102
  in-vitro fertilization, 65
  pregnancy, 58, 65, 93, 118
Rhythm City, 107
romance, 6, 63, 66, 99, 113, 117–119, 125
Ruga, Athi-Patra
  Future White Women of Azania, 44, 154
  Versatile Queen Ivy (persona), 44
rupture, 28, 42

Sachs, Albie, 28, 151
same-sex (same-gender)
  activity, 62
  adoption, 2
  attraction, 1, 58, 130
  desire, 15, 82, 129
  intimacy, 91, 134
  marriage, 2, 6, 12
  object choice, 122
Sangoma, 118
Sassen, Robyn, 94, 153
Schneider, Rebecca, 152
Seig, Katrin, 31
Semenya, Caster, 165
Senelick, Laurence, 25, 150
Sesotho, 8
sexual identity, 61–62, 64, 127, 132
sexual minority, 1
sexual orientation, 1–2, 6, 24, 61–64, 78–79, 143
sexual trauma, 20, 103
sexual violence
  corrective, 20, 61, 64, 75, 77–81, 86, 88, 92, 96, 99, 104, 159
  curative, 20, 61, 81
  narratives, 80, 161
  rape, 7, 20, 61–62, 64–65, 68, 75, 77–81, 84–89, 92–96, 98–100, 102–104, 138
Simelane, Eudy, 93
soap opera (soapie), 6, 11, 14, 20–21, 106–110, 112–119, 121, 123–126, 128, 130, 133–135
soccer, 6, 13–14, 18–19, 46–48, 53, 56, 58–60, 83, 93, 136
Sontag, Susan, 152
South African Broadcasting Corporation (SABC), 11, 106, 163
Soweto, 27, 56, 99, 103, 146, 149
Soweto Theatre, 99, 103
Spivak, Gayatri Chakravorty, 78
squatter camp, 13, 37, 39–40
Stanislavski, Constantin, 154
strangeness, 24, 26, 36–37, 39–41, 59, 78–79, 81, 87, 95, 104
Steyn, Melissa, 29
subjectivity, 34, 36, 50, 77, 81, 83
"swagga," 53–55, 57–58, 71, 88, 138, 141

taboo, 24, 104
Tamale, Sylvia 17–18, 149
tattoos, 57
Taylor, Diana, 81
television, 9–12, 22, 32, 91, 106–108, 110–113, 115–116, 126, 133
theater
  American, 11
  audience, 44
  community, 9, 11
  dance, 75, 99
  industry, 33
  live, 9, 108
  musical, 11
  postapartheid, 11
  practitioners, 35
  scholarship, 12, 108
  South African, 43
  as space, 10, 31, 36, 74, 96
  street, 141–142
  struggle, 10, 43, 147
Thomas, Kylie, 87

toyi-toyi, 10, 147
tradition, 2, 14–15, 30, 32, 36, 40, 49–50, 61, 67, 69–72, 79, 91, 93, 98, 101–102, 110–111, 118, 132
transgression
  boundaries, 33, 70
  gender, 33
  as performance, 20
  racial, 33
transnational, 4, 55–57, 59, 61, 74, 99, 105
Trinh, T. Minh-Ha, 127
Truth and Reconciliation Commission, 104
Turner, Victor, 156
Tutu, Desmond, 5, 8, 30–31, 42, 146–147

Ubuntu, 10, 30, 42, 151
Uganda, 17, 49, 77
United Christian Democratic Party, 49
urban, 13, 15, 35, 37, 50, 54, 74, 91, 111, 113, 140
Uys, Peter-Dirk
  African Times, 43
  Evita Beduidenhout (persona), 22–24, 27–35, 41, 43
  Evita's Free Speech, 43
  MacBeki, 43
  The Merry Wives of Zuma, 43

Vaid-Menon, Alok, 12
Van der Vlies, Andrew, 86
violence, 3–4, 6–7, 11, 13, 20, 22, 27, 36, 40–42, 47–48, 61, 64–65, 75–84, 87, 89, 91–95, 98, 102–105, 132, 138, 166
virginity, 37
visibility
  hypervisibility, 75, 79–81, 86, 88–89, 104
  invisibility, 6, 17, 61, 79–81, 83, 86, 89, 94, 96, 103–104, 110, 126–127, 133, 135, 138
  representation, 5–6, 8, 11, 15, 20, 49, 60, 62, 64, 71, 75, 78, 81, 83, 86, 88–89, 91, 100, 103–105, 113, 118, 126, 138–139
Vosloorus, 47, 53, 56, 58, 73, 139
voting, 22, 24, 138, 151

Walder, David, 9
Western Cape, 34, 43
white, 3, 6–15, 18–19, 22–37, 40–46, 51–52, 59, 62, 73, 77–78, 81, 83, 89, 91, 93, 95, 98, 101, 103, 107, 111, 121, 138, 140

Xaluva, Zolisa, 106
!Xam, 8
Xhosa (iXhosa), 8, 22, 93, 98, 116, 132
Xingwana, Lulu, 82–83, 91

Yuval-Davis, Nira, 49

Zondi, Mlondolozi, 52
Zondo, Senzo (character), 106–109, 111, 117–121, 124, 126, 128–135
Zulu (isiZulu), 8, 22, 27, 39, 48, 67, 70, 102
Zuma, Jacob, 10, 43, 137, 148, 159